LANGUAGE AND LITERACY SERIES

Dorothy S. Strickland, FOUNDING EDITOR
Celia Genishi and Donna E. Alvermann, SERIES EDITORS

ADVISORY BOARD: Richard Allington, Kathryn Au, Bernice Cullinan, Colette Daiute, Anne Haas Dyson,
Carole Edelsky, Shirley Brice Heath, Connie Juel, Susan Lytle, Timothy Shanahan

For volumes in the NCRLL Collection (edited by JoBeth Allen and Donna E. Alvermann) and the Practitioners Bookshelf Series (edited by Celia Genishi and Donna E. Alvermann), please visit www.tcpress.com.

Teaching Vocabulary to English Language Learners

Michael F. Graves

Diane August

Jeannette Mancilla-Martinez

Foreword by Catherine E. Snow

TEACHERS COLLEGE PRESS

TEACHERS COLLEGE | COLUMBIA UNIVERSITY
NEW YORK AND LONDON

Center for Applied Linguistics
Washington, DC

International Reading Association
Newark, DE

TESOL International Association
Alexandria, VA

Published simultaneously by Teachers College Press, 1234 Amsterdam Avenue, New York, NY 10027; the Center for Applied Linguistics, 4646 40th Street NW, Washington, DC 20016-1859; the International Reading Association, 800 Barksdale Road, Newark, DE 19711; and the TESOL International Association, 1925 Ballenger Avenue, Suite 550, Alexandria, VA 22314-6820.

Library of Congress Cataloging-in-Publication Data

Graves, Michael F.
  Teaching vocabulary to English language learners / Michael F. Graves, Diane August, Jeannette Mancilla-Martinez ; foreword by Catherine Snow.
    p. cm.— (Language and literacy series)
  Includes bibliographical references and index.
  ISBN 978-0-8077-5375-0 (pbk.)
    1. English language—Study and teaching—Foreign speakers. 2. Vocabulary—Study and teaching. I. August, Diane. II. Mancilla-Martinez, Jeannette. III. Title.
  PE1128.A2G682 2012
  428.0071—dc23   2012023129

ISBN 978-0-8077-5375-0 (paperback)

Printed on acid-free paper
Manufactured in the United States of America

20   19   18   17   16   15   14   13   8   7   6   5   4   3   2   1

For the millions of English language learners who strive daily to master English, and for the teachers who guide and support them.

Contents

Foreword

For the covert clan of lexicophiliacs to which I confess membership, words are endlessly fascinating. Is it not worthy of contemplation that *recess* can mean both "time out" and "niche"? Does English need another word for *corner*, to match the very different meanings expressed in Spanish by "esquina" (street corner) and "rincon" (corner of a room)? How do children learn that *mouth* and *bath* and *breath* get turned into verbs via vowel and/or voicing changes, when the vast majority of short Germanic-origin nouns require no change at all to be used as verbs (e.g., *knee, glue, table, bat, pencil, book,* and thousands more)? Have you ever considered how *considerable* came to have the primary meaning "to a high degree" rather than the much more straightforward "worthy of consideration"? Is it weird or normal that *comfortable*, originally a feature of the objects that offered comfort (e.g., a comfortable bed), is now predicated of people experiencing comfort (e.g., "Sal feels really comfortable in her new job")? What exactly is the difference between a *foreword* and a *prologue* (Greek for "before+word")? Is it stupid to misspell *foreword* as *forward,* or is that insightful? For lexicophiliacs with high standards, it is actually the latter. But if this entire paragraph has bored and/or puzzled you, you are probably not a lexicophiliac.

But even so, you use, read, write, and learn words all the time. And if you are a teacher, you are probably worried about whether your students are learning words fast and well enough. In 2005, the Strategic Education Research Partnership established its first field site in the Boston Public Schools (BPS). Tom Payzant, then superintendent in BPS, had asked us to figure out why reading comprehension was not progressing more effectively during the middle grades. When we interviewed teachers to get their views on the situation, we heard two recurrent messages: "My students can read all the words in their texts, but often don't know what they mean" and, simultaneously and paradoxically, "I teach vocabulary all the time." So if teachers are teaching vocabulary, why do students not know the words they need to read their texts? Our observations suggested that teachers were teaching the words of their disciplines, but no one was attending to the challenge of teaching the ubiquitous, all-purpose academic words that are crucial to text comprehension. Students who had not had the opportunity to learn those words from conversations with parents or from wide reading were faced with texts they had no hope of understanding. They desperately needed wider-ranging vocabulary instruction, and their teachers desperately needed ideas for tackling their students' massive vocabulary deficits.

Anyone faced with that challenge should experience jubilation at the appearance of this book. It lays out in readable prose and logical order the basic facts about word learning, the research-based principles of good vocabulary teaching, and concrete examples of the practices that exemplify those principles. The most challenging, and probably the most powerful, of the principles identified is "providing a rich and varied language experience." Doing so, of course, requires thinking beyond vocabulary to content—identifying rich, lexicogenic topics to talk about, identifying the teachable words that are most connected to those topics, and devising activities that promote use of those words by teacher and students. Adults who themselves have large vocabularies and well-developed word consciousness have an easier time providing the rich and varied language experience language learners need. Ultimately, some students may themselves end up as full-fledged lexicophiliacs, obsessed with crossword puzzles and Scrabble, seeking etymologies online, punning painfully, and recycling Greek and Latin roots into neologisms with abandon. Or, at a bare minimum, they will at least understand their texts.

Catherine E. Snow
Cambridge, MA

PERMISSIONS AND ACKNOWLEDGMENTS

Figure 3.1: Adapted from Hayes, D. P., & Ahrens, M. (1988). Vocabulary simplification for children: A special case of "motherese"? *Journal of Child Language, 15*, 395–410.

In Chapter 3, discussion of Judith Viorst's *Alexander and the Terrible, Horrible, No Good, Very Bad Day* is from August, D., & Vockly, M. (2002). *Spanish to English: Reading and Writing for English Language Learners.* Washington, DC: National Center on Education and the Economy and the University of Pittsburgh.

Figure 3.3: From Graves, M. F., Sales, G. C., & Ruda, M. (2008). *The First 4,000 Words.* Minneapolis, Seward Inc. Available at thefirst4000words.com.

Figure 4.1: From Sales, G., & Graves, M. F. (2009b). *Listening Vocabulary Test.* Minneapolis, MN: Seward Inc.

Figure 4.2: Sample Reading Vocabulary Placement Test Item for Help. From Sales, G., & Graves, M. F. (2009c). *Reading Vocabulary Test.* Minneapolis, MN: Seward Inc.

Figure 4.3: Listening item adapted from Center for Applied Linguistics. (2011). *Acquisition of vocabulary in English vocabulary assessment (AVEVA).* Unpublished assessment instrument. Reading item adapted from Center for Applied Linguistics. (2011). *Test of academic vocabulary in English (TAVE).* Unpublished assessment instrument.

Figure 5.2: Twenty Most Frequent Prefixes. Adapted from White, T. G., Sowell, J., & Yanagihara, A. (1989). Teaching elementary students to use word-part clues. *The Reading Teacher, 42*, 302–308.

Figures 5.5, 5.8, 5.14, and 5.16: Adapted from Sales, G. C., & Graves, M. F. (2012). *Word Learning Strategies.* Minneapolis, MN: Seward Inc.

Figure 6.1: From Scott, J. A., Blackstone, T., Cross, S., Jones, A., Skobel, B., Wells, J., et al. (1996, May). *The Power of Language: Creating Contexts Which Enrich Children's Understanding and Use of Words.* Microworkshop conducted at the meeting of the International Reading Association, New Orleans.

Figures 7.1 and 7.2: From August, D., & Barr, C. (2010). *Effect of VIOLETS on the vocabulary growth of young children* (Tech. Rep. No. 1). Baltimore, MD: Ready at Five.

Figures 7.4–7.8: From August, D., Artzi, L., & Massoud, L. (2011). *Acquisition of vocabulary in English curriculum.* Unpublished curriculum. Washington, DC: Center for Applied Linguistics.

Figures 7.10 and 7.11: Copyright 2006 Strategic Education Research Partnership. http://word-generation.org

Figures 7.12 and 7.13: From August, D., Duguay, A., Lombard, M., & Powell, J. (2010). *Quality English and Science Teaching (QuEST) curriculum.* Unpublished curriculum. Washington, DC: Center for Applied Linguistics.

The First 4,000 Words: Keys to Success in School program described in Chapter 3 was developed with a grant from the SBIR program of the Institute of Education Sciences, U.S. Department of Education, through contract #ED-07-CO-0043 to Seward Inc. The contents of these materials do not necessarily represent the positions or policies of these agencies, and readers should not assume endorsement of these materials by the federal government.

We thank Greg Sales, Melanie Ruda, and other members of the Seward team for their work in developing The First 4,000 Words.

The Word Learning Strategies program described in Chapter 5 was developed with a grant from the SBIR program supported by the Institute of Education Sciences, U.S. Department of Education, through contract #ED-IES-09-C-0013 to Seward Inc. The contents of these materials do not necessarily represent the positions or policies of these agencies, and readers should not assume endorsement of these materials by the federal government.

We thank Greg Sales, Melanie Ruda, and other members of the Seward team for their work in developing Word Learning Strategies.

The Vocabulary Improvement and Oral Language Enrichment Through Stories project (VIOLETS) described in Chapter 7 is supported by Ready at Five with funds from Maryland State Department of Education, Division of Early Childhood Development. The contents of these materials do not necessarily represent the positions or policies of these agencies, and readers should not assume endorsement of these materials by the federal government.

We thank Cheryl Dressler and Louise Corwin, who collaborated on the VIOLETS project.

The Acquiring Vocabulary in English (AVE) effort was supported by Grant Number P01HD03950 from the *Eunice Kennedy Shriver* National Institute of Child Health and Human Development to the Center for Applied Linguistics. The content is solely the responsibility of the authors and does not necessarily represent the official views of the National Institute of Child Health and Human Development or the National Institutes of Health.

We thank Lauren Artzi, Chris Barr, Lindsey Massoud, and Kat Kramer, who collaborated on the AVE project.

The Quality English and Science Teaching project (QuEST) is conducted by the Center for Applied Linguistics under the auspices of the Center for Research on the Educational Achievement and Teaching of English Language Learners (CREATE) through Grant Number R305A050056 from the Institute of Education Sciences, U.S. Department of Education, awarded to the University of Houston. The information and materials included here do not necessarily represent the positions or policies of the Department of Education, and readers should not assume endorsement by the federal government.

We thank Lauren Artzi, Annie Duguay, Jennifer Powell, Michelle Lombard, and Aileen Bach, who have collaborated in the development of the QuEST materials.

CHAPTER 1

Introduction

An important finding that emerges from the research [on language-minority children] is that word-level skills in literacy—such as decoding, word recognition and spelling—are often taught well enough to allow language-minority students to attain levels of performance equal to those of native English speakers. However, this is not the case for text-level skills—reading comprehension and writing. Language-minority students rarely approach the same levels of proficiency in text-level skills achieved by native English speakers. The research suggests one reason for the disparity between word- and text-level skills among language-minority students is their English vocabulary.

Diane August and Timothy Shanahan,
ESL and Reading Researchers

It is estimated that native English speakers acquire something like 3,000 new words every school year (Nagy & Anderson, 1984). This increase in vocabulary accounts for a significant portion of their language and reading comprehension growth. As more words are acquired, students are able to draw finer distinctions in meaning among words, develop a stronger understanding of how words work together, and increase their sensitivity to context and communicative intent. In turn, this growing sophistication with language aids vocabulary development, making it possible to acquire words through exposure to text and conversation.

Helping English language learners (ELLs) catch up and keep up with the steady growth experienced by their English-proficient peers over years of exposure to their native tongue is imperative. We use the term *English language learners* (ELLs) to refer to students who come from homes where a language other than English is spoken and who are still acquiring proficiency in English (August & Shanahan, 2006a). Research suggests that ELLs can indeed experience accelerated growth in vocabulary, but this requires systematic and long-term vocabulary instruction (Carlo, August, & Snow, 2005). Unfortunately, recent studies suggest that the amount of instructional time devoted to vocabulary development is simply insufficient to support the level of growth needed to close the vocabulary gap between ELLs and their English-proficient peers. A Reading First impact evaluation reported that 1st-grade reading teachers spent approximately 8 minutes of their daily reading block—about 13% of instructional time—on vocabulary instruction, and 2nd-grade teachers spent approximately 12 minutes of their daily reading block—about 20% of instructional time (Gamse, Jacob, Horst, Boulay, & Unlu, 2008). A recent study of a large number of kindergarten and 1st-grade classrooms in urban and border schools in California and Texas serving ELLs reported that vocabulary instruction comprised less than 7% of the total instructional time (Saunders, Foorman, & Carlson, 2006).

The findings of over 100 years of vocabulary research on native English speakers include the following:

- Vocabulary knowledge is one of the best indicators of verbal ability (Sternberg, 1987; Terman, 1916).
- Vocabulary knowledge contributes to young children's phonological awareness, which in turn contributes to their word recognition (Goswami, 2001; Nagy, 2005).
- Vocabulary knowledge in kindergarten and 1st grade is a significant predictor of reading comprehension in the middle and secondary grades (Cunningham & Stanovich, 1998; Scarborough, 1998).
- Vocabulary difficulty strongly influences the readability of text (Chall & Dale, 1995; Klare, 1984).
- Teaching vocabulary can improve reading comprehension (Baumann, 2005; Beck, Perfetti, & McKeown, 1982).
- Growing up in poverty can seriously restrict the vocabulary children learn before beginning school and make attaining an adequate vocabulary a challenging task (Coyne, Simmons, & Kame'enui, 2004; Hart & Risley, 1995; Templin, 1957; White, Graves, & Slater, 1990).
- Lack of vocabulary can be a crucial factor underlying the school failure of disadvantaged students (Becker, 1977; Biemiller, 1999).

Fortunately, since vocabulary is so important, we know a great deal about vocabulary development and about how to teach vocabulary to native English-speaking students. As we just mentioned, over 100 years of research led to the above findings, as well as to a wealth of other conclusions. Research on the development of vocabulary in ELLs mirrors many of these findings. However, research related to effective vocabulary instruction for ELLs is much more recent, and there is much less of it. Fortunately, the research we do have on instruction for ELLs suggests that much of what we have learned about teaching vocabulary to native English speakers also applies to teaching ELLs, but that some adjustments will strengthen instruction for ELLs (August & Gray, 2010; August & Shanahan, 2010a; August & Snow, 2007; Gersten & Baker, 2000; Goldenberg, 2008; Goldenberg & Coleman, 2010; Saville-Troike, 1984). The research also provides guidance about the techniques that are valuable for ELLs (August, Carlo, Dressler, & Snow, 2005; Carlo et al., 2004). We review the research on vocabulary learning and vocabulary instruction for both native English speakers and ELLs in some detail in Chapter 2. At this point, however, we introduce two crucial facts about vocabulary—facts to keep in mind as you read this book and plan vocabulary instruction for ELLs.

First, the vocabulary learning task is enormous! Estimates of vocabulary size vary greatly, but a reasonable estimate based on a substantial body of past and more recent scholarship (Anderson & Nagy, 1992; Anglin, 1993a, 1993b; Hiebert & Cervetti, 2012; Miller & Wakefield, 1993; Nagy & Anderson, 1984; Nagy & Herman, 1987; Snow & Kim, 2007; Stahl & Nagy, 2006; White, Graves, & Slater, 1990) is this: The books and other reading materials used by schoolchildren include over 180,000 different words. The average child who speaks English as her native language enters school with a very small reading vocabulary, typically consisting largely of environmental print. Once in school, however, this child's reading vocabulary is likely to soar at a rate of 3,000–4,000 words a year, leading to a reading vocabulary of something like 25,000 words by 8th grade, and a reading vocabulary of something like 50,000 words by the end of high school.

Second, these figures are for native English speakers and for linguistically advantaged students, students who grow up in English-speaking homes filled with language that nourishes their growing vocabularies. Although we have very little detailed information on the sizes of ELLs' vocabularies, both common sense and the data we do have suggest that there is a tremendous range in the sizes of their vocabularies (August et al., 2005; Proctor, Carlo, August, & Snow, 2005; Snow & Kim, 2007; Swanson, Saez, & Gerber, 2006) and that the vocabulary gap is quite wide. A considerable number of recent studies that report oral language outcomes on standardized tests indicate that ELLs' performance is significantly below the average performance of native English speakers on vocabulary and other oral language proficiency outcomes such as listening comprehension, memory for sentences, and verbal analogies (Cirino, Pollard-Durodola, Foorman, Carlson, & Francis, 2007; Gonzalez et al., 2011; Mancilla-Martinez & Lesaux, 2011; Manis, Lindsey, & Bailey, 2004; Oller & Eilers, 2002; Proctor et al., 2005; San Francisco, Mo, Carlo, August, & Snow, 2006; Vaughn et al., 2006). Results from a recent study suggest a developmental lag in ELLs' patterns of growth, from the preschool years through early adolescence, in oral language, relative to national norms (Mancilla-Martinez & Lesaux, 2011).

We also know that many children from low-income families enter school with vocabularies much smaller than those of their middle-class counterparts (Biemiller & Slonim, 2001; Hart & Risley, 1995, 2003; Templin, 1957; White, Graves, & Slater, 1990). ELLs from low-income families have notably lower levels of vocabulary than those who are middle-class (Oller & Eilers, 2002). As many educators have noted, it is tremendously important to find ways to bolster the oral and reading vocabularies of all students who enter school with small stores of words (August et al., 2005; Becker, 1977; Biemiller, 1999, 2009; Carlo, 2007; Chall, Jacobs, & Baldwin, 1990; Cunningham & Stanovich, 1998; Elley, 1991; Graves, 2006; Hirsch, 2003; Mancilla-Martinez & Lesaux, 2010, 2011; Nation, 2001; National Reading Panel, 2000; RAND Reading Study Group, 2002; Schmitt, 2000; Snow & Kim, 2007).

A FOUR-PART VOCABULARY PROGRAM

This book presents a comprehensive plan for vocabulary instruction for ELLs, one broad enough to include instruction for students who are just beginning to build their English vocabularies and for students whose English vocabularies are approaching those of native speakers. Specifically, the book describes a four-pronged vocabulary program that one of us began developing 30 years ago and continues to elaborate and refine (Graves, 2006, 2009a, 2009b). The program has the following four components:

- providing rich and varied language experiences;
- teaching individual words;
- teaching word-learning strategies; and
- fostering word consciousness.

It is similar to programs described by Baumann and Kame'enui (2004); Kame'enui & Baumann, 2012), Blachowicz, Fisher, Ogle, and Watts-Taffe (2006), and Stahl and Nagy (2006); was recently validated in a study by Baumann, Ware, and Edwards (2007); and serves as the framework for current studies by August and Snow (2008) and Baumann, Blachowicz, Mangak, Graves, & Oleynik (2009). In the next several sections, we briefly discuss each component and the rationale behind it.

Providing Rich and Varied Language Experiences

One way to build students' vocabularies is to immerse them in a rich array of language experiences so that they learn words through listening, speaking, reading, and writing. In kindergarten and the primary grades and for ELLs in the early stages of learning English vocabulary, listening and speaking are particularly important for promoting vocabulary growth (Beck, McKeown, & Kucan, 2003). In the intermediate grades, the middle grades, and secondary school, discussion continues to be important. Students of all ages need to engage frequently in authentic discussions—give-and-take conversations in which they are given the opportunity to thoughtfully discuss topics (Applebee, Langer, Nystrand, & Gamoran, 2003; Beck & McKeown, 2006; Guthrie & Humenick, 2004). Increasingly from the intermediate grades on, and as students become increasingly proficient with English vocabulary, reading becomes a principal language experience for increasing their vocabularies (Cunningham & Stanovich, 1998). If we can substantially increase the reading students do, we can substantially increase the words they learn (Anderson, 1996; Anderson & Nagy, 1992; Krashen, 2001; Stahl, 1998).

Teaching Individual Words

Another way to help students increase their vocabularies is to teach them individual words. To be sure, the size of the vocabulary that students will eventually attain means that we cannot teach all of the words they need to learn. However, the fact that we cannot teach all of the words students need to learn does not mean that we cannot and should not teach some of them. Fortunately, research has revealed a good deal about effective—and ineffective—approaches to teaching individual words (Beck, McKeown, & Omanson, 1987; Graves, 2009a; Mezynski, 1983; Stahl & Fairbanks, 1986). Vocabulary instruction is most effective when learners are given both definitional and contextual information, when learners actively process the new word meanings, and when they experience multiple encounters with words. Said somewhat differently, vocabulary instruction is most effective—and most likely to influence students' comprehension—when it is rich, deep, and extended. At the same time, because there are so many words to teach, not all of them can or should receive rich, deep, and extended instruction. Thus, there is a need for rich, deep, and extended instruction on some words and less robust, introductory instruction on others.

Teaching Word-Learning Strategies

A third approach to helping students increase their vocabularies is to teach word-learning strategies. One widely recommended strategy is that of using word parts to unlock the meanings of unknown words, and doing so is well-supported by research (Baumann, Font, Edwards, & Boland, 2005; Carlyle, 2007). If students can use their knowledge of prefixes, suffixes, and roots to recognize and understand the various members of word families—for example *indicate, indicates, indicated, indicating, indication,* and *indicator*—the number of individual words they need to learn is significantly reduced. Using context to infer word meanings is another widely recommended strategy. As Sternberg (1987) has forcefully pointed out, "Most vocabulary is learned from context." If we can improve students' abilities to use context to glean word meanings, they will markedly increase their vocabularies. Using the dictionary and similar reference tools is a third recommended approach, and many students need assistance in more effectively using these tools (Graves, 2006; Stahl & Nagy, 2006). Dealing with multiword units is another task ELLs need to master. Finally, for Spanish-speaking ELLs and others whose native language shares etymological roots with English, learning to use cognate knowledge can be a powerful word-learning strategy (August et al., 2005; Bravo, Hiebert, & Pearson, 2007; Carlo, August, & Snow, 2005).

Fostering Word Consciousness

The last component of the four-part program is fostering word consciousness. The term *word consciousness* refers to an awareness of and interest in words and their meanings. Word consciousness involves both a cognitive and an affective stance toward words and integrates metacognition about words, motivation to learn words, and a deep and lasting interest in words (Graves & Watts-Taffe, 2008; Scott, Skobel, & Wells, 2008).

Students who are word conscious are aware of the words around them—those they read and hear and those they write and speak. This awareness involves an appreciation of the power of words, an understanding of why certain words are used instead of others, and a sense of the words that could be used in place of those selected by a writer or speaker. It also involves, as Scott and Nagy (2004) emphasize, recognition of the communicative power of words, of the differences between spoken and written language, and of the particular importance of word choice in written language. And it involves an interest in learning and using new words and becoming more skillful and precise in word usage.

With something like 50,000 words to learn and with most of this word learning taking place incidentally as students are reading and listening, a positive disposition toward word learning is crucial. Word consciousness exists at many levels of complexity and sophistication, and can and should be fostered among preschoolers as well as among students in and beyond high school.

THE LIKELY EFFECT OF THE COMMON CORE STATE
STANDARDS ON VOCABULARY INSTRUCTION FOR ELLs

The Common Core State Standards for English Language Arts & Literacy in History/ Social Studies, Science, and Technical Subjects (CCSS, 2010a) are a set of standards for K–12 students developed by the Council of Chief State School Officers and the Governors Association Center for Best Practices. The *Standards* are designed to define the knowledge and skills needed to succeed in college or the workplace.

Although they leave room for local innovation and do not specify how teachers should teach, the *Standards* are very likely to have a profound effect on education in the United States. At the present time, 45 of the 50 states and the District of Columbia have adopted the *Standards*, and two consortia are developing tests that will assess students' mastery of them. The tests are expected to be widely used, and teachers, schools, and districts are expected to do their best to prepare students to succeed on them.

The question here is how the *Standards* will affect vocabulary instruction for ELLs. We believe that the answer is "markedly," and we see three features of them that are likely to bring about this marked effect.

First, vocabulary is very prominently featured. Vocabulary is referred to almost 200 times in the *Standards*. It is included at all grade levels and in all strands of the document: in reading, in writing, in speaking and listening, and in language. And it is included in both the English Language Arts section and in the Literacy in History/Social Studies, Science, and Technology section.

Second, one central purpose of the *Standards* is to ensure that all students, regardless of where they live and go to school or their linguistic backgrounds, develop the knowledge and skills specified. Regarding their application to ELLs, the *Standards* specifically state that while it is "beyond the scope of the *Standards* to define the full range of supports appropriate for English language learners . . . , all students must have the opportunity to learn and meet the same high standards."

Third, another central purpose of the *Standards* is to make education more rigorous. A large part of this rigor is to be achieved by using more canonical texts, more complex texts, and more informational texts. All this means texts with more challenging vocabulary—vocabulary that will require significant scaffolding for many ELLs.

In addition to considering the *Common Core Standards*, it is also important to consider the *Pre K–12 English Language Proficiency Standards*, which were published by Teachers of English to Speakers of Other Languages (TESOL) in 2006. While the *Common Core Standards* do not give specific attention to the needs of ELLs, the *TESOL Standards* were developed specifically for ELLs. As noted on the TESOL website—www.tesol.org—the standards "were developed through a collaborative process involving hundreds of ESL teachers, researchers, administrators, and language arts specialists . . . [to] provide national coherence for students and the educators who serve them." As the website further indicates, the standards "acknowledge the central role of language in the achievement of content and highlight the learning styles and particular instructional and assessment needs of learners who are still developing proficiency in English." These standards are quite detailed and provide information on five curricular areas (social/intercultural interactions, language arts, mathematics, science, and social studies), five grade-level clusters (PreK–K, 1–3, 4–5, 6–8, and 9–12), five language proficiency levels (starting, emerging, developing, expanding, and bridging), and four language domains (listening, speaking, reading, and writing).

AN OVERVIEW OF THIS BOOK

This opening chapter has discussed the importance of vocabulary for ELLs, noted the huge number of words to be learned and the fact that many ELLs' vocabularies are considerably smaller than those of their native English-speaking peers, and briefly described the four-part program that is described in detail in this book. The remainder of the book consists of six chapters, each of which is briefly described below.

Chapter 2, "Learning Words in a Second Language," begins with a discussion of the vocabulary learning task ELLs face; moves to a discussion of the role of individual, home, school, and instructional context in developing English vocabulary in ELLs; and concludes with a discussion of effective vocabulary instruction. The discussion of effective instruction includes information on providing rich and varied language experiences, teaching individual words, teaching word-learning strategies, fostering word consciousness, and important considerations for ELLs.

Chapter 3, "Providing Rich and Varied Language Experiences," deals with the first part of the four-part program. The first section of the chapter stresses the importance of promoting incidental word learning and discusses ways of doing so through listening, discussion, reading, and writing. The second section describes ways of directly building children's oral vocabularies using shared book reading—a procedure that is particularly useful for building the oral vocabularies of primary-grade ELLs and older ELLs who enter school with much smaller vocabularies than their English-only peers.

Chapter 4, "Teaching Individual Words," describes the second part of the four-part program. The first section of the chapter discusses foundational issues for ELLs, such as the number of words they must learn, levels of word knowledge, the various word-learning tasks that different words represent, identifying and selecting vocabulary to teach, and some principles of vocabulary instruction. The second and much longer section presents detailed descriptions of specific procedures for providing introductory instruction, stronger and more powerful instruction, and repetition and review.

Chapter 5, "Teaching Word-Learning Strategies," describes the third part of the program. This chapter describes powerful procedures for teaching ELLs to use word parts, context, cognates, and the dictionary in learning English words. It also discusses dealing with multiword units, describes strategies students can use in dealing with unknown words, suggests some personal approaches students can take to building their vocabularies, and considers when word-learning strategies should be taught.

Chapter 6, "Promoting Word Consciousness," deals with the fourth and final part of the program. This chapter describes various approaches to get ELLs interested and excited about words. The approaches include creating a word-rich environment, recognizing and promoting adept diction, promoting word play, fostering word consciousness through writing, involving students in original investigations, and teaching students about words.

Chapter 7, "Empirically Validated Vocabulary Programs for English Language Learners," describes four programs of vocabulary instruction for ELLs that have been evaluated in formal studies. Particular attention is given to how the methods build on what we know about effective first-language vocabulary instruction and highlight modifications that appear to benefit ELLs.

The book concludes with a list of children's literature cited, a list of references, and a detailed index.

OTHER SOURCES OF INFORMATION ON INSTRUCTION FOR ENGLISH LANGUAGE LEARNERS

There are, of course, myriad other sources of information on teaching ELLs. Here we highlight four of these other sources, our four co-publishers: The Center for Applied Linguistics (CAL), the International Reading Association (IRA), Teachers College Press, and Teachers of English to Speakers of Other Languages (TESOL).

CAL (www.cal.org) is a private, nonprofit professional organization that "provides a range of research-based information, tools, and resources related to language and culture." Their catalog currently lists over 200 publications on topics related to language education, linguistics, policy, and cultural education. While many of these are text-based, CAL publications also include audios, videos, software, and CDs. Additionally, CAL personnel "conduct research, develop instructional materials and language tests, provide technical assistance and professional development, conduct needs assessment and program evaluations, and disseminate information and resources related to language and culture."

IRA (www.reading.org) is a nonprofit professional organization dedicated to "improving the quality of reading instruction, disseminating research and information about reading, [and] encouraging the lifetime habit of reading." Their catalog currently lists over 150 books, brochures, and videos on topics relating to reading and literacy more generally, including a number of publications focusing on English language learners. IRA also holds an annual conference, as well as regional and state conferences, and publishes *The Reading Teacher* (a journal for elementary teachers), *The Journal of Adolescent Literacy*, and *Reading Research Quarterly*.

Teachers College Press (www.tcpress.com) is a university press that currently publishes well over 500 books dealing with a wide variety of educational topics. Teachers College Press books seek to "expand the dialogue between theory and practice" by, for example, "looking at education, learning, and service in diverse ways" and "providing substantive resources for all of the participants in the educational process" (for example, teachers, teacher educators, researchers, administrators, parents, and students). Included in their catalog are books on English language learners and a series of books on language and literacy.

TESOL (www.tesol.org) is a professional organization whose mission is to "advance professional expertise in English language teaching and learning for speakers of other languages worldwide." Their catalog currently includes over 100 books on a range of topics of interest to English language teaching professionals. TESOL also holds an annual convention and publishes *TESOL Quarterly* (a print journal for teachers and researchers), *TESOL Journal* (a practitioner-oriented electronic journal), position statements on various issues related to language learning, and the PreK–12 English Language Proficiency standards we described previously, as well as several other sets of standards.

CHAPTER 2

Learning Words in a Second Language

I went into the word and I found love.

> —From a 5th-grade Spanish-speaking student who had learned to use first-language cognate knowledge and second-language morphological knowledge to infer the meaning of an unknown English word *amorous*

Is word learning different in a second language? Clearly, we believe it is different in some ways. We would not have written this book if we thought otherwise. Research and theory about the vocabulary acquisition and instruction of native English speakers has been very influential in shaping the way we think about how to teach vocabulary to second-language learners, but research and theory on bilingualism and second-language acquisition also suggest that there are important differences between instruction in a first language and in a second that we need to attend to in order to increase instructional effectiveness and efficiency. One source of differences between first- and second-language vocabulary development stems from learners' degree of proficiency in the second language. A second stems from learners' level of proficiency in the mother tongue. State-reported data indicate that there were an estimated 5.3 million English language learners enrolled in U.S. public schools (preK through grade 12) for the 2008–2009 school year. This number represents approximately 10.8% of total public school student enrollment (National Center for English Language Acquisition, 2011a). Additional data indicate that the number of ELLs in U.S. public schools increased 51% between the 1998–1999 and 2008–2009 school years, with increases in 11 states of over 200% (National Center for English Language Acquisition, 2011b).

In this chapter, we take up three major topics: First, we consider the vocabulary learning task that students face across the K–12 years. Then we consider the role of individual, home, school, and instructional context in second-language vocabulary development. Finally, we turn to the main theme of the chapter, effective vocabulary instruction.

THE VOCABULARY LEARNING TASK STUDENTS FACE

What Is a Word?

Vocabulary can be classified as receptive (words we understand when others use them) or productive (words we use ourselves). Vocabulary can also be classified as oral or written. Thus, each of us has four vocabularies: Words we understand when we hear them (receptive/oral), words we can read (receptive/written), words we use in our speech (productive/oral), and words we use in our writing (productive/written). The four vocabularies overlap but are not the same, and the relationships among them change over time. Children entering school, for example, have larger oral than reading vocabularies in their first language. Literate adults, on the other hand, have larger reading than oral vocabularies. And both children and adults have larger receptive vocabularies than productive ones; that is, they understand more words than they use in their speech or writing. The emphasis in this book will be on reading vocabulary. However, all four types of vocabulary are important, and we will give some attention to each of them.

In order to talk about vocabulary size—the very important matter of how many words students know and need to learn—it is necessary to decide just what we will call a word. When written, words are groups of letters separated by white space. Thus, *the* is a word, *apple* another word, *predawn* another, *perpendicular* another, and *houseboat* still another. By this same definition, however, *want, wants, wanted,* and *wanting* are each separate words, though their only real difference is how they are grammatically inflected. Therefore, for the most part, when we are considering how many words students know or need to learn, we will use the term *word* to refer to *word families*. By *word families*, we mean the basic word and all of its inflected forms. Thus, we count the forms *want, wants, wanted,* and *wanting* as a single word.

Another convention we follow in talking about the size of the learning task is to count graphic forms with different meanings as a single word. Thus, *key* referring to the door key, *key* the musical term, and *key* meaning a small island are considered one word. Doing so definitely underestimates the size of the learning task, but it is necessary because this convention has been followed in virtually all studies of vocabulary size.

What Does It Mean to Know a Word?

Given the assumption that second-language word learning is influenced by knowledge of first-language words, it is necessary to carefully consider what it means to know a word for an ELL. Several researchers have weighed in on this issue. Recently, Beck, McKeown, and Kucan (2002) suggested this continuum of word knowledge for native English speakers:

- No knowledge.
- General sense, such as knowing *mendacious* has a negative connotation.
- Narrow, context-bound knowledge, such as knowing that a *radiant* bride is a beautifully smiling happy one, but unable to describe an individual in a different context as radiant.
- Having knowledge of a word but not being able to recall it readily enough to apply it in appropriate situations.
- Rich, decontextualized knowledge of a word's meaning, its relationship to other words, and its extension to metaphorical uses, such as understanding what someone is doing when they are *devouring* a book. (Beck et al., 2002, p. 10)

Previously, Cronbach (1942) noted that knowing a word involves the ability to select situations in which it is appropriately applied, recall different meanings of the word, and recognize exactly in which situations the word does and does not apply. Calfee and Drum (1986) noted that knowing a word well "involves depth of meaning; precision of meaning; facile access (think of Scrabble and crossword puzzle experts); the ability to articulate one's understanding; flexibility in the application of the knowledge of a word; the appreciation of metaphor, analogy, word play; the ability to recognize a synonym, to define, to use a word expressively." And Nagy and Scott (2000) further underscored the complexity of what it means to know a word when they discussed five aspects of the complexity of word knowledge—incrementality, polysemy, multidimensionality, interrelatedness, and heterogeneity—attributes that we discuss in Chapter 6.

Our understanding of the levels of word knowledge needs to be modified somewhat when applied to ELLs. For some ELLs, learning English words may be less orderly and incremental than for native English speakers (for example, learning may not directly follow Beck, McKeown, and Kucan's [2002] continuum). ELLs whose first language shares cognates with English may recognize a word form in English, and if they know the meaning of the word in their first language, they may know the English meanings that overlap with the meanings in their first language. While this complicates our understanding of what it means to know a word, it can potentially simplify the process of second-language vocabulary instruction. To the extent that we can identify those words an ELL knows well in his first language, we can expedite learning by helping him apply first-language cognate knowledge to uncovering word meanings in a second language and focusing less on conceptual development and more on the word's other possible meanings in English, as well as its usage.

How Many Words Are There?

In the most serious attempt to get a reliable estimate of how many words there are in contemporary American English, Nagy and Anderson (1984) completed a study appropriately titled "How Many Words Are There in Printed School English." As part of the study, they investigated the number of words in printed English school texts, using as their source the *American Heritage Word Frequency Book* (Carroll, Davies, & Richman, 1971), which is a highly regarded compilation of the words occurring in books and other material likely to be used by children in grades 3–9. Based on careful study and a number of calculations, Nagy and Anderson (1984) concluded that printed school English contains about 88,000 word families. Subsequent to the original study, Anderson and Nagy (1992) again considered the size of printed school English vocabulary and concluded that if proper nouns, multiple meanings of words, and idioms were included, their estimate would increase to 180,000 word families.

More recently, Zeno, Ivens, Millard, and Duvvuri (1995) produced *The Educator's Word Frequency Guide,* essentially an updated version of the *Word Frequency Book,* based on a much larger corpus of material used in kindergarten through college. Although no one has yet calculated the number of word families in the *Educa-*

tor's Word Frequency Guide, since the number of entries in the *Guide* is considerably larger than the number in the *Word Frequency Book,* it is reasonable to assume that an estimate of word families based on the *Guide* would be well over 180,000.

Note that these are not estimates of the size of individual students' vocabularies; they are estimates of the total number of words in the myriad texts students might encounter. Note also that many of these words are extremely rare and that no single student will encounter all of them, much less learn all of them. Still, realizing that there are this many words that could be taught is important. It is abundantly clear that we cannot directly teach all of them.

How Many Words Do Students Learn?

As noted in Chapter 1, estimates of the number of words in native English-speaking students' reading vocabularies vary considerably depending on how the estimate is made. Many of these estimates can be dismissed or at least very strongly questioned because of such factors as the size of the dictionary from which words were sampled, the definition of what constitutes a word, the method of testing, the sampling procedures used, and such ad hoc requirements as that a word appear in a number of different dictionaries (Graves, 1986; Lorge & Chall, 1963).

The most unbiased estimate of the size of native English-speaking students' reading vocabularies comes, in our judgment, from work done by Nagy and Herman (1987). Using data gathered from the Nagy and Anderson (1984) study, Nagy and Herman recalibrated earlier estimates and concluded that 3rd-graders' reading vocabularies average about 10,000 words, that 12th-graders' reading vocabularies average about 40,000 words, and that schoolchildren therefore learn about 3,000 words each year. These figures refer to word families as previously described, but they do not include idioms, other multiword units, multiple meanings, or proper nouns, which would raise the figure considerably. All in all, our best estimate—based on the work of Anderson and Nagy (1992); Anglin (1993b); Miller and Wakefield (1993); Nagy and Anderson (1984); Nagy and Herman (1987); and White, Graves, and Slater (1990)—is that average 12th-graders know something like 50,000 word families and learn from 3,000 to 4,000 words each year. These figures, however, are for native English speakers. ELLs, of course, have smaller English vocabularies. Moreover, the vocabularies of ELLs vary tremendously depending on their levels of first-language literacy development and second-language proficiency. The goal is to help all students develop an extensive vocabulary—something like 50,000 words—over their years in school. Based on this goal, many ELLs face a huge word-learning task.

There is one other crucial fact about the vocabulary-learning task that students face: The English language includes a very large number of infrequent words and a very small number of frequent words. Here are some examples of just how important frequent words are: The 100 most frequent words account for about 50% of the words in a typical text; the 1,000 most frequent words for about 70%; and the 5,000 most frequent words for about 80% (Hiebert, 2005). If a student does not know these very frequent words, he will be repeatedly stumbling over the words in anything other than a book with severely controlled vocabulary.

As we see it, the bottom line with respect to the number of words students eventually learn and what to do about helping them learn them is this: There are far too many words to teach all of them directly. There is a much smaller number of frequent words, and these can be taught directly. Teaching 2,000 to 4,000 of the most frequent word families directly, or at least ensuring that all children know these words as soon as possible, is a feasible task. In Chapter 3, we will discuss ways of selecting and teaching these very frequent words; and in Chapter 4, we will suggest how to select and teach less frequent words.

With regard to ELLs, several studies have shown that while ELLs' vocabulary growth rates are similar to and may even surpass those of native English speakers, they are typically 2 to 3 years behind native English-speaking students in vocabulary knowledge, and a large vocabulary gap remains (Mancilla-Martinez & Lesaux, 2011). Additionally, some data indicate that the sequence in which ELLs learn words is similar to that in which native English speakers learn them (Biemiller, 2005). We can draw some important conclusions from this information: It is crucial to provide early, systematic, effective vocabulary instruction for ELLs to enable them to catch up to their native English-speaking peers as soon as possible, thus enabling them to take advantage of grade-appropriate instruction across the content areas.

THE ROLE OF INDIVIDUAL, HOME, SCHOOL, AND INSTRUCTIONAL FACTORS IN THE DEVELOPMENT OF ENGLISH VOCABULARY IN ELLs

Here we consider English proficiency and vocabulary learning, the role of first-language proficiency in English vocabulary learning, the role of home and school factors, and the role of instructional factors.

English Proficiency and Vocabulary Learning

We know that ELLs move along a continuum of English proficiency, with overlapping stages of language acquisition (Ellis, 1982). This means that teachers can use instructional strategies that scaffold students' incomplete knowledge of the language system to a greater or lesser extent depending on their degree of English proficiency.

ELLs face various types of linguistic demands when learning second-language words. At the most emergent stages of English proficiency, the task of orally segmenting words in a sentence poses challenges, as this task is tied to knowledge about phonological, syntactic, and lexical features in the language. The silences and pauses we think we hear between words in a language are not actually there in reality. In natural language, the speech signal is a continuous stream of sound. There are no pauses. As proficient English speakers, we "hear" pauses because we apply our knowledge of phonology, grammar, and words to appropriately segment the utterance. You have probably experienced this phenomenon when listening to someone speaking in a language you do not speak and been left with the impression that words in that language are very, very long!

To acquire word meanings incidentally from mere exposure to a language, learners need to be able to perceive individual words. The ability to do this develops in close relation to phonological and grammatical knowledge. Also, to acquire word meanings from context, as often occurs in first-language acquisition, learners need to be able to exploit the grammatical and semantic cues surrounding the unfamiliar word. A learner needs to know the meaning of the words that surround the unfamiliar word as well as how the words relate to one another. This can only happen in conjunction with ELLs' development of English proficiency. The development of English proficiency takes time, but can be expedited with direct and systematic second-language vocabulary instruction. Hence, we will not spend much effort reviewing research on learners' incidental acquisition of second-language vocabulary aside from acknowledging that it happens when learners have access to the second language (thankfully!) and that we can help move this natural process along by providing students with access to rich and varied communicative experiences that involve native speakers of the language students are acquiring (August & Shanahan, 2006a). Instead, we will focus primarily on what we know about promoting second-language word learning through classroom instruction that is deliberate and systematic.

The Role of First-Language Proficiency in English Vocabulary Learning

We mentioned earlier that the learning experiences ELLs have experienced through their first language influences their learning of a second language. ELLs' proficiency in their home language can vary a great deal depending on their age, exposure to their home language in out of school settings, and the amount of formal schooling in their home language. Some students will be able to use oral and written skills developed in their home language for use across a wide range of communicative situations, while others may possess only rudimentary knowledge that supports communication in quite restricted social situations, such as family routines. The degree of influence of the first language on second-language word learning is likely to be greater for learners with high levels of proficiency in their first language than it will be for learners with more limited proficiency in their first language. Over the past 30 years, researchers studying bilingual memory have produced a great deal of evidence suggesting that the lexicons of bilingual individuals are highly interconnected across their two languages. After years of controversy regarding the nature of bilingual memory organization, a consensus model has been developed that characterizes bilingual memory as consisting of separate lexical systems that map onto shared semantic representations (Chen & Leung, 1989; Kroll & Curley, 1988; Kroll & Sholl, 1992; Potter, So, Von Eckardt, & Feldman, 1984). Additionally, Kroll and her colleagues have provided a model that captures the manner in which lexical access develops from reliance on translation during early stages of second-language learning to direct access to conceptual representations at more advanced levels of proficiency.

There is also a growing body of literature on ELLs that suggests that the use of cognate identification strategies for inferring the meaning of unfamiliar words in text has a positive effect on vocabulary acquisition for ELLs (for example, Dressler

& Kamil, 2006). Cognates are words that have similar spellings, meaning, and sometimes similar pronunciations across two languages. Research suggests that ELLs can use their knowledge of word meanings and spellings in their first language to infer the meaning of unfamiliar English words. Hence, having a broad vocabulary in the first language may facilitate the learning of English words, provided of course that the first language is etymologically related to English (or has borrowed many words from English or other similar languages) and thus contains words that are similar to English words in spelling and meaning.

The Role of Home and School Factors

Socioeconomic status consistently predicts cognitive and academic outcomes among both native English speakers and ELLs (Biemiller & Slonim, 2001; Cobo-Lewis, Pearson, Eilers, & Umbel, 2002; Hart & Risley, 1995, 2003; Lara-Cinisomo et al., 2004; Neuman, 2008), with children from low-income homes performing less well than their more economically advantaged peers. Social class differences that give higher-income children better access to language-related literacy experiences include ownership of books and other reading materials (Raz & Bryant, 1990), availability of books through public libraries (Neuman, 2006), frequency of shared reading (Adams, 1990; Neuman, Caperelli, & Kee, 1998), and opportunities to engage in experiences that build conceptual knowledge needed for understanding text (Neuman, 2008). And it is an unfortunate fact that many ELLs come from lower-SES backgrounds. These children's less developed oral language proficiency is therefore not surprising.

However, with high-quality instruction, the effects of SES on ELLs can be mitigated (August & Shanahan, 2006a; D'Angiulli, Siegel, &, Maggi, 2004). One method that has been successful in bolstering the vocabularies of less advantaged children is shared book reading, in which adults read aloud to children, periodically stopping to highlight and discuss individual words as well as other aspects of what they are reading. Shared book reading highlights language not often heard orally in classrooms and not encountered by young children or less skilled readers in the texts that they are able to read. It also offers adults meaningful contexts in which to discuss new words and provide students with opportunities to engage in conversational interactions that support vocabulary and comprehension (Coyne, Kame'enui, Simmons, & Harn, 2004; De Temple & Snow, 2003). Several studies on interactive shared reading will be reviewed in the section below on providing rich and varied language experiences.

Research on the relationship between language use in the home and ELLs' literacy development in their first or second language generally indicates that children's proficiency is related to family language preferences (Duursma et al., 2007). On average, children from families who prefer to use English at home tend to have larger English vocabularies, and children from families with a preference for Spanish at home tend to have higher Spanish vocabularies. However, as was the case with SES, the nature of the home and school practices influences this relationship (August & Shanahan, 2006a); high-quality first-language home experiences and high-quality second-language school experiences enhance literacy development. For example, a recent study showed no differences in English vocabulary acquisition for young low-SES Hmong- and Spanish-speaking children engaged in first-language home storybook reading and English school storybook reading compared with a similar group of students who participated in home and school storybook reading in English only (T. Roberts, 2008). Both groups learned a substantial number of new words. However, in order for increased home book reading to lead to increases in vocabulary and comprehension among older ELLs, it is important to carefully consider the match between the readers' ability and texts being read, as well as the goals for parental involvement (Kim & Guryan, 2010).

The Role of Instructional Context

The literature on the amount of vocabulary instruction in classrooms consists of a handful of studies. In one study of vocabulary instruction in 4th- through 8th-grade classrooms in Canada, Scott, Jamieson-Noel, and Asselin (2003) found that about 12% of the time in language arts classrooms was devoted to vocabulary instruction, but only 1.4% of the time was spent on vocabulary instruction in other academic subjects. They also found that most instruction involved mentioning meanings and assigning vocabulary to be learned, rather than providing more effective vocabulary instruction based on recent research in the area.

Foorman, Goldenberg, Carlson, Saunders, and Pollard-Durodola (2004) examined the biliteracy and bilingual development of approximately 850 mostly Hispanic children in kindergarten through 2nd grade who were enrolled in English immersion, dual-language, or transitional bilingual programs in two urban sites and one border site in Texas and in one urban site in California. As part of the study, the authors examined the amount of time teachers spent in various activities during the reading/language arts and language development blocks. Findings indicated that there were big differences between the states. Irrespective of language model, teachers in California allocated much more time to oral language development in each grade (ranging from 30% to 87%) than teachers in Texas (ranging from 7% to 27%), where teachers focused more on word work and working with text. Where oral language instruction did take place, it consisted of oral language/discussion, English language strategies, Spanish language, and vocabulary. A study by Mora-Harding (2009) of the instructional practices used by 36 teachers in nine South Florida public elementary schools serving high numbers of Spanish-speaking students indicated that teachers spent only 6% of the time devoted to the English Language Arts block on instructional strategies involving vocabulary.

Considering studies of the vocabulary instruction observed in actual classrooms, it appears that there remains a great deal of room for improvement, both in terms of time spent on instruction and in methods. The sorts of powerful vocabulary instruction documented in the research described in the next section of the chapter needs to become more common, vocabulary instruction needs to become more frequent in academic areas such as science and social studies (see, for example, Torres & Zeidler, 2002), and something needs to be done to help students with relatively small vocabularies catch up with their classmates. Given the focus on vocabulary acquisition in the Common Core State Standards, we are hopeful that these changes will begin to take place in the near future.

EFFECTIVE VOCABULARY INSTRUCTION

In this section, we first briefly characterize the research on effective vocabulary instruction for ELLs and then describe a multifaceted approach to vocabulary instruction that consists of the following components: providing rich and varied language experiences, teaching individual words, teaching word-learning strategies, and fostering word consciousness.

While we know a great deal about teaching vocabulary to native English-speaking students, and while the topic of vocabulary occupies an increasingly significant place in second-language theory and pedagogy, we know far less about teaching vocabulary to ELLs. In a review of peer-reviewed research conducted between 1980 and 2009, a limited number of experimental studies were located that focused on vocabulary outcomes for ELLs (Avila & Sadoski, 1996; Biemiller & Boote, 2006; Block, 2008; Bos, Allen, & Scanlon, 1989; Carlo et al., 2004; Collins, 2006; Elley, 1991; Filippini, 2007; Giambo & McKinney, 2004; Gunn, Smolkowski, Biglan, Black, & Blair, 2005; Neuman & Koskinen, 1992; Pérez, 1981; Perozzi, 1985; T. Roberts, 2008; Roberts & Neal, 2004; Townsend & Collins, 2009; Ulanoff & Pucci, 1999; Vaughn, Cirino, et al., 2006; Vaughn, Mathes, et al., 2006; Weitz, 2003; Zhang & Schumm, 2000). Many of the instructional approaches that were used in these studies built on approaches proposed for first-language learners (Graves, 2006; National Reading Panel, 2000; Stahl & Nagy, 2006). However, there were exceptions. For example, a study by Giambo and McKinney (2004) found improved vocabulary for ELL kindergartners with phonemic awareness instruction, perhaps because this program included the introduction of some new words; and at early stages of language acquisition, high-quality English interactions may be effective in promoting vocabulary development.

While most studies built on methods used with English-proficient students, many studies also restructured the instructional tasks to better meet the specific needs of ELLs (e.g., Avila & Sadoski, 1996; Bos, Allen, & Scanlon, 1989; Carlo et al., 2004; Filippini, 2007; Klinger & Vaughn, 2000; Perozzi, 1985; T. Roberts, 2008; Townsend & Collins, 2009; Ulanoff & Pucci, 1999; Vaughn, Cirino, et al., 2006; Vaughn, Mathes, et al., 2006) by using students' first language to help them learn vocabulary in English, providing additional scaffolding and reinforcement, and differentiating instruction, topics that are discussed further at the end of this chapter. In the remainder of this section, we list each of the four components of a comprehensive vocabulary program listed above and described in Chapter 1 and make a series of research-based generalizations, supporting each generalization with a representative study or several studies.

Throughout the activities that take place during comprehensive vocabulary instruction, students should be given ample opportunities and encouraged to communicate with English-proficient speakers for it is in this way that second languages are predominately acquired (Ellis, 2005).

Providing Rich and Varied Language Experiences

Language is primarily acquired incidentally, through listening, talking, and reading. Thus, to the extent possible, teachers need to immerse students in language-rich environments that provide them with many opportunities to acquire language. Children can be exposed to rich language through having text read aloud to them, their own reading of texts, and media such as television.

Shared Book Reading. As noted in the Introduction, one method that has been used frequently and successfully to develop vocabulary in children is shared book reading in which adults read aloud to children, periodically stopping to highlight and discuss individual words as well as other aspects of what they are reading. Research with native English speakers indicates that this method has an impact on oral language outcomes, including vocabulary, grammar, and listening comprehension (Wasik & Bond, 2001; Zevenbergen & Whitehurst, 2003). The same appears to be the case for ELLs (Biemiller & Boote, 2006; Carlo et al., 2004; T. Roberts, 2008; Roberts & Neal, 2004; Silverman, 2007). In a study with young ELLs, Roberts and Neal (2004) compared small-group comprehension-oriented instruction, which consisted of shared book reading, vocabulary instruction, and comprehension activities, with emergent literacy instruction, which consisted of naming and writing letters and recognizing and generating rhymes. Findings indicated that children in the comprehension-oriented instruction outperformed children in the emergent literacy instruction in vocabulary and print concepts, while emergent literacy instruction resulted in better letter-naming and writing. Additionally, English oral proficiency was more correlated with the comprehension-related skills than with the decoding-related skills.

There is evidence that shared book reading can be an effective component for programs for older learners as well. In a study conducted by Carlo et al. (2004), a 15-week intervention was designed to build breadth and depth of vocabulary knowledge and reading comprehension in 254 bilingual and native English-speaking children from nine 5th-grade classrooms in four schools in California, Virginia, and Massachusetts. The intervention used immigration as a theme. Each weekly lesson began with shared reading of one of a variety of text genres, including newspaper articles, diaries, first-hand documentation of the immigrant experience, historical accounts, and fiction. In accordance with research indicating that words are best learned from rich semantic contexts, target words were selected from the brief, engaging reading passages. Twelve words that students at this level were likely to encounter repeatedly across texts in different domains were introduced each week. Although there were relatively few words introduced each week, activities helped children make semantic links to other words and concepts and thus to attain a deeper and richer understanding of each word's meaning, as well as to learn other words and concepts related to the target words. The lessons also taught students to infer meanings from context and to use roots, affixes, cognates, morphological relationships, and comprehension monitoring. All the strategy instruction used the reading passages as a springboard. Findings indicated that the ELLs did better in generating sentences that conveyed different meanings of multi-meaning words, in completing cloze passages, on tests of knowledge of word meanings, and on measures of word association and morphological knowledge. On a cloze test used to evaluate comprehension, students showed significant improvement, but the impact on comprehension was much lower than on vocabulary. These results indicate that this multifaceted training led to improved knowledge of the words studied.

In Chapter 3, we discuss several shared book readings in some detail. We want to note that this is an extremely important type of vocabulary instruction for children who enter school with relatively small vocabularies and that a number of studies have shown that shared book reading can successfully teach word meanings. However, these results must be taken as encouraging rather than definitive. All of the studies have been relatively short, and few of them have taught anything like the number of words that less advantaged students need to learn in order to catch up to their more advantaged peers. Instruction that successfully bridges this gap will need to extend over several years and help students acquire many more words than have been acquired in studies thus far.

Independent Reading. One great advantage of independent reading is that it has the potential to expose learners to massive amounts of vocabulary in a variety of registers that may not be available through spoken language. This clearly affords rich learning opportunities. There is ample evidence to show that incidental learning of vocabulary through reading does occur for both native English-speaking students and ELLs.

For example, Nagy, Anderson, and Herman (1987) had English proficient students read four natural passages and found that the probability of students learning a word well enough to answer a multiple-choice question was .05. They went on to note that even though the probability of learning a word from context is small, given the volume of texts students can potentially read, they could learn a very large number of words from context. Based on their findings, they estimated that the average middle-grade child learns between 800 and 1,200 words from context annually. As a cautionary note, the authors also pointed out that their study revealed "no learning from context for words at the highest level of conceptual difficulty."

Based on a meta-analysis of 20 studies that examined how native English-speaking students learn from context when not directly prompted to do so, Swanborn and de Glopper (1999) concluded that students can and do learn words incidentally, and that the probability of learning a word from one exposure in a naturally occurring context is .15. They also showed that students at higher grade levels and students with higher reading ability are better able to use context, and that texts containing fewer unknown words better facilitate learning from context.

Research conducted with ELLs indicates that silent sustained reading in which students select and regularly read books of their choice for a period of time each day leads to improvements in comprehension and oral language development (Elley, 1991; Tudor & Hafiz, 1989).

With regard to ELLs, an important question is what students learn about vocabulary through reading. Schmitt (2010, p. 30) argues that "incidental vocabulary learning from reading is more likely to push words to a partial rather than a full level of mastery, and that any recall learning is more prone to forgetting than recognition learning." Additionally, incidental acquisition appears to include only content words—function words are generally not attended to. These limitations may explain why even very advanced second-language learners continue to manifest lexical errors in such areas as the use of prepositions and collocations. Finally, research with ELLs indicates that independent reading along with structured support for comprehension and language development facilitates ELLs' language development to a greater degree than reading that is not accompanied by such activities (Laufer, 2003).

A related issue concerns the number of exposures to a word or expression needed for incidental acquisition to occur. Summarizing the research, Schmitt (2010, p. 31) concluded that "8–10 reading exposures may give learners a reasonable chance of acquiring an initial receptive knowledge of words." However, the number is likely to be highly variable depending on a variety of factors such as the language proficiency of the readers, the difficulty of the texts, and the conceptual difficulty of the words. It will also depend on the depth of processing involved when readers encounter words. "Exposure" may involve no more than fleeting attention to a word, or it may involve more deliberate attempts to process the form and meaning of the word.

All in all, these studies of learning from context show that context can produce learning of word meanings for both native English speakers and ELLs, that the probability of learning a word from a single occurrence is low, and that the probability of learning a word from context increases substantially with additional occurrences of the word. In giving students books to read on their own, it is important to ensure that the texts are ones they can read with accuracy, fluency, and good comprehension.

Television. Research with native English speakers indicates that educational television programs can be a source of language learning for these students (Linebarger, 2000; Van Evra, 1998). Several studies have also found that exposing ELLs to high-quality television can also be effective in developing their vocabulary. For example, Neuman and Koskinen (1992) found that middle-grade ELLs who watched captioned episodes of *3-2-1 Contact,* a high-quality science program, outperformed their classmates who just read from their science textbooks on measures of word recognition, understanding sentences, and word meaning. In addition, these students also performed better than their classmates who watched the television program without captions. It should also be noted that only ELLs with sufficient English proficiency benefited from the television programming, indicating the need to consider this variable when designing instruction.

In a similar study, Uchikoshi (2005) found that watching *Arthur*, a television program that emphasizes narrative storytelling, improved Spanish-speaking kindergarten ELLs' oral language development more than watching *Between the Lions*, a television program emphasizing phonics. Taken together, these studies indicate that ELLs may benefit from increased exposure to rich language experiences using media such as television. It seems likely that similar material presented digitally on the Web and on the various pad devices now available will have similar results.

Teaching Individual Words

There is a large, robust, easily interpretable, and very consistent body of research on teaching individual words to native English-speaking students as well as a number of summaries of the research on vocabulary instruction. These include traditional reviews of research by Petty, Herold, and Stoll (1968), Graves

(1986), Mezynski (1983), Beck and McKeown (1991), Blachowicz and Fisher (2000), the National Reading Panel (2000), and Graves and Silverman (2010), and a meta-analysis by Stahl and Fairbanks (1986). As noted above, the research on ELLs is less robust but is generally consistent with the first-language research.

These studies lead to several generalizations. In organizing them, we proceed from considering effects that can be achieved by brief and relatively shallow instruction to effects that can be achieved from more lengthy and more robust instruction.

Some vocabulary instruction is better than no instruction (Petty, Herold, & Stoll, 1968). Although this is a commonsense finding, it is not a trivial one. It means that vocabulary instruction typically works. However, thin instruction—for example, giving students a set of words and asking them to look up the words in the dictionary, or giving them a set of words and their definitions—only serves to teach the basic meanings of the words. That is, simply giving students definitions of words will not result in their learning rich and full meanings. For example, recent findings from research conducted by August (2010) found that 2nd-grade Spanish-speaking ELLs learned vocabulary from exposure to the vocabulary with comprehensible definitions embedded in text, but did not learn vocabulary that they merely heard in the context of a shared book reading lesson. In this study, the vocabulary words taught in various conditions were matched for difficulty level, so findings are attributable to method rather than word types.

Instruction that incorporates both definitional information and contextual information is likely to be more effective than instruction incorporating only one sort of information (Mezynski, 1983; Stahl & Fairbanks, 1986). While simply having students work with definitions of words can improve their word knowledge, giving them both definitional information and contextual information, has repeatedly proven to be a stronger approach. In fact, except in situations where there are far too many unknown words in an upcoming selection to teach and you are forced to simply give students a glossary, using a procedure that gives students both definitional and contextual information is the thinnest approach we recommend.

Two recent studies with ELLs have shown the advantages of including both definitions and context. In one of them August (2010) found that 2nd-grade Spanish-speaking ELLs learned vocabulary from exposure to the vocabulary with comprehensible definitions embedded in the text during shared book reading, but learned the words less well than they did with instruction that included both definitions and context. Various activities were used to develop context for the targeted vocabulary, including introducing it as a lesson objective, using picture cards to clarify its meaning, reinforcing it through discussion during daily shared interactive reading, and reviewing it through the use of glossaries. In another study (August, Artzi, & Mazrum, 2010) in which 30 teachers in 18 schools implemented an intervention to develop the academic vocabulary of 509 3rd- and 4th-grade ELLs, findings indicated that instruction that included both definitions and context was much more effective than instruction in which students were only provided with child-friendly definitions of the target academic vocabulary. Again, various activities were used to develop context for the targeted vocabulary, including introducing it as a lesson objective; using picture cards to clarify its meaning; reinforcing it through discussion during daily shared interactive reading; and reviewing it through the use of glossaries and concept maps.

Instruction that involves activating prior knowledge and comparing and contrasting word meanings is likely to be more powerful than simple combinations of contextual information and definitions (Baumann, Edwards, Boland, Olejnik, & Kame'enui, 2003; Beck & McKeown, 1991). Such instruction has also been shown to improve comprehension of selections containing the words taught. The best known and most widely researched techniques falling in this category are semantic mapping (Heimlich & Pittelman, 1986) and semantic feature analysis (Pittelman, Heimlich, Berglund, & French, 1991). In a study with upper-elementary-grade, learning-disabled, bilingual students, Bos, Allen, and Scanlon (1989) found that semantic/feature analysis led to significantly higher vocabulary scores than more traditional vocabulary instruction, and that semantic mapping led to significantly higher comprehension scores than more traditional vocabulary instruction.

More lengthy and robust instruction that involves explicit teaching that includes both contextual and definitional information, multiple exposures to target words in varied contexts, and experiences that promote deep processing of words meanings is likely to be more powerful than less time-consuming and less robust instruction. Working with native English speakers, Beck and McKeown and their colleagues have developed, refined, and repeatedly tested several forms of rich vocabulary instruction that involve students in extensive and varied experiences with words (Beck & McKeown, 2004; Beck, Perfetti, & McKeown, 1982; McKeown, Beck, Omanson, & Perfetti, 1983; McKeown, Beck, Omanson, & Pople, 1985). Researchers who work with ELLs (August, Artzi, & Mazrum, 2010; August et al., 2009; Calderón et al., 2005; Carlo et al., 2004; Lawrence, Capotosto, Branum-Martin, White, & Snow, 2011; Mancilla-Martinez, 2010; Silverman, 2007; Snow, Lawrence, & White, 2009) have also developed, refined, and tested forms of rich vocabulary instruction that generally have consisted of:

- introducing words through the rich context of authentic children's literature or grade-appropriate expository text;
- clear, student-friendly definitions and explanations of target words;
- questions and prompts to help students think critically about the meaning of words;
- examples of how words are used in other contexts;
- opportunities for younger children to act out the meaning of words when applicable;
- visual aids illustrating the meaning of words in authentic contexts other than the book in which the word was introduced;
- encouragement for students to pronounce, spell, and write about words;

- opportunities for students to compare and contrast words;
- repetition and reinforcement of the target words;
- and activities that develop word consciousness such as listening for word meanings as text is read aloud.

A series of recent studies (Dalton, Proctor, Uccelli, Mo, & Snow, 2011; Proctor, Dalton, & Grisham, 2007; Proctor, Uccelli, Dalton, & Snow, 2009; Proctor, Dalton, et al., 2011) with Spanish-English bilinguals and native English-speaking 4th- and 5th-grade students in high-poverty schools has investigated the effects of rich vocabulary instruction delivered via the Internet. In one intervention (Proctor, Dalton, et al., 2011), students read eight multimedia texts and received embedded vocabulary instruction on 40 "power" words. The intervention, termed Improving Comprehension Online (ICON), embodied a variety of features, including

> Spanish translations of all texts and directions; human read-alouds of each text in English and Spanish; English monolingual and Spanish-English bilingual pedagogical "coaches"who provided assistance with using the system and responding to prompts; a revisable electronic work-log that collected student responses; a multimedia glossary; and pictures illustrating the narrative and informational text content. (Proctor, Dalton et al., 2011, p. 524)

In comparison to a control group, there were significant intervention effects on a standardized measure of vocabulary and researcher-developed measures of vocabulary depth, but not on comprehension or on researcher-developed measures of vocabulary breadth.

Taken together, these studies clearly show that rich instruction in which students have multiple thoughtful encounters with words is very worthwhile, and that more encounters with words produce better learning than fewer encounters. However, it needs to be remembered that rich instruction comes at a huge cost. Instruction of this kind may require up to 30 minutes per word and involves activities outside of class as well as in class. Considering the number of words that ELLs need to learn to close the gap with their native English-speaking peers, we cannot provide rich instruction for all of the words we need to teach.

Teaching Word-Learning Strategies

The three word-learning strategies most frequently recommended for native English speakers are teaching students to use context to infer the meanings of unknown words, teaching students to use word parts to glean word meanings, and teaching students to use the dictionary. There is a fair amount of research on using context and word parts (Baumann, Font, Edwards, & Boland, 2005; Beck & McKeown, 1991; Fukkink & de Glopper, 1998; Graves, 1986; Kuhn & Stahl, 1998; Swanborn & de Glopper, 1999), but very little research on teaching students to use the dictionary. The second-language research literature is much more limited, but has investigated teaching students these strategies as well as helping students use cognate knowledge to uncover unknown word meanings of second-language cognates (Shanahan & Beck, 2006; August & Shanahan, 2010a). As was the case for other vocabulary methods, the second-language studies generally taught strategies as part of a multifaceted vocabulary program, making it difficult to disentangle the effects of strategy instruction from that of other methods. Nevertheless, like all students, ELLs must master word-learning strategies—using context, using word parts, using the dictionary, and using first cognate knowledge when students' native language shares cognates with English. However, mastering word-learning strategies is particularly important for ELLs because they have so many words to learn (Carlo, August, & Snow, 2005).

Context Clues. As Sternberg (1987) suggests, "Most vocabulary is learned from context." In our judgment, and in the judgment of most other vocabulary researchers, no other explanation can account for the huge number of words students learn. Relevant studies on context clues include descriptive research on students' ability to use context to learn the meanings of unknown words, a topic that was discussed in the section above on rich and varied language experiences. The next question for educators is, "Can students be taught to better use context to learn the meanings of unknown words?" As Baumann, Edwards, Boland, Olejnik, and Kame'enui (2003) point out, not all instruction in using context clues has been successful. In fact, teaching students to use context clues is a challenging task. Still, there have been some notable successes.

Two studies by Baumann and his associates (Baumann et al., 2002; Baumann, Edwards, Boland, Olejnik, & Kame'enui, 2003) are the most ambitious to date. In both studies, native English-speaking students were taught contextual analysis and morphological analysis. In the 2002 study, results indicated that students in both the contextual group and the morphemic group were better able to glean the meanings of transfer words on an immediate test, but not on a delayed test. In the 2003 study, results indicated that students receiving the experimental treatment were more successful at inferring the meanings of novel affixed words and at inferring the meanings of morphologically and contextually decipherable words on a delayed test, but not on an immediate test.

Fukkink and de Glopper (1998) conducted a meta-analysis of 21 studies of instruction in context clues with native English speakers. In their analysis, they distinguished five types of instruction, including:

1. instruction centering on one or more context-type clues,
2. instruction in which students are asked to complete cloze tests,
3. instruction focused on developing a general strategy to infer word meaning from context with explicit reference to clue types,
4. instruction directed at helping students develop a general schema to conceptualize a definition, and
5. instruction involving practice only, without any specific guidance about how to infer the meanings of the words.

Findings indicated a significant positive effect (medium effect size of .43) for instruction deriving word meaning from context. Of the five types, clue instruction was superior to the other types.

In a recent study with ELLs by Carlo et al. (2004), inferring meaning from context was one of several strategies taught. During interactive reading, teachers read books aloud, discussed chunks of each page as they read, and used think-aloud procedures to model how context could be used to infer the meaning of unknown words. Students then practiced inferring meaning for those target vocabulary words whose meaning could be inferred from context. In an activity subsequent to the interactive reading, students worked in pairs using context clues in a new set of sentences to figure out which target words belonged in each sentence.

Unfortunately, it is clear that both native English speakers and ELLs experience considerable problems in inferring meaning from context. Frantzen (2003) identified a number of reasons why this is the case for ELLs and concluded that students should maintain a "healthy skepticism about the trustworthiness of contexts because they can suggest a variety of meaning" (p. 185). She argued that students need to make efforts to verify the inferences they make based on context, a position supported by her finding that students exhibited higher rates of retention from inferring when they also consulted a dictionary.

Given the limited amount of research with ELLs and the fact that context instruction for ELLs has generally been one component of a multifaceted vocabulary program, it is difficult to reach any definite conclusion about the usefulness of such instruction. It seems unlikely that such training will work for ELLs when they are confronted with texts that are too linguistically difficult for them, as they are unlikely to be able to process sufficient information from context to guess the meaning of a word. However, training in inferring meaning from context may be effective if the text level is controlled. Finally, any consideration of a role for strategy training needs to distinguish the role it plays in fostering comprehension of a text and the role it plays in vocabulary acquisition. It cannot be assumed that the guessing from context that assists comprehension will necessarily result in the acquisition of new words. If a word can be guessed easily, little attention to its form is needed with the result that it may not be retained. If the aim is to increase vocabulary through reading, vocabulary acquisition might be enhanced if ELLs are motivated to attend to words they don't know and use all the resources at hand to determine a word's meaning, including context as well as the other strategies listed below.

Word Parts. Considerations about teaching word parts can be conveniently grouped according to three questions: What elements might we consider teaching? What elements do students know? And what are the effects of instruction in these elements? Here we consider each of these in turn.

The elements that we might consider teaching students are the same for both native English speakers and ELLs and include inflections, derivational suffixes, prefixes, and Latin and Greek roots. Inflections are suffixes that modify a base word by changing grammatical features such as tense, number, and aspect. Examples include the plural marker *-s* in *houses* and the past tense marker *-ed* in *wanted*. Inflections do not change the part of speech or the basic meaning of the word. Derivational suffixes are suffixes that modify root words, changing the part of speech and to some extent meaning. Examples include *-less* in *worthless* and *-able* in *adorable*. Prefixes are elements that are attached to the beginnings of words and change the word's meaning. Examples include *un-* in *unhappy* and *re-* in *replay*. Latin and Greek roots are non-English words that are sometimes used as parts of English words. Examples include *tract* meaning "pull," as in *attract* and *extract*, and *voc* meaning "call," as in *advocate* and *equivocate*.

Children learning in their first language learn inflectional suffixes well before entering school and thus do not need to be taught them. Conversely, 1st-grade children show little competence in recognizing derivational suffixes, and although competence increases with age, even some high school students show little knowledge of some of them. There is some evidence that derivational suffixes can be taught, and thus these suffixes are a reasonable target of instruction as students progress through school. Many upper-elementary students do not know even the most common prefixes, and there is good evidence that prefixes can and should be taught in the upper-elementary grades (White, Power, & White, 1989). The situation with Latin and Greek roots is more problematic for the following reasons: There are hundreds of roots that might be taught; most roots are not used in a great many English words; the relationship between the original Greek or Latin meaning of a root and its meaning in an English word might be vague; and roots are variously spelled, making them difficult for students to notice in words. Nevertheless, the CCSS recommends that students begin using common, grade-appropriate Latin and Greek roots as clues to word meanings in the 4th grade.

ELLs will not have learned as many inflectional suffixes as native English speakers prior to school entry. A recent study with 4th- and 5th-grade Spanish-speaking ELLs (Kieffer & Lesaux, 2007) examined the role of derivational suffixes in students' reading comprehension and found that between 4th and 5th grade, awareness of these derivational suffixes became a more significant predictor of reading comprehension.

Although not all studies conducted with English-proficient students focusing on the use of word parts to unlock the meanings of unknown words have produced positive results, in general the results have been good. A recent meta-analysis of three types of morphological awareness interventions in English—those that focused on awareness of inflections, derivational suffixes, and compound words for school-age children synthesized data from 17 published and unpublished studies (Goodwin & Ahn, 2010) and found an overall effect of .44 on literacy outcomes, with significant effects for morphological awareness, vocabulary, phonological awareness, phonological recoding, and reading comprehension. Eleven studies had vocabulary outcomes with a large and significant effect size of 1.04. The Goodwin and Ahn review identified 14 teaching strategies. The most common was teaching students the meaning of prefixes, suffixes, and roots as well as to identify these units within morphologically complex words. Other interventions taught children to build morphologically complex words from cards containing prefixes, roots, and suffixes (Berninger et al., 2003); taught morphological patterns and rules (Roberts, F. A., 2008); helped students identify the words within compound words (Lovett et al., 2000); taught the grammatical role of morphemes (Nunes et al., 2006); helped students break words into morphemes (Harris, 2007); and taught about word origin (Henry, Calfee, & Avelar-LaSalle, 1989).

In one recent study (Lesaux, Kieffer, Faller, & Kelley, 2010), a text-based academic language program was implemented in classrooms with high numbers of ELLs and former ELLs. Students were exposed to words in text, were introduced to additional meanings of the words, engaged in morphological analysis of different forms of the words, and used the words in their own writing. Findings indicated that students learned the meanings of the words they were taught and improved in morphological awareness. The principles that guided Lesaux and her colleagues' morphology instruction were: teach morphology in the context of rich, explicit vocabulary instruction; teach students to use morphology as a cognitive strategy with explicit steps; teach the underlying morphological knowledge both explicitly and in context; and for Spanish-speaking students, teach morphology in relation to cognate instruction.

As with previous methods described in this chapter, it is impossible to determine which aspects of morphological instruction are most effective in improving literacy outcomes because too many studies involved morphological strategies from multiple categories (Goodwin & Ahn, 2010).

The Dictionary. Relevant studies here include investigations of what students understand from typical dictionary entries and investigations of how to improve dictionary entries. For native English speakers, dictionary definitions alone are not sufficient to help students understand word meaning, because the definitions are deliberately decontextualized. While there are no studies with ELLs, we posit that this is even more true for ELLs because of their limited depth and breadth of vocabulary knowledge.

In one study illustrating the difficulty native English speakers have with dictionary definitions, Miller and Gildea (1987) investigated the ability of 5th- and 6th-grade students to generate appropriate sentences after reading traditional dictionary definitions. Results indicated that over 60% of the sentences students constructed were judged to be odd, often because students appeared to select only a fragment of the definition on which to base their sentence. For example, based on the dictionary definition of *eroding* including the phrase "eating out," one student generated the sentence, "My family erodes a lot." In another study with 4th- and 6th-grade English-speaking students, Scott and Nagy (1997) investigated the effects of modifying traditional definitions by using everyday English that clarified the subject and object of the verb being defined, rather than the conventional format, and by including an illustrative example. Results indicated that neither type of modification significantly affected students' performance, and that even the performance of high-ability 6th-grade students was far from perfect.

A study by McKeown (1993) with 5th-grade native English speakers was more successful. She examined the effects of traditional definitions and definitions revised in a very systematic and principled way, creating what she called "student-friendly" definitions. For example, the traditional definition for *conspicuous* was "easily seen," while the revised definition was, "describes something you notice right away because it stands out." Students showed improvement in a task that required them to write sentences after reading traditional and revised definitions, and on a task requiring them to answer questions about the meaning of words.

In summary, using the dictionary to define words is possible but difficult, even for native English speakers, and some traditional dictionary entries can be improved significantly. Given these results, it appears that ensuring all students, including ELLs, use newer dictionaries that have been revised to ensure second-language definitions are student friendly would be important. For ELLs, dictionaries that provide entries in students' first language, student-friendly first-language definitions, student-friendly English definitions, and examples of the target words in sentences that further clarified target word meaning might be helpful. Additionally, teaching ELLs to more effectively use dictionaries to learn word meanings might be useful. See Chapter 5 on word learning strategies for information about dictionary use.

Using Cognate Knowledge. Recognizing and using cognates—words that are similar in the student's native language and in English—has been shown to be an important strategy for ELLs whose first language shares cognates with English (Kamil & Hiebert, 2005). ELLs' ability to use cognate knowledge is mediated by developmental factors, the typological or perceived distance between the first and second languages, and students' knowledge of the word's meaning in their first language (Dressler & Kamil, 2006).

Teaching children to take advantage of their cognate knowledge can be a powerful tool for Spanish-speaking ELLs, because many English words that are cognates with Spanish are high-frequency Spanish words, but low-frequency English words. Thus, students are likely to know both the concept and the label in Spanish but lack the English label. Moreover, many cognates (*infirm/enfermo; profound/profundo*; and *fortunate/afortunado*) are important to know, are characteristic of mature language users, and appear frequently across a variety of domains.

Several studies have examined the effect of teaching students to use their first-language knowledge in inferring the meaning of unknown second-language words that are cognates (August, 2009; August, Branum-Martin, Cardenas-Hagan, & Francis, 2009; Carlo et al., 2004). For example, in the Vocabulary Improvement Project (Carlo et al., 2004), English-proficient and Spanish-speaking ELLs worked together to figure out which words in their reading passages were cognates and to jointly define them. In a study designed to assess the extent to which students in the Vocabulary Improvement Project used their knowledge of cognates in inferring word meaning, Dressler, Carlo, Snow, August, and White (2011) found that cognate performance depended to some extent on the characteristics of cognate pairs, including the degree of phonological transparency between the cognates and the degree of orthographic overlap shared by the cognate pair. Additionally, their findings indicate that even students who are not literate, but are orally proficient in Spanish, might benefit from instruction in cognate awareness.

It is important to acknowledge that while in most cases cognate knowledge is helpful, in some cases it may result in ELLs inferring the wrong meaning to unknown words, as when words are false cognates (look and sound alike in both languages but do not have any of the same meanings) or when the words share some meanings in common but not the meaning required in a particular context (García, 1991).

Fostering Word Consciousness

Scott and Nagy (2004) suggest that word consciousness can be thought of as the metacognitive or metalinguistic knowledge that a learner brings to the task of learning, as well as an interest in and awareness of words. Word consciousness includes several types of metalinguistic awareness such as morphological awareness, syntactic awareness, and semantic awareness, which help students acquire specific words. It also entails a facility for learning words in general. An awareness of words involves "an appreciation of the power of words, an understanding of why certain words are used instead of others, a sense of the words that could be used in place of those selected by a writer or speaker," and cognizance of first encounters with words (Graves & Watts-Taffe, 2008).

Word consciousness is a concept that has only relatively recently been articulated. As a consequence, there is little research that directly demonstrates the effectiveness of word consciousness. Nevertheless, there are various sorts of evidence that strongly suggest its importance. For one thing, vocabulary theorists and researchers (Anderson & Nagy, 1992; Baumann & Kame'enui, 2004; Beck, McKeown, & Kucan, 2002, 2008; Blachowicz & Fisher, 2004; Graves, 2006; Scott & Nagy, 2004; Stahl & Nagy, 2006) strongly support the inclusion of word consciousness as an integral and necessary part of an effective vocabulary program.

Another sort of evidence is the importance of motivation to all learning and for all students (Malloy, Marinak, & Gambrell, 2010), from kindergartners (Pressley et al., 2003b) to high school seniors (National Research Council, 2004). Students simply do not learn much unless they are motivated to do so, and if they are going to accomplish the huge task of learning something like 50,000 words by the time they graduate from high school, they absolutely must be motivated to do so.

Still another sort of evidence comes from vocabulary studies. In a series of relatively informal studies undertaken over a 7-year term, Scott and her colleagues (Scott, Butler, & Asselin, 1996; Scott & Nagy, 2004; Scott, Skobel, & Wells, 2008) investigated the effects of a project called The Gift of Words, in which they provided students with an enriched focus on words in their reading, writing, and discussion. Results supported the effectiveness of this program on students' use of interesting words in their writing and on students' awareness and interest in words more generally. In other studies, word consciousness was an important part of multifaceted vocabulary programs designed to improve native English speakers' reading vocabulary and reading comprehension (Beck, McKeown, & Omanson, 1987), native English speakers' use of vocabulary in their writing (Duin & Graves, 1987), and ELLs' general proficiency in vocabulary (Carlo et al., 2004; Lesaux et al., 2010). All of these programs produced positive results.

In summary, while word consciousness is a recently articulated concept and does not have an extensive research base, experts in the field, the importance of motivation to learning, and several research studies support including it as a component of the vocabulary curriculum.

Important Considerations for ELLs

For a number of years, vocabulary received relatively little attention in second-language instruction, with grammar being the major focus (Folse, 2004; Long & Richards, 2001). Recently, however, that situation has changed; while experimental research focused on developing vocabulary in ELLs is limited, vocabulary occupies an increasingly significant place in second-language theory and pedagogy (August & Shanahan, 2006a). As we have already noted, much of the instruction appropriate for teaching vocabulary to students who are native speakers of English suggests an appropriate place to start in teaching vocabulary to ELLs (Graves, 2006). However, as we have also noted, there are some special factors to consider.

Bootstrapping on first-language knowledge and skills. The first special factor is that many ELLs have a well-developed first language that can be used to support learning in the second language. There are instructional routines that, although focused on the teaching of English vocabulary, make effective use of the students' first language. Examples of these include previewing and/or reviewing storybook reading in students' first language (T. Roberts, 2008; Roberts & Neal, 2004; Ulanoff & Pucci, 1999), teaching vocabulary in students' first language prior to teaching it in their second (Perozzi, 1985), conducting instructional conversations that permit some interpretation to take place in the home language (August, 2009), using bilingual glossaries for the targeted vocabulary (August et al., 2009; Carlo et al., 2004), and providing instruction in the transfer of cognate knowledge from a first language to a second (August et al., 2009; Carlo et al., 2004).

Foundational English vocabulary. Another important factor to consider is that ELLs need to develop a basic oral and reading vocabulary of the most frequent English words. Many of these words are words that native English speakers will have in their vocabulary when they enter school. Several second-language scholars suggest a list of about 2,000 words (Cummins, 2003; Nation, 2001; Schmitt, 2000), and the most commonly recommended list is *The General Service List* (West, 1936/1953). More recently, Sales and Graves (2009c) have suggested a somewhat larger and much more recent list, *The First 4,000 Words,* based on the work of Hiebert (2005) and Zeno, Ivens, Millard, and Duvvuri's (1995) *Word Frequency Guide.* As Folse (2004) has noted and as we will discuss in Chapter 4, there are several other lists that can also be useful, and using a list does not necessarily mean simply teaching the words from the beginning of the list to the end. Teachers can use lists, for example, as guides to what words to teach and what words probably do not need to be taught.

Of course, students need a vocabulary much larger than 2,000–4,000 words. To succeed in school and once they leave school, students need a large vocabulary that includes academic English (Cummins, 2003; Snow, Lawrence, & White, 2009), a vocabulary of words that are used in school texts and other readings for students and adults. Although native English speakers also need a large vocabulary of academic English, it is likely to be easier for native speakers to acquire these words because they already have foundational English vocabulary that helps them learn from context.

It is now becoming clear that vocabulary knowledge also involves knowledge of multiword units. Simpson-Vlach and Ellis (2010) have set out a pedagogically useful list of formulaic sequences for academic speech and writing for adults. First, they identified frequently occurring 3-, 4-, and 5-word units in a representative body of oral and written academic English. They then constructed a measure of teaching worth based partly on frequency, partly on teachers' evaluations of whether the units constituted formulaic expressions and were worth teaching, and partly on a measure that indicates the extent to which the items appear in a coherent sequence. The result was a core list of academic sequences, as well as separate lists for oral and written sequences sorted into functional groupings, including referential expressions (for example, *based on, such as the*), stance expressions (for example, *the importance of, tell me what*), and discourse-organizing expressions (for example, *what happens is, in order to*). At present, we know of no intervention studies that explore effective methods to teach ELLs in elementary and secondary schools high-frequency multiword units. However, researchers at the Center for Applied Linguistics have developed a list of educationally relevant multiword units that appear frequently in text in grades K–12, which may form the basis for intervention studies (August, 2011).

Repetition and reinforcement. Reinforcement of learned material that provides students with repeated exposures to words, concepts, and skills has been long known to be effective for strengthening learning. Reinforcement may be particularly important for ELLs because many ELLs will have less exposure to English words outside the school environment than their native English-speaking peers. In studies on vocabulary, reinforcement often takes the form of revisiting material in ways that differ from the initial encounter. For example, in a study with young ELLs, Roberts and Neal (2004) reinforced the meanings of new vocabulary through the use of real-life objects, drama, art activities, and fostering understanding of the important events in a story through a picture-sequencing activity. Carlo et al. (2004) reinforced word knowledge through several post-reading activities with target vocabulary, including cloze tasks that drew students' attention to the multiple meanings of some words, word association tasks, synonym/antonym tasks, and semantic feature analysis. They also recycled words learned in earlier lessons in later ones. Part of the success of these instructional efforts was surely the amount of guided and varied repetition students received.

Scaffolding. Scaffolding refers to support that teachers provide to students to allow them to successfully carry out tasks that are beyond their independent abilities. With the teacher's guidance and support, students are able to increase or extend their academic skills. For students learning content in a new language, scaffolding is particularly important (August & Shanahan, 2008; Graves & Fitzgerald, 2009). Across the experimental studies reviewed here, various scaffolding methods were used. Examples included using guides and materials that explicitly address concepts in basal readers that might be confusing for second-language learners (Pérez, 1981); creating opportunities for children to act out meanings of words and using visual aids that illustrate the meanings of words in authentic contexts other than the book in which the word is introduced (August et al., 2009; Silverman, 2007); aligning independent reading materials to children's level of reading and second-language proficiency with support prior to and during reading, and creating opportunities for teacher-student interaction around books to make them comprehensible during reading (August et al., 2009); and providing a model of a process, task, or assignment before requiring students to undertake it, previewing material prior to questioning students, and using graphic organizers (August, 2010).

Differentiating instruction. It is important to keep in mind that students' development of literacy is influenced by a range of individual factors, including age of arrival in a new country, educational history, SES, and cognitive capacity (August & Shanahan, 2006a). This point is highlighted by the differential effects of instruction on students of different ages (such as the differences in word learning described in this book), with differing degrees of English proficiency (Neuman & Koskinen, 1992), and varied ability to read (Block, 2008).

The studies examined here provide clues as to how to successfully differentiate instruction for individual ELLs:

- by building on first-language proficiency and literacy (Carlo et al., 2004),
- by considering levels of English proficiency as well as levels of first-language literacy (Saunders, 1999),
- by accommodating the needs of older learners who have recently arrived in the United States (August et al., 2009), and
- by taking into account individual differences in learning ability and rates (Gunn et al., 2005).

However, given the diverse needs of children, there is very little experimental research that provides specific guidance about how to accommodate the diverse needs of students within a single classroom or school.

A FINAL WORD

Given the difficulty of deciding just what will be counted as a word and what level of word knowledge should count as knowing a word, it is difficult to say exactly how many words students know or need to learn. However, there is good evidence that the texts and other reading materials students could encounter over the 13 years of schooling contain over 180,000 word families, that average students learn to read something like 3,000–4,000 words each year, and that average students acquire reading vocabularies in the neighborhood of 50,000 words by the time they graduate from high school. To accomplish this very significant task, students need all the help that we can give them. There is also good evidence that

ELLs need even more of our assistance if they are to catch up with their native English-speaking peers in knowledge of English vocabulary.

Although the vocabulary instruction provided in schools has typically not been strong, either for native English speakers or for ELLs, it is improving. Providing ELLs with the assistance they need in building rich and powerful vocabularies means several things. First, it means assuring that ELLs acquire a basic vocabulary of the more frequent words, a vocabulary of about 4,000 words. While this is only a fraction of the words they must eventually learn, the 4,000 or so more frequent words account for approximately 75% of the words students will meet, even in adult texts, and an even larger percentage of the words students will encounter in texts for the lower grades and in oral English. Second, it means teaching a number of words beyond these 4,000 very frequent words. For the most part, these will be medium-frequency words or words for understanding what ELLs are read-ing, listening to, or otherwise studying in class. Third, it means teaching ELLs word-learning strategies—using word parts, context, cognates, and the diction-ary to glean word meanings. Powerful instruction is needed to teach these strate-gies. Fourth, it means assisting ELLs in becoming word-conscious, kindling their interest and enjoyment in words and furthering their metalinguistic awareness of words so that they become eager and knowledgeable word learners. Fifth, it means organizing classrooms and schools in ways that give ELLs opportunities to interact with native speakers of English (Ellis & Wells, 1980; Johnson & Swain, 1998). Finally, it is important to remember that the assistance we provide for ELLs can build on effective instructional methods used for native English-speaking stu-dents but that many ELLs will need to be taught more words, will need to spend more time on vocabulary, and will need instruction that builds on their strengths and takes into consideration the fact that they are learning in a second language.

Providing Rich and Varied Language Experiences

We undertook 2 1/2 years of observing 42 families for an hour each month to learn about what typically went on in homes with 1- and 2-year-old children learning to talk. The data showed us that ordinary families differ immensely in the amount of experience with language and interaction they regularly provide their children and that differences in children's experiences are strongly linked to children's language accomplishments.

Betty Hart and Todd Risley,
Early Childhood Researchers

In this very brief summary of their findings, Hart and Risley are talking about the vastly different preschool language experiences of English-only children, experiences that vary hugely depending on the volume of language they hear in their homes. However, although there are indeed vast differences in the preschool language experiences of English-only children, these are nothing compared to differences between the early English-language experiences of English-only children and those of English language learners. While many ELLs come from homes where a language besides English is spoken and are advantaged in this way, many have had less exposure to English than children in homes where only English is spoken. Not surprisingly, therefore, many young ELLs have English vocabularies far smaller than those of their English-only classmates from similar homes (Vagh, Pan, & Mancilla-Martinez, 2009). It is therefore crucial that we do everything possible to provide ELLs with rich and varied language experiences in English—rich experiences in listening, discussion, reading, and writing. This of course does not preclude the continued development of children's first language, an important asset that should be nurtured throughout their lives.

This chapter has two aims. First, it describes approaches to promoting incidental word learning that should be used with all ELLs. Second, it describes a procedure for directly building oral vocabularies for those ELLs who enter school with oral English vocabularies that are considerably smaller than those of their English-only peers—an approach we term "shared book reading."

PROMOTING INCIDENTAL WORD LEARNING

Children cannot build rich and powerful vocabularies without reading a great deal. In fact, over time, wide reading makes the single largest contribution to vocabulary development, more than do listening, discussion, or writing (Cunning-ham & Stanovich, 1998). However, wide reading is by no means the only language experience students need to build rich and deep vocabularies. In addition to read-ing widely, students need other language experiences: They need to hear spoken language in a wide variety of situations. They need to engage in frequent discus-sions in which they interact with other students, with teachers, and with other mature or more proficient language users in real communicative situations. And they need to write frequently, for writing provides the opportunity and the incen-tive to focus closely on words and choose just those words that will best convey their intended message to the intended audience. In the remainder of this section of the chapter, we discuss promoting incidental word learning though listening, discussion, reading, and writing. In the earliest years, there will be more listening and discussion; in the later years, more reading and writing. For ELLs learning in English, even in the later years, there should continue to be many opportunities for listening and discussion as well as reading and writing. Moreover, opportuni-ties for reading and writing should begin as early as possible.

Listening

In promoting students' incidental word learning through listening, your most powerful tools are the vocabulary you use in the classroom and your oral reading. Whatever grade or proficiency level you teach, it is worthwhile making a deliber-ate effort to include some new and somewhat challenging words in your interac-tions with students. Selecting just which words to focus on is a challenging task, and it is a topic we discuss in some detail in Chapter 4. Briefly, however, by "new and somewhat challenging words," we generally mean words that are fairly fre-quent, that are used by mature language users, and that students are likely to encounter in the texts they will read in upcoming years. Of course, the words you want to introduce to students differ from one grade and proficiency level to another. The ones to focus on are those that are not known by many students at the level you are teaching and are thus a bit of a stretch, but not too much of one. For beginning ELLs, these might be words like *favorite* and *locate*. For intermediate ELLs, they might be ones like *deliberately* and *minimum*. And for advanced ELLs, they might be ones like *complex* and *optional*. Note that at this point we are not talk-ing about teaching these words; we are simply suggesting using somewhat chal-lenging words from time to time, occasionally pausing to explain their meanings but often just letting students hear them. For example, if you have recently taught the word obvious and a 4th-grade ELL with intermediate skills announced that the answer to the math question was obvious, it would be a good idea to tell her that *obvious* is a great word to describe an answer that is easy to supply. Similarly, you might tell a group of 7th-graders with advanced skills who have just come in from lunch and brought with them their cafeteria conversations that all those *decibels* are not needed in classroom. The goal is to expose students to some new, fairly fre-quent, and somewhat challenging words and to pique their interest in such words.

As we just explained, the other major opportunity for building students' listening vocabulary comes when you are reading to them. Reading to children from books that they find interesting and enjoyable and that include a few new and somewhat challenging words deserves considerable attention and should be a daily activity in the primary grades, and one that continues beyond the primary grades. The importance of reading to children has been recognized for a number of years. In 1985, the Commission on Reading, a group of scholars assembled by the National Academy of Education and the National Institute of Education, concluded that "the single most important activity for building the knowledge required for eventual success in reading is reading aloud to children." Moreover, the report continued, "it is a practice that should continue throughout the grades" (Anderson, Hiebert, Scott, & Wilkinson, 1985). Shortly after this, long-time proponent of reading aloud to children Jim Trelease (1989) observed that "a large part of the educational research and practice of the last twenty years confirms conclusively that the best way to raise a reader is to read to that child." Solid support for reading aloud to students continues today with, for example, the National Educational Association sponsoring a Read Across America Day each spring. Something to keep firmly in mind when reading to ELLs is to use scaffolding techniques to help ensure that children understand what they are hearing. Such techniques include pointing to the pictures as the book is being read, pausing to define words, stopping to summarize short passages, and asking children ongoing questions to ensure that they have grasped the meaning of the text. Of course, a variety of new technologies make it possible for children to hear a story read without a teacher having to read it.

Discussion

In addition to being read to, children need to engage in a good deal of discussion, give-and-take conversations in which real issues are considered (Duke, Pearson, Strachan, & Billman, 2011). Discussion gives children an opportunity to take an active role in building their receptive and expressive vocabularies. There is evidence, however, that discussion, particularly high-quality discussion, is not prominent in U.S. schools. This is particularly the case in schools serving ELLs (Torgesen et al., 2007).

There are several characteristics of good discussions. Among those identified by Applebee, Langer, Nystrand, and Gamoran (2003) are these four:

- Asking questions that elicit actual discussion, not simply right and wrong answers.
- Creating free exchanges of information that last longer than 30 seconds.
- Verbally encouraging students, modeling how to take a position, and showing students how to express opinions or explore personal reactions.
- Making connections across time and subjects.

Additionally, for ELLs as for all students, while it is important to expose students to grade-appropriate text, it is important to use scaffolding techniques to help these students understand the text. In some cases (particularly with informational text) it will be important to build the requisite background knowledge before students encounter the text (August & Shanahan, 2010a).

ELLs are likely to benefit from conversations they have with native English speakers. Casual conversations will of course be of some benefit, but it is also important to engage ELLs in discussions that will prompt them to use academic language. The key to having discussions that will prompt students to use more academic language is to select appropriate topics and to ensure rich discussion across the content areas. If students are going to use sophisticated words, they need to discuss sophisticated ideas. This means talking about academic topics that students have some familiarity with—topics they are reading about, investigating in the library and on the Internet, and probably writing about. Such discussions might focus on science topics such as the ecology of freshwater lakes, social studies topics such as barriers to ordinary people running for public office, and sophisticated literary topics such as the motivations that prompt a character's actions. One good source of discussion topics is the list of informational texts suggested in Appendix B of the Common Core State Standards (CCSS, 2010a).

Reading

In promoting students' incidental word learning through reading, considerations include recognizing the importance of wide reading, helping students select books that will promote vocabulary growth, and facilitating and encouraging their reading widely. Most words are learned from context, and the richest context for building vocabulary in students beyond the primary grades is books. Books, as Stahl and Stahl (2004) so aptly put it, are "where the words are," a fact well illustrated in Figure 3.1. As can be seen, even children's books contain about one-third more rare words than prime-time adult TV shows and nearly twice as many rare words as adult conversational speech. If we want to help students increase their vocabularies, we need to get them to read more (Anderson, Wilson, & Fielding, 1988; Elley, 1996; Trelease, 2006). Some reading, of course, can and should be done in class. We very strongly recommend some sort of in-class independent reading program in the elementary grades, particularly if the students are not avid readers. But there is only so much class time available. To really build their vocabularies, students need to read a lot outside of school. Unfortunately, both our informal conversations with teachers and students and empirical evidence indicate that many children do very little reading outside of school (Anderson et al., 1988; Baer, Baldi, Ayotte, & Green, 2007; National Center for Educational Statistics, 1992; National Endowment for the Arts, 2007). For example, in their study of how 5th-grade students spend their time out of school, Anderson and his colleagues (1988) found that 50% of the children read from books less than 4 minutes a day and 30% of the children read from books less than 2 minutes a day. Similarly, data gathered by the National Center for Educational Statistics (1992) show that about one-fourth of the students questioned reported reading no books outside of school in the previous month. These students, the ones who read no books outside of school or read books outside of school for only a few minutes a day, are almost certainly those most in need of building their vocabularies. Moreover, data reported by the National Endowment for the Arts (2007) indicate that teens and young adults are reading less today than they did in the past.

The starting point for encouraging wide reading is a well-stocked classroom library, a library with books that you know well, books appropriate for the various

FIGURE 3.1. Frequency of Rare Words in Various Sources

	Rare Words per 1,000
I. Printed texts	
Abstracts of scientific articles	128.0
Newspapers	68.3
Popular magazines	65.7
Adult books	52.7
Children's books	30.9
Preschool books	16.3
II. Television texts	
Prime-time adult shows	22.7
Prime-time children's shows	20.2
Mister Rogers and *Sesame Street*	2.0
III. Adult speech	
Expert witness testimony	28.4
College graduates' talk to friends/spouses	17.3

Source: Adapted from Hayes & Ahrens, 1988.

levels of readers in your classroom, and books that include appropriately challenging vocabulary. As Figure 3.1 suggests, newspapers and magazines are also valuable parts of the classroom library and are likely to contain the sort of challenging words students need to learn. Additionally, some students already have access to Kindles, iPads, and similar devices, and soon these devices may be available in many classrooms. They can provide students with convenient access to a huge variety of books and other resources. While ELLs often face the problem that books in their first language are not widely available, the new devices will make it more likely that students will have access to many more materials produced in their first languages. Thus, one task that teachers, schools, and communities face is doing everything possible to make texts presented via a variety of media widely and conveniently available for students.

While nothing can replace the immediacy and convenience of a classroom library, as children progress through elementary school and into the secondary grades, school and community libraries become increasingly important. Unfortunately, in poorer neighborhoods, classroom libraries, school libraries, and even community libraries are likely to have very meager resources (Neuman & Celano, 2001).

Of course, books need to be at an appropriate reading level. Several quantitative tools exist to help you select the proper level of texts for students, including the Dale-Chall Readability formula (Chall & Dale, 1995); the Lexile Framework for Reading, available at lexile.com; and Coh-Metrix, available at cohmetrix.memphis.edu/. The latter may be the best indicator for ELLs reading in English because it focuses on the cohesiveness of a text rather than solely on word familiarity and sentence length.

But just having books at the appropriate level available is not enough. Something must be done to entice children to read the books. Many possibilities exist here. Teachers of young children can read books aloud and then invite children to take the books home to reread. Teachers at all grade levels can read parts of books in class and encourage students to read the rest of the book at home. Teachers at all grade levels can give book talks that preview and advertise books the same way movie trailers advertise upcoming films. Students can be encouraged to share the books they read with each other. Teachers can become familiar with individual students' interests and with individual books and thus recommend particular books to particular students. Students can be required to do some reasonable amount of reading outside of class. Also, some sort of in-class independent reading activity can be undertaken, particularly for students who, even with all of your efforts, are not likely to do much reading outside of school. Whether you call it DEAR (Drop Everything and Read), SSR (Sustained Silent Reading), or USSR (Uninterrupted Sustained Silent Reading), for students who do not read out of school, some sort of ongoing, structured, long-term in-school silent reading program is something to consider. Recent research with ELLs indicates that encouraging students to read has improved literacy outcomes (August & Shanahan, 2006a). For example, in one study (Tudor & Hariz, 1989), providing extensive additional reading time outside the school day resulted in gains for a treatment group of 10- and 11-year-old ELLs but not a control group.

Finally, since most words are learned from context, it is important to give ELLs strategies they can use to help learn word meanings when reading in their second language. Researchers have identified a variety of strategies that older readers employ when they elect to process a word. Among the many strategies available are using first-language cognate knowledge, knowledge about word parts, information beyond sentence boundaries, background knowledge, and dictionaries (Paribakht & Wesche, 1999). We discuss these and other word-learning strategies in detail in Chapter 5.

Writing

The keys to promoting students' independent word learning through writing are similar to those for promoting discussion. Students need to write about topics that they care about and that are at least somewhat sophisticated. Additionally, as noted in the CCSS, students should be encouraged to write about the content they are studying. They also need to write with a purpose and for an audience. This is the case because it is only when you are writing with a real purpose and for an audience that you have identified and care about that you are likely to ask the most important questions about the words you use in your writing. Here, for example, are some questions you might pose about words to intermediate or advanced ELLs:

- Is this the best word to get across my meaning?
- Is the word precise enough?
- Is it appropriately formal or informal?
- Is it a word my reader will know?

- Is it a word my reader will find interesting?
- Have I used it too much? Should I use a synonym?

Similar but simpler questions can be used with younger or less advanced students. The goal is to get students to realize that the words they use in their writing are very important, that the words they use will affect both the clarity of what they write and the reaction their writing receives from others, and that they should choose words wisely, honing their word choices as one of the last steps in editing their writing.

DIRECTLY BUILDING PRIMARY-GRADE ELLs' ORAL VOCABULARIES

In this second major section of the chapter, we turn from the matter of indirectly promoting word learning, something that is necessary for all ELLs and at all grade levels, to directly building children's oral vocabularies, something that is particularly necessary in the primary grades and continues for many ELLs beyond the primary grades, especially for ELLs who enter school with much smaller vocabularies than their English-only peers. In kindergarten, most children can't read. And in 1st and 2nd grade, they certainly do not read a lot. If children are going to learn a significant number of new words, they are going to have to learn them through oral language activities. And the most powerful oral language activity that has been developed for use in classrooms is shared book reading, which can be done with human readers or with computer-based instruction.

Over the past 30 years, there have been a number of naturalistic studies of mothers reading to their preschool children. And over the past 20 years, there have been a number of experimental studies in which researchers, teachers, parents, and aides used specific procedures in reading to children with the goal of building their vocabularies, comprehension, and language skills more generally. Here, we call both the informal procedures mothers use and the more formal ones used in school "shared book reading." The findings of studies on both types of shared book reading are very positive and highly consistent and serve to highlight the characteristics of effective approaches to building oral vocabulary in this way. Below, we discuss these characteristics and give some examples of them, drawing heavily on the work of De Temple and Snow (2003) as well as our own synthesis of the literature.

Before continuing, however, we should note that for some ELLs, shared book reading in their first language followed by reading in English is more effective than reading only in English (T. Roberts, 2008). Skills and knowledge acquired in a first language will transfer to English (Genesee, Geva, Dressler, & Kamil, 2006). Also, when shared book reading is done in English, it is important to scaffold instruction to ensure that ELLs understand the story (August & Shanahan, 2010a).

Commonalities of Effective Shared Book Reading

The various types of shared book reading have a good deal in common. Here we list those commonalities. After that, we identify four shared book reading programs and describe one of them in some detail.

Effective shared book reading is interactive. That is, both the reader and the children play active roles. The reader frequently pauses, prompts children to respond, and follows up those responses with answers and perhaps more prompts. Children respond to the prompts or questions, elaborate in some of their responses, and perhaps ask questions of their own. Additionally, the interactions are frequently supportive and instructive (Weizman & Snow, 2001). In other words, the reader scaffolds children's efforts to understand the words and the text, as illustrated in the following excerpt of an adult discussing a segment of Judith Viorst's *Alexander and the Terrible, Horrible, No Good, Very Bad Day* (1972) with two 1st-grade ELLs.

Teacher: Can you remember why he was having a horrible day?
Luis: He wanted to go to Australia.
Teacher: Why did he want to go there?
Priscilla: Some people had nice things so he had terrible things and that's why he wanted to go to Australia.
Teacher: Can you remember some of the terrible things?
Luis: He had to sleep in his striped pajamas.
Priscilla: And he hates it.
Teacher: Any other reasons he had a horrible day?
Priscilla: His brother; they had shoes and I forget what else.
Teacher: And they had shoes and his shoes weren't as nice.
Luis: He didn't want to sleep with his tiger.

Effective shared book reading involves reading the book several times. This allows the children and the reader to revisit the same topic and the same words several times, and it allows the children to begin actively using some of the words they have heard and perhaps had explained in previous readings.

Effective shared book reading directly focuses children's attention on a relatively small number of words. In some cases, the word work comes before the reading, in some cases during the first reading, in some cases during subsequent readings, and in some cases after the book has been read.

Effective shared book reading requires the adult readers to read fluently. Skilled adult readers effectively engage children with their animated and lively reading style.

Effective shared book reading requires carefully selected books. The books need to be interesting and enjoyable for children, and they need to include some challenging words that are worth studying and will enhance children's vocabularies.

There are, as we have noted, several different programs of shared book reading developed for native English-speaking children. One of the earliest programs developed was Dialogic Reading (Whitehurst et al., 1988, 1994; Zevenbergen & Whitehurst, 2003). This is a one-to-one picture-book shared book reading technique designed for preschoolers. It can be used by teachers, teacher aides, other caregivers, and parents to foster vocabulary development and language development more generally. There are two videotapes designed to train parents and teachers to use dialogic reading (*Read Together, Talk Together* [Parent Video], 2002a,; [Teacher Training Video], 2002b). Words in Context (Biemiller, 2001, 2009; Biemiller & Boote, 2006) is a shared book reading technique intended for kindergarten through 2nd-grade children. The procedure includes some very direct instruction, more direct than that provided in some of the other approaches. Also, Words in Context differs from some of the other approaches in that vocabulary development is the sole concern. Another and much different shared reading program, *Text Talk*, was developed by Beck and McKeown (2007) and is available as a commercial program (Beck et al., 2005). The program is particularly strong in providing robust and interesting instruction. It differs from other shared reading programs in that it teaches considerably more sophisticated words. Still another program—*The First 4,000 Words*—is described just below. Additionally, in Chapter 7, where we describe several empirically validated vocabulary programs for ELLs in some detail, we describe the *Acquisition of Vocabulary in English* program (August, 2011), a program in which shared book reading plays a major part.

The First 4,000 Words

The First 4,000 Words (Fehr et al., 2011; Graves, Sales, & Davison, 2009; Graves, Sales, & Ruda, 2008; Sales & Graves, 2009c) is an individualized, Web-based program for ensuring that ELLs and other 1st- through 4th-grade children with very small oral vocabularies learn the ~4,000 most frequent English words. Results of a pilot study that taught 100 words indicated that students in the Web-based treatment condition significantly ($p < .01$) outperformed students in the control condition, with an effect size of 1.1 (Fehr et al., 2011). Results on a second study in which students completed as much of the entire program as they could in approximately 2 months indicated that students who studied a word missed on the pretest were 1.6 times more likely to answer it correctly on the posttest if they encountered it in the online lesson than if they did not (Davison, 2011).

The program is based on the fact that the English language includes a relatively small number of frequent words, which together make up the vast majority of running words in anything children read. For example, the first 100 words account for about 50% of the words students will encounter, the first 1,000 words about 70%, and the first 5,000 words about 80%. Just how important it is to know these words is shown in Figure 3.2, which shows an intermediate-grade text and how much of it children could read if they knew the 500, 1,000, 2,000, or 4,000 most frequent English words.

As can be seen, even with a vocabulary of only 500 words, a student could read a lot of the words in this text. However, she would not be able to read nearly enough words to comprehend it. Once a student has acquired a vocabulary of

FIGURE 3.2. Intermediate-Grade Passage Showing What Students Could Read If They Knew the Most Frequent 500, 1,000, 2,000, and 4,000 Words

Panel 1: Knowing only the 500 most frequent words, a student could read only the words shown here:

Could it be an _____? The year before, _____ had seen one for the first time when his mother took him to a _____ _____ in _____, _____ _____. He had _____, _____, as the _____ a _____ by _____ on the _____ of a _____ that was _____ on the _____. Now _____ an _____ was right here in _____, and about to _____ over his house. Not _____ to _____ a thing, _____ the _____ and _____ up the _____ of the house to its _____. From there he had a good _____ of the _____, _____ the _____ place. And in the _____, _____ ever_____, he saw the _____.

Panel 2: Knowing the 1,000 most frequent words, a student could read the words shown in this version:

Could it be an _____? The year before, _____ had seen one for the first time when his mother took him to a _____ in _____, _____. He had watched, _____, as the _____ gave a _____ by _____ on the _____ of a _____ that was _____ on the ground. Now maybe an _____ was right here in _____, and about to _____ over his house. Not _____ to _____ a thing, _____ opened the window and _____ up the _____ of the house to its _____. From there he had a good view of the _____ River, _____ past the _____ place. And in the sky, coming ever _____, he saw the _____.

Panel 3: Knowing the 2,000 most frequent words, a student could read the words shown in this version:

Could it be an airplane? The year before, Charles had seen one for the first time when his mother took him to a flying _____ in _____, Virginia. He had watched, _____, as the _____ gave a _____ by _____ oranges on the _____ of a _____ that was _____ on the ground. Now maybe an airplane was right here in _____, and about to fly over his house. Not _____ to _____a thing, Charles opened the window and climbed up the _____ roof of the house to its _____. From there he had a good view of the _____ River, _____ past the _____ place. And in the sky, coming ever closer, he saw the plane.

Panel 4: Knowing the 4,000 words, a student would be able to read all the words in the version below that are not in italics:

Could it be an airplane? The year before, Charles had seen one for the first time when his mother took him to a flying *exhibition* in Fort *Myer,* Virginia. He had watched, *enthralled,* as the pilot gave a bombing *demonstration* by dropping oranges on the outline of a *battleship* that was traced on the ground. Now maybe an airplane was right here in Minnesota, and about to fly over his house. Not wanting to miss a thing, Charles opened the window and climbed up the sloping roof of the house to its peak. From there he had a good view of the Mississippi River, flowing *languidly* past the *Lindbergh* place. And in the sky, coming ever closer, he saw the plane. (Giblin, 1997, p. 3) about 4,000 words—with the help of the teacher and some use context—she can begin to comprehend texts of this sort. The purpose of *The First 4,000 Words* program is to help students build the basic oral vocabulary they need to support a basic reading vocabulary.

The specific words used in *The First 4,000 Words* program is a set of approximately 3,600 words taken from *The Educator's Word Frequency Guide* (Zeno, Ivens, Millard, & Duvvuri, 1995), the most recent large-scale word frequency count of American English, and modified from work conducted by Hiebert (2005). The complete word list and additional information on the program are available at thefirst4000words.com.

This is how the program works:

- Students are pretested in intact classrooms with a paper-and-pencil test to see which students qualify for the program. Even in classrooms with a number of ELLs, many of the students will already know these words, and only a half a dozen or so students are likely to qualify for the program.
- Based on their pretest results, qualified students are placed in the program at the level at which they know about 80% of the words.
- Students move through the program at their own pace, and can move up or back depending on their performance on online pretests on each of 360 units, each of which deals with 10 words.
- In each unit, students are only taught those of the 10 words that the online pretest indicates they do not know.
- Following the pretest, the student participates in three shared reading experiences. In Shared Reading 1, the passage is visible to the student with the missed words highlighted, and it is read to the student without interruption. In Shared Reading 2, the student has a variety of options for interactive work with the words she missed. In Shared Reading 3, the student listens to the story again and has four options: listen to a sentence again, listen to the definition of a word, hear the passage again, or move on.
- The shared reading experiences are followed by two games centering on the words missed and a unit posttest that is identical to the unit pretest. If a student does well on the posttest, she moves on to the next 10-word unit. If she does not do well, she participates in a remediation activity.

The four panels in Figures 3.3 show various aspects of the program.

Panel One shows the Treehouse Studio. This is where the student is pretested on the 10 words from each unit. In this example, the student hears the word *clock* and presses the picture of the clock to show her understanding.

Panel Two shows the Cozy Cave, the virtual environment in which the shared reading is done. The student begins her shared reading experience with each story by clicking on the image of the Cozy Cave.

Panel Three shows the second of the three shared reading sessions. The student missed six words on the unit pretest—*build, everyone, fire, remember, table,* and

FIGURE 3.3. The Treehouse Studio, the Cozy Cave, a Shared Book Reading Lesson, and a Word Game

Panel One: The treehouse studio

Panel Two: The cozy cave

Panel Three: A shared book reading lesson

Panel Four: A word game

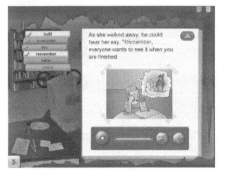

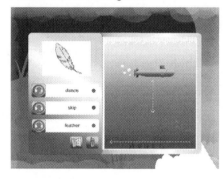

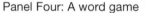

voice—and thus concentrates on these words. In this example, the student clicked on *remember,* and the sentence you see appeared on the screen and was read aloud to her. The student then has the options of clicking on the button at the bottom left and saying the word, clicking on the microphone button and hearing what she said, and clicking on the check button to see if she got it correct. Work with the other words is similar.

Finally, Panel Four shows a typical game following the three shared readings. Clicking on the correct word, in this case *feather*, makes the submarine go faster and deeper, earning points that show up on a counter. It the student wants to hear a word, she clicks on the microphone button. If she wants a hint, she clicks on either of the help buttons at the bottom.

While assisting English learners in learning the 4,000 most frequent English words is going to take a considerable period of time—months and years, not days and weeks—doing so is well worth the time spent. Without these words, there are few texts a student can read; with these words, the world of reading opens up to her. Of course, most children will not start at the beginning of the list; they will know many of the most frequent words and begin at some point well into the list.

A FINAL WORD

Building English language learners' English vocabularies is extremely important, and building young ELLs' oral vocabularies is especially important. Schools have not given much attention to building students' oral vocabularies, at least up until very recently. While many students need help building oral vocabularies, doing so is particularly important for ELLs who arrive at school with small vocabularies. We can help all children—whether they are ELLs or native English speakers—build their oral vocabularies by reading aloud to them, using some sophisticated vocabulary in talking to them, complimenting and encouraging them when they use words well, and discussing sophisticated topics that invite and even demand sophisticated vocabulary. We can also help all children build their reading vocabularies by having them read and write frequently. And we can particularly help ELLs who enter school with small vocabularies by using shared book reading activities such as Dialogic Reading, Words in Context, *Text Talk,* and *The First 4,000 Words.*

In concluding this chapter, we want to note that most of the approaches to increasing the oral vocabularies of all children we described are easily implemented. Unfortunately, as we have already noted but want to stress, this is not the case with shared book reading. Programs like Dialogic Reading, Words in Context, and *The First 4,000 Words* require that children most in need of oral vocabulary be identified, that they receive something like 30 minutes of special instruction per day, and that they receive this instruction over a considerable period of time—months and even years. This is difficult and time-consuming, and therefore costly, but is it something that ELLs with very small vocabularies desperately need.

CHAPTER 4

Teaching Individual Words

Consider the power that a name gives a child. Now this is a table and that a chair. . . . Having a name for something means that one has some degree of control. . . . As children get more words, they get more control over their environment. . . . Language and reading both act as the tools of thought to bring representation to a new level and to allow the formation of new relationships and organizations. . . . To expand a child's vocabulary is to teach that child to think about the world.

Steven Stahl and Katherine Dougherty Stahl,
Vocabulary Scholars

Stahl and Stahl (2004) composed this eloquent statement about the importance of words while thinking about all children and not just English language learners. But it is particularly important to recognize its truth for this rapidly growing population of learners. As ELLs' vocabularies grow—in either their native language or in English—so, too, do their abilities to think about their world and to exercise some control over it. And as their English vocabularies grow, so does their skill in comprehending English and in communicating with other English speakers, in school or out. Over their years of schooling, ELLs are faced with learning a truly astounding number of English words, many more than we could possibly teach them one by one. However, the fact that ELLs need to learn more words than we can possibly teach them clearly does not mean that we should not teach them some words. In fact, it is vital to teach ELLs a lot of words.

Teaching individual words pays a number of important dividends. First, and most obviously, teaching a student a word leaves him with one fewer word to learn independently. Second, teaching individual words gives students a store of words that they can use to explore and understand their environment. Third, teaching individual words can increase students' comprehension of selections containing those words. Fourth, teaching individual words can increase the power and overall quality of students' speech, writing, and communications skills. Finally, and very importantly, teaching individual words demonstrates our interest in words, and teaching them in engaging and interesting ways fosters students' interest in words. It is for this reason that the Common Core State Standards specify that students should acquire and use accurately a range of general academic and domain-specific words and phrases sufficient for reading, writing, and speaking.

In this chapter, we describe a variety of effective ways to teach individual words. Using different teaching methods is important for several reasons. For one thing, different words represent different learning tasks. For example, some of the words you teach will be words that are in students' listening vocabularies but that they don't recognize in print; others will be words that they know in their first language but not in their second; and still others will be words that are not in students' listening vocabularies and that represent new and difficult concepts. For another thing, in different situations you will have different goals for teaching a word. In one case, for example, you may just want to introduce a word so that students have some idea of what it means when they see it in an upcoming passage. In another, you will want to give students deep, rich, and lasting meanings for a word. Yet another reason for using different ways of teaching words is that some students will learn best from some methods while other students will learn best from other methods. And yet one more reason for using different methods is to provide some variety for both your students and yourself.

This chapter is divided into four parts. In the first part, Preliminaries on Teaching Individual Words, we discuss several factors to consider as you plan instruction for individual words. In the next three parts, we describe and give examples of Introductory Instruction, Stronger and More Powerful Instruction, and Repetition and Review.

PRELIMINARIES ON TEACHING INDIVIDUAL WORDS

We begin by briefly reviewing three ideas we have previously discussed. First, the task ELLs face in learning English words is a huge one: When proper nouns, multiple meanings, idioms, and other multiword units are considered, the English language consists of something like 180,000 words. ELLs need to learn as many English words as native English speakers, but often they begin the acquisition process later. It is very important that they catch up as quickly as possible so that they can understand what they read and hear in English. This does not mean that they should stop acquiring vocabulary in their first language. For children whose first language shares cognates with English, first-language knowledge is extremely helpful in learning second-language vocabulary. And, of course, bilingualism itself is a real asset.

Second, while no student learns all the words in the English lexicon, achieving students do learn a large number of them. The average native English speaker has learned something like 50,000 word families by the time he graduates from high school.

Third, we can teach words in varying depths: We can provide students with a general sense of the word's meaning, context-bound knowledge, basic knowledge that can be used in a variety of situations, or rich and decontextualized knowledge. How thoroughly we teach a word will depend on how thoroughly students need to know it and how much time we have available. Given the number of words to be learned, it is impossible to always teach meanings in depth.

Now we turn to four new topics: Word-Learning Tasks Students Face, Assessing Word Knowledge, Selecting Words to Teach, and Providing Student-Friendly Definitions.

...g Tasks Students Face

As we have noted, all word-learning tasks are not the same. Word-learning tasks differ depending on such matters as how much students already know about the words to be taught, how well you want them to learn the words, and what you want them to be able to do with the words afterwards. Elsewhere, one of us (Graves, 2009a) has described eight different tasks. Here, we consider four of the most important ones.

Learning a Basic Oral Vocabulary. As noted, many ELLs arrive in school with very limited English vocabularies. For such children, building a basic oral vocabulary of the most frequent English words is of utmost importance, and they need to acquire this vocabulary just as soon as possible. Because learning a basic oral vocabulary is so important, we discussed it at length in Chapter 3; it will not be considered further in this chapter.

Learning More Nuanced Meanings for Known Words. As students are in the process of learning words, they often at first acquire simple and perhaps partial meanings. One major task with ELLs is helping them refine and extend these partial meanings.

Learning New Words Representing Known Concepts. A third word-learning task students face is learning words that are in neither their oral nor their reading vocabularies but for which they have an available concept. For example, the word *flounder* meaning to struggle helplessly is unlikely to be known to many beginning and intermediate ELLs, and the word *ensemble* meaning a group of musicians is unlikely to be familiar to at least some advanced ELLs. But in both cases the concepts are familiar. With words like *flounder* and *ensemble*, students do not need to internalize a new concept. It is for this category of word that first-language cognate knowledge can be most helpful. Students can use their first-language knowledge to figure out the meaning of an English cognate, provided that they have the concept.

Learning New Words Representing New Concepts. A fourth word-learning task students face—and a very demanding one—is learning words that are in neither their oral nor their reading vocabularies and for which they do not have an available concept. Learning the full meanings of such words as *equation, impeach,* and *mammal* is likely to require most ELLs in the elementary grades to develop new concepts, while learning the full meanings of such words as *mass, enzyme,* and *fascist* will require most ELLs in high school to develop new concepts. Note, too, that students whose backgrounds differ from those of the majority culture will have internalized a set of concepts that is at least somewhat different from the set internalized by students in the majority culture. Thus, some words that represent known concepts for native English speakers will represent unknown concepts for some ELLs.

Assessing Word Knowledge

If you are going to spend your time and your ELLs' time teaching individual words, you need to know how your ELLs' vocabularies compare to those of their grade-level peers. You can get some idea of the size of your ELLs' English vocabularies relative to those of the general population of students in the United States by using a commercial test such as the Peabody Picture Vocabulary Test (Dunn & Dunn, 2007) or the Gates-MacGinitie Reading Tests (MacGinitie, MacGinitie, Maria, Dreyer, & Hughes, 2000), both of which are available for a range of ages. By 2014 additional tests—state tests aligned with the CCSS—will be available to measure vocabulary knowledge.

You can also get some idea of your students' knowledge of specific sets of words by using tests of specific sets of words. Here, we describe several tests that can be useful for this purpose.

The Listening Vocabulary Test and the Reading Vocabulary Test. The Listening Vocabulary Test (Sales & Graves, 2009a) is a 40-item, group-administered test that assesses students' knowledge of the most frequent ~4,000 English words. It is intended for elementary students who are not likely to have the majority of the most frequent 4,000 English words in their oral vocabularies. Although it was designed to be used as part of *The First 4,000 Words* instructional program described in Chapter 3 (Graves, Sales, & Ruda, 2008), it can also be used independently of that program. The administrator says a word and children choose the best response from a set of four pictures. The test takes about 30 minutes to give, but because it is given to the class as a whole it is not nearly as time-consuming as individually administered assessments. There are no norms available for the test, but data gathered during its construction indicated that the scores of ELLs were distinctly below those of English-only students. For example, while English-only students knew about 90% of the most frequent 1,000 words on the test, ELLs knew only about 70% of these same words (Graves, Sales, & Davison, 2009). An item from the test is shown in Figure 4.1. The word being tested is *different*.

A companion group-administered test, The Reading Vocabulary Test (Sales & Graves, 2009b), assesses students' ability to read the most frequent ~4,000 English words. It is designed for elementary students who are not likely to have the majority of the 4,000 most frequent words in their reading vocabularies. It too contains 40 items. In taking the test, students view a single picture representing each word and select a word from one of four written alternatives. An item from this test is shown in Figure 4.2. The word being tested is *help*.

Teacher-Made Tests. Another option for testing vocabulary knowledge is to construct and administer your own test. Typically, you construct such a test from a specific group of words, often the potentially difficult words in an upcoming reading selection, a set of words you have taught, or the glossary of a textbook you are planning to teach. This makes it possible to draw conclusions such as, "Elena has not learned the vocabulary I have instructed" or "It looks like my class knows

FIGURE 4.1. Sample Listening Vocabulary Test Item for *Different*

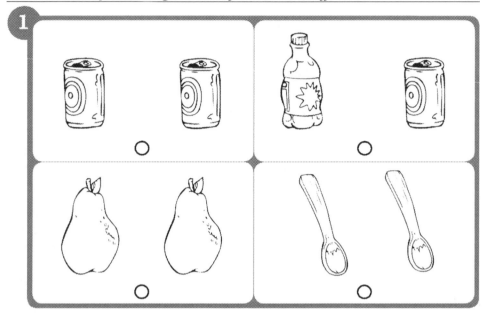

FIGURE 4.2. Sample Reading Vocabulary Test Item for *Help*

about half of the words that are glossed in our health text." One way to construct such a test is to create items that provide a definition without the target word and/ or a sentence that uses the target word in context. Students select the answer from a list of words that includes all the tested target words and several distractors. In constructing such a test, we suggest the following guidelines:

1. Provide a clear and concise definition and context-rich sentence, doing everything you can to keep the words in the definition and in the sentence simpler than the word you are testing.

2. Avoid giving away the correct answer with clues not related to a word's mean-
    ing (e.g., the use of "an" or "a" before a blank lets students know that the
    target word is a noun).
3. While the distractors should be distinctly wrong, they should not be obviously
    wrong.

Examples of two formats for teacher-made tests—one you might use with students who are not proficient English readers and one you might use with students who can read independently in English—are shown in Figure 4.3. These
assessments were developed by researchers at the Center for Applied Linguistics
to assess ELLs' knowledge before and following instructional interventions (Artzi,
Kenyon, August, Barr, Massoud, & Dressler, in preparation). The first assessment
shows what teachers read to students. Students themselves have only the picture
and the choices in front of them. In the second assessment, students read the assessment on their own. In both cases, teachers explain the assessment and students
practice with several easy items before they take the actual assessment.

In addition to testing students on their word knowledge, you can use a test to
inform your knowledge of your students' general levels of vocabulary knowledge.
In constructing such a test, include five or so words you are pretty sure most of
your students know, five or so words you are pretty sure most of them don't know,
and five or so you are uncertain about. If students know most of the words you
think they do, don't know most of those you think they don't, and know some of
the words you are uncertain about, then you have pretty good knowledge of their
vocabularies. If some other pattern occurs, then you need to work to improve your
understanding of which words your students do and don't know.

Student Self-Reporting. When time constraints make it impossible to create an
actual test, there is a satisfactory alternative. Simply create, duplicate, and hand
out a list of words. Give students the list, and explain what they are to do and the
purpose of the exercise. What they are to do is put a check mark beside the words
they know. The purpose of their doing so—and it's really important to stress this—
is for them to indicate whether they know each word so that you can teach those
they don't know. It is not to give them a grade or in any way penalize them for
not knowing some of them. Research showed that English-only students are quite
adept and truthful in identifying words they don't know in this way (White, Slater, & Graves, 1989). Although we have very little information on ELLs' ability at
this task, a study by one of us that included self-assessment of real and nonsense
words suggests that ELLs are also able to differentiate between words they know
and do not know (Mancilla-Martinez, 2010).

Selecting Words to Teach

Once you have gained some information about your students' vocabularies
through assessments, you still have the crucial and challenging task of selecting
just which words to teach. As we explain below, we believe that word lists can

FIGURE 4.3. Teacher-Made Test Items

Listening Item

Put your finger on number 10: This staircase leads to nowhere, which is *weird*. When something is *weird*, is it "harsh," "strange," or "current"? Listen again and bubble in the word that means *weird*: "harsh," "strange," or "current"?

10

Wierd		
O	O	O
Harsh	strange	current

Reading Item

Directions: Fill in the blanks in the sentences below with one of the words from the box. Each word can be used only once.

sustain	convince	infer	concept	factor	contrast
stable	internal	establish	abandon	region	block

1. If something is _____ , it is inside something or someone. *Example: The house has an _____ patio.*

2. To _____ means to keep something going. *Example: I ate a big breakfast to _____ myself during the long run.*

3. A _____ is a general understanding about something. *Example: He understands the _____ of multiplication.*

4. To _____ means to stop something from happening. *Example: I tried to walk home from school on the path but a fallen tree _____ the path.*

5. To _____ means to identify the differences between things. *Example: I can tell the twins apart when _____ their different hairstyles.*

6. A _____ is a part of a country. *Example: I live in the southern _____ of the country.*

7. To _____ means to decide if something is true because of the facts you have. *Example: I _____ that it is cold outside because I see the children wearing warm coats and hats.*

8. If something is _____ it stays the same. *Example: The temperature outside was _____ , it didn't go up or down.*

9. To _____ something means to no longer use it. *Example: The children _____ the playground for the winter because it is too cold to play.*

10. A _____ is one of the things that influence something. Example: *Strong winds were a _____ in the spread of the fire.*

sometimes play a role here—particularly for ELLs with very small English vocabularies—but that much of the vocabulary you teach will come from selections students are reading in your classroom.

Word Lists. Although myriad word lists exist, we see three of them as particularly useful. The most basic list we recommend is one we have already mentioned, *The First 4,000 Words* (Graves, Sales, & Ruda, 2008). It is a slightly modified version of Hiebert's Word Zones™ list (2005) and is simply a list of the roughly 4,000 most frequent word families from the most recent large-scale frequency count of American English, *The Educator's Word Frequency Guide* (Zeno, Ivens, Millard, & Duvvuri, 1995). The words are ordered by frequency, so you can identify and work with smaller sets—the first 500 words or first 1,000 words, for example—if smaller sets fit your needs. The list is available as a PDF at *thefirst4000words.com*. Although many English-only students come to school with all of these words already in their oral vocabularies and will learn to read them over the first several years of school, many ELLs may need to learn these words in English and will need help in getting them into both their oral vocabularies and their reading vocabularies. As Figure 3.2 in Chapter 3 shows, knowing them is essential to reading any but the most basic text.

Marzano (2004) has created a very different list, one that includes content-area words useful at various grade levels. The list as a whole consists of 7,923 terms taken from national standards documents and representing 11 subject areas (math, science, language arts, history, geography, civics, economics, health, physical education, the arts, and technology). The terms in each of these areas are further classified into four grade-level ranges (K–2, 3–5, 6–8, and 9–12). Thus, in all Marzano presents 44 different lists (K–2 math, K–2 science, K–2 language arts, etc.). Examples include *guest speaker* and *picture book* from K–2 language arts; *dividend* and *equilateral triangle* from 3-5 math, and *dollar diplomacy* and *Eisenhower Doctrine* from 6-8 history. As you can see from this example, the list includes multiword phrases and proper words, elements not often included in word lists but certainly elements students need to learn.

The final list we describe here, The Academic Word List (Coxhead, 2000), is an empirically derived list of words that are not among the most frequent 2,000 English words, that are not content-specific words, and that do not appear frequently in narrative texts, but that do appear frequently in expository texts on subjects like history, biology, and psychology. Although the list was constructed using college-level texts, it is divided into 10 sublists, with the first sublist containing the more frequent words and therefore the words most likely to be appropriate for pre-college students. In fact, a few vocabulary programs involving ELLs—Snow, Lawrence, and White (2009), Mancilla-Martinez (2010), Lesaux, Kieffer, Faller, and Kelley (2010), August, Branum-Martin, Cardenas-Hagan, and Francis, 2009—have taught words from this list. It is available as a PDF at www.victoria.ac.nz/lals/resources/academicwordlist/sublists.aspx.

An Online Resource to Identify High-Frequency Words. One very useful online resource for identifying high-frequency words is Word Sift, developed by researchers at Stanford University (http://www.wordsift.com/). Word Sift was created to help teachers, particularly those who work with ELLs, identify vocabulary that appears frequently in the texts they are teaching. When chunks of text are cut and pasted into Word Sift, it identifies the 50 most frequent words in the text, excluding function words. It then displays these words in a Tag Cloud, a visual display that lists the 50 most frequent words alphabetically and indicates the frequency of each word by showing more frequent words in larger type and less frequent ones in smaller type. A sample tag cloud, constructed from the first few pages of Kevin Beals's *Earthworms Underground* (2007), a 3rd–4th-grade science book, is shown in Figure 4.4. Word Sift also enables teachers to mark and sort different lists of words according to instructional purposes. The cloud can, for example, be sorted to show the words' frequency in printed English from common-to-rare and rare-to-common, and it can indicate which of the 50 words shown occur on the Academic Word List, the General Service List (West, 1936/1953), and Marzano's list of content-area vocabulary. Still other functions are described on the Word Sift site itself, which can be used free of charge.

Selecting Specific Words to Teach. Word lists can certainly be of use in identifying vocabulary you might teach. Sometimes, if you are teaching basic vocabulary as is done with *The First 4,000 Words* program described in Chapter 3 or a research-based intervention like those of Snow et al. (2009), Mancilla-Martinez (2010), Lesaux et al. (2010), and August (2011) that we mentioned earlier in this chapter or some of those we describe in Chapter 7, a word list may be your principal source of words to teach. More often, however, you are likely to choose the words you teach from the selections students are reading, using a procedure in which you go through an upcoming selection deciding (1) which words are likely to be unfamiliar to students, (2) which of these are important, and (3) which of these you will actually teach.

In doing so, you may find it helpful to make use of word lists as one source of information influencing what you teach. For example, if you are teaching social studies to intermediate ELLs, you might check the content terms you are considering teaching against Marzano's grade 3–5 or grade 6–8 history list and consider giving particular attention to words that appear on Marzano's list. Or you might use Word Sift or the Academic Word List to help you locate useful words in the text you are teaching.

Unfortunately, many reading selections will contain more difficult words than you have time to teach. Thus, once you have identified potentially difficult vocabulary in a selection students are going to read, there is still the matter of deciding just which ones you will teach. The answers to five questions should be helpful.

- *Is understanding the word important to understanding the selection in which it appears?* If the answer is "yes," the word is a good candidate for instruction. If the answer is "no," then other words are probably more important to teach.
- *Does the word represent an important concept in the subject being studied?* This question applies primarily to informational text. Even if a word is not important to understanding the particular selection being read, it

FIGURE 4.4. Tag Cloud from the Opening Pages of *Earthworms Underground*

Absorbadaptationair**animal**bellybookbreath
breathecantcolddanger**dry**earth**earth**
wormeatfindgo**habitat**
helphighhotimaginelifelike**live**lotmatter**moisture**movemovingneed
organismpersonplaceplantprotectreproduce**seeskinsoil**survive
thinktree**underground**wetwon'tworld

may be worth teaching because it represents an important concept in the discipline.

- *Are students able to use context, structural-analysis skills, or cognate knowledge to discover the word's meaning?* If they can use these skills, then they should be allowed to practice them. Doing so will both help them hone these skills and reduce the number of words you need to teach.

- *Can working with this word be useful in furthering students' context, cognate, structural-analysis, or dictionary skills?* If the answer here is "yes," then your working with the word can serve two purposes: It can aid students in learning the word, and it can help them acquire a strategy they can use in learning other words. You might, for example, decide to teach the word *regenerate* because students need to master the prefix *re-*.

- *How useful is this word outside of the reading selection currently being taught?* The more frequently a word appears in material students read, the more important it is for them to know the word. Additionally, the more frequent a word is, the greater the chances that students will retain the word once you teach it.

As a comment on these five questions, we need to note that they are not independent. In fact, the answer to one question may suggest that a word should be taught, while the answer to another may suggest that it should not. Selecting vocabulary to teach is a challenging and, at least, partly a subjective task. Ultimately, you will need to use your best judgment about which words to teach based on the demands of the reading selection and the needs of your students.

Providing Student-Friendly Definitions

Virtually all effective vocabulary instruction is likely to include a definition. And not any definition will do. Instructional definitions should be what

Beck, McKeown, and Kucan (2002, 2008) have described as "student friendly." Traditional dictionary definitions are often brief, phrased in ways that provide little information to learners, and include words that are more difficult than the word being defined. Such definitions are of little use to students, including ELLs, trying to learn an unknown word. Student-friendly definitions, by contrast, are longer, often written in complete sentences, phrased in ways that are as helpful as possible to second-language learners, and do not include words more difficult than the word being defined. Also, sentences that give an example of the thing named can be a useful add-on to a student-friendly definition. Figure 4.5 shows some examples of both traditional and student-friendly definitions. For ELLs, providing a visual that represents a word and a sentence that explains how it represents the word may be crucial in helping them understand the word's meaning. Finally, providing the word in a child's first language and a brief first-language definition is extremely helpful. Examples of these methods appear below in the section on Definition Plus Rich Context and a Picture. For examples of student-friendly definitions take a look at the *Collins COBUILD New Student's Dictionary* (2005). While most dictionaries do not use student-friendly definitions, the *Collins COBUILD* was developed specifically for ELLs and includes largely student-friendly definitions. Another source of student-friendly definitions and sentences that use the target word in context is Wordsmyth (http://www.wordsmyth.net/).

This concludes our discussion of preliminaries to teaching individual words. The next three sections of the chapter present specific teaching procedures.

INTRODUCTORY INSTRUCTION

As we have explained, the most powerful vocabulary instruction is time-consuming. Unfortunately, with something like 50,000 words ELLs need to learn, you cannot always spend a lot of time on each word you teach. Moreover, often you do not need to. Frequently, it is appropriate and sufficient to give students introductory instruction, instruction that will start them on the long road to learning rich and deep meanings. Here, we describe four types of introductory instruction.

Building Children's Oral Vocabularies

Building children's oral vocabularies was the major topic of Chapter 3 and will not be dealt with in this chapter. However, we do want to once again stress that for ELLs who enter school with small oral English vocabularies, building their oral vocabularies is of utmost importance. As explained in Chapter 3, one important vehicle for doing so is shared book reading, in which teachers read aloud and discuss passages with students. Another way to increase ELLs' oral vocabulary is to create lots of opportunities for them to speak with native English speakers (Johnson, 1983; Klinger & Vaughn, 2000).

FIGURE 4.5. Traditional and Student-Friendly Definitions

Traditional Definitions

Dazzling: Bright enough to deprive someone of sight temporarily. (*Microsoft Word 2004 for Mac*)
Climate: The prevailing weather conditions of a particular region. (*American Heritage Dictionary*, 2001)
Contagious: Transmissible by direct or indirect contact; communicable. (*American Heritage Dictionary*, 2001)

Student-Friendly Definitions

Dazzling: If something is dazzling, it is so bright that it is hard to look at. After lots of long, dark winter days, sunshine on a sunny day is dazzling. (modified from Beck et al., 2002, p. 55)
Climate: Climate is the usual weather of a place.
Contagious: A contagious illness is an illness that you can get by touching people or things that have the illness. The flu is a very contagious illness.

Teaching Students to Read Known Words

The simplest vocabulary teaching task is that of teaching students to read English words that are already in their oral vocabularies. In this case, the student already knows the English word's meaning, he can understand it when he hears it, and he can probably (although not necessarily) use it in speaking. But he can't read it. The basic task for the student is to associate what is unknown, the written word, with what is already known, the spoken word. To establish this association, the student needs to see the word at the same time that it is pronounced. Once this association is established, the student needs to rehearse it repeatedly so that the relationship becomes automatic. Reading digital text sometimes makes this sort of instruction readily available to the student because he may be able to click on the word to hear it pronounced and access its definition.

Providing Glossaries

Providing glossaries is one of the least time-consuming and least interruptive vocabulary teaching techniques available. Glossing can be particularly useful for words that are concrete, infrequent, and not crucial to understanding the text. It entails just three steps:

- Identify key words in a selection students will be reading that they may not know.
- Write a student-friendly definition for each word.
- Give students the glossary, explain how to use it, and model using it yourself.

If possible, glossaries should include translation equivalents in the native language to help students fully understand word meanings.

Glossaries can be created for both fiction and nonfiction selections. For example, a glossary for an intermediate-grade science chapter on ecology might include the words *succession, species,* and *community.* A glossary for intermediate-grade narrative text, on the other hand, is likely to include high-frequency general academic vocabulary like *influence, obviously, constantly, precious,* and *scarcely.* For ELLs, glossaries may need to be created for short passages as well as longer ones.

One of the advantages of glossaries is that they can include quite a few words, more than you would be likely to include with a more direct teaching technique.

Definition Plus Rich Context and a Picture

Unlike Providing Glossaries, the Definition Plus Rich Context and a Picture procedure requires direct teaching on your part. Still, it is a simple and straightforward procedure.

- Create a student-friendly definition and a rich context for the word.
- Display the target word and its definition and have students repeat the word several times. For younger children you can engage students in letter-sound activities that call attention to the written and spoken forms of a word.
- Including an image of the target word whenever possible can markedly improve students' understanding of a word, make the instruction more interesting, and better cement the word in students' memories. Pictures are very helpful and can even be used for abstract terms by finding a picture that demonstrates a word's meaning. With the availability of pictures on the Internet, you have easy access to a huge collection of pictures. It is, of course, very important to select pictures carefully so that they clearly convey the particular meaning of a word.
- Providing opportunities for students to briefly discuss the word can help them remember it, although doing so probably moves the approach out of the Introductory category into the Stronger and More Powerful category. You can pose questions that require students to discuss words in relation to the text they are reading or their personal experience or ask questions that require students to actively analyze words. For ELLs with lower levels of English proficiency, it is helpful to provide sentence stems. For example, in working with the word *lovely*, you might provide the stem "On my walk, I saw a _____." The use of Partner Talk is another way of providing students with an opportunity to use the word in context. In Partner Talk, teachers pair less English-proficient students with students who are more proficient. The teacher poses a question, and then asks student pairs to think for a moment and answer the question. Finally, the teacher asks several pairs to report out their responses. In some cases the teacher can have each partner report on the other partner's response.

FIGURE 4.6. Definition Plus Rich Context and a Picture for the Word *Interpret*

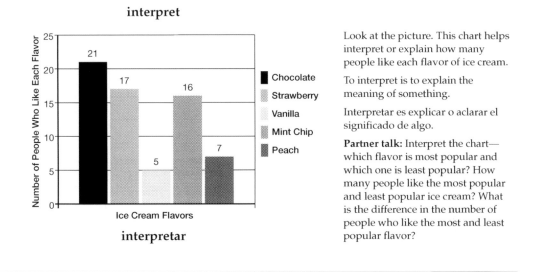

interpret

Look at the picture. This chart helps interpret or explain how many people like each flavor of ice cream.

To interpret is to explain the meaning of something.

Interpretar es explicar o aclarar el significado de algo.

Partner talk: Interpret the chart—which flavor is most popular and which one is least popular? How many people like the most popular and least popular ice cream? What is the difference in the number of people who like the most and least popular flavor?

interpretar

- Providing a native-language equivalent of the target word and its definition is very helpful. If the students' first language shares cognates with English, you can explain the nature of cognates and let students know (or ask them to figure out) which target words are cognates.

A Definition Plus Rich Context and a Picture item for the word *interpret* that might be used with students with fairly advanced proficiency is shown in Figure 4.6, and an item for the word *enthusiasm* that might be used with students with more basic proficiency is shown in Figure 4.7. Note that when used with students with less proficiency, the procedure is more involved and includes some of the elements of rich and powerful instruction.

STRONGER AND MORE POWERFUL INSTRUCTION

As we explained in Chapter 2, we know a great deal about how to create rich and powerful vocabulary instruction. Here are the general principles we listed earlier, reproduced in an abbreviated form:

- Involve students in active and deep processing of the words.
- Provide students with multiple exposures to the words.
- Review, rehearse, and remind students about the words in various contexts over time.
- Involve students in discussions of the words' meanings.
- Spend a significant amount of time on the words, involving students in actively grappling with their meanings.

FIGURE 4.7. Definition Plus Rich Context and a Picture for the Word *Enthusiasm*

enthusiasm

entusiasmo

A word we are going to learn is *enthusiasm*. Enthusiasm is being very excited about or interested in something.

Enthusiasm en español es *entusiasmo*. Si tienes entusiasmo, significa que tienes mucho interés en algo.

Enthusiasm and *entusiasmo* are cognates. They sound alike and have similar meanings.

Whole-class response: Let's all say *enthusiasm* three times.

Let's look at a picture that helps us understand the word *enthusiasm*. The boys and girls are cheering with enthusiasm because their team won.

Model: I play soccer with enthusiasm. I have an interest in soccer because I like running and kicking the ball and trying to beat the other team.

Partner talk: What do you do with enthusiasm? Why? Use the following phrase in your answer: "I… with enthusiasm because…"

Rephrase and Repeat (R&R): Rephrase student's response and have the class repeat the response.

Point to the letters in *enthusiasm*: Let's all spell the word *enthusiasm*. What do the letters say?

As we read, I want you to listen for the word *enthusiasm*. If you hear it, touch your nose!

In this section of the chapter, we describe five rich and powerful techniques for teaching the meanings of individual words. While these techniques build on effective practice for native English speakers, there are alterations that will make them particularly effective for ELLs. First, it is often helpful to introduce these words through the techniques described in the previous section. Second, it is important to provide additional teacher explanation (which can be in students' first language if necessary and possible) to ensure that students understand the procedures and content of the activity and to provide models of the task before requiring students to undertake it (August & Shanahan, 2010a). Third, throughout this activity, if students don't have the requisite second-language vocabulary, you might consider providing bilingual dictionaries, allowing students to respond in their first language and translating for them, and including first-language equivalents for each of the target vocabulary words. Fourth, ensure that ELLs understand the word and the concept it represents through checking student work, asking questions, or administering short, targeted assessments. Fifth, it is important to give ELLs opportunities to interact in English with English-proficient speakers through ongoing discussion with the teacher and peers. As mentioned before, pairing less English-proficient students with more English-proficient students during these activities and explicitly calling for partner work is another good way to provide lots of opportunities for interaction in English.

Each of the rich and powerful techniques we describe here take significant amounts of time, and with all of them the time you spend will pay off in power-

FIGURE 4.8. Four Squares Example for the Word *Buoyant*

buoyant	boats canoes balloons capped bottles
A thing that is buoyant floats	bricks steel nails marbles

ful learning. In general, we have listed the less time-consuming and less power-ful techniques first and the more time-consuming and more powerful ones later. However, all of them are quite powerful and fairly time-consuming.

Four Squares

Four Squares (Schwartz & Raphael, 1985; Stahl & Nagy, 2006) is a straightfor-ward procedure for teaching individual words and the concepts they represent. It is particularly easy to use because it does not require much preparation. Begin Four Squares by asking students to fold a blank piece of paper into four parts or simply draw lines to divide the paper up into four equal sections. At the same time, display a four-square matrix like that shown in Figure 4.8, but blank.

- Have students write the word to be defined in the upper left quadrant. Provide them with a student-friendly definition of the word, but don't have them write it down because they will later be writing their own def-initions. You might ask them to add the first-language equivalent. Here, we use the word *buoyant* in the example shown in Figure 4.8.
- Ask students for some examples of things that are buoyant and record them in the upper right quadrant.
- Some possible responses are shown in the upper right quadrant of Fig-ure 4.8. If you get a response that seems incorrect, lead the class toward a more accurate response. You don't want students to record misinfor-mation.
- After several students have had an opportunity to give examples and you have enough examples to illustrate the concept, ask students for some non-examples, some things that are not buoyant. Record these in the lower right quadrant as shown in Figure 4.8. Again, question any re-sponses that don't seem to work, and record only useful non-examples.
- Finally, ask students to compose their own definitions of *buoyant* and write these in the lower left quadrant of their individual four-square sheets. Once they have done this, have students share their definitions, and add at least one of them to the class four-square sheet.

Four Squares is a good example of a technique that you can expand on as you choose. You can, for example, solicit more examples and non-examples, ask students to explain why their examples and non-examples are good ones, or work with students to make their definitions more precise.

Venn Diagrams

Venn Diagrams (Nagy, 1988) differ from the Four Squares approach in that with Venn Diagrams you compare two terms, in the process figuring out which characteristics are exclusive to one term, which are exclusive to the other term, and which are shared. This method often works well for content-area terms for important concepts you want students to master. Before completing a Venn Diagram, students should have acquired the background knowledge related to each term. As is the case with Four Squares, the procedure is straightforward.

- Choose two terms with overlapping meanings, such as *short stories* and *essays*, both of which are writing forms.
- Draw an empty Venn Diagram, two overlapping circles, on the chalkboard, overhead, Smart Board, or LCD.
- Discuss the characteristics unique to each term and those common to both of them, and fill in the Venn Diagram accordingly.

A Venn Diagram for the terms *plant cells* and *animal cells* is shown in Figure 4.9. As with any activity, the first time you use Venn Diagrams, you will want to model the procedure, thinking aloud as you complete a portion of the diagram. Students might then work in pairs to complete the Venn Diagram. Finally, check students' Venn diagrams and make sure they correct any mistakes in their diagrams.

Semantic Mapping

Semantic Mapping is a method that has been used extensively with English-only students and is described at length in an IRA monograph (Heimlich & Pittelman, 1986). Here is the basic version of this approach:

- Put a word representing a central concept in the middle of the chalkboard or on some projection device.
- Surround the target word with categories related to the word. For example, in discussing trees, you might include conifers, shade trees, and potential problems for trees. Work as a group to fill in examples for each of the categories.
- Ask students to work in pairs or groups, listing as many words for each category as they can. If possible, make sure that lower-proficient ELLs have access to a more proficient English speaker.
- As a group, discuss with students the central concept, the other words, the categories, and their interrelationships.

FIGURE 4.9. Venn Diagram for the Terms *Plant Cells* and *Animal Cells*

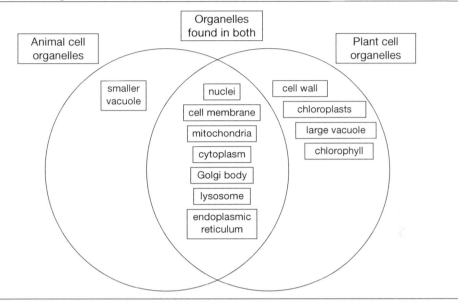

- Add this information to the semantic map displayed for the class.
- Have students add this information to their semantic maps.

Figure 4.10 shows a semantic map for Pioneers on the Oregon Trail.

What is particularly important to recognize about Semantic Mapping is that it is both a vocabulary technique and a technique to build comprehension. For example, one likely occasion for using Semantic Mapping with the concept *electronics* is as a review after students have read and discussed an informational text on electronics. Completing a semantic map after reading a selection gives students a chance to share and solidify what they have learned. Semantic mapping does a good deal more than simply teach the terms; it involves students in working with the overall meaning of the selection.

A slightly different kind of map, something that might be called a Semantic Map by some and a Concept Map by others, is shown in Figure 4.11. A Concept Map can be used to explore or consolidate information about a topic, and it too is both a vocabulary technique and a comprehension technique. It consists of cells that contain a term and links. The links are labeled and denote the relationship between cells and can have arrows that denote the direction of the relationship. One benefit of Concept Maps is that they can be used to tie concepts together across several units of study. A sample Concept Map focusing on the Earth's surface and events that change it is shown in Figure 4.11.

Vocabulary Self-Selection Strategy

The Vocabulary Self-Selection Strategy (Haggard, 1986; Ruddell & Shearer, 2002) differs from the techniques we have described thus far in that it is specifi-

FIGURE 4.10. Semantic Map for *Pioneers on the Oregon Trail*

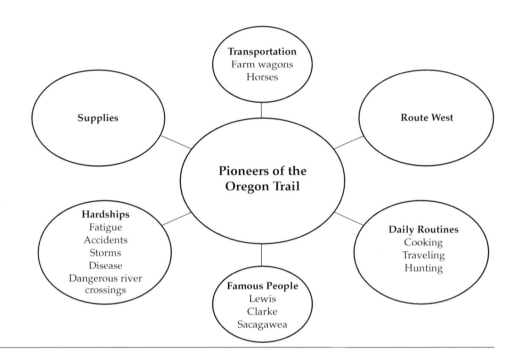

cally designed so that students, rather than the teacher, select the words to study. Because of this, it is particularly likely to get students interested and excited about words. Here is how it is typically done:

- Emphasize the importance of vocabulary and the importance of students taking charge of their own learning.
- Ask each student to select five or so words that they do not initially know the meaning of, want to study, and think important for the class to learn. Review the methods they can use to figure out the kinds of words to select and review their choices with them. Frequently, a particular set of words is studied for a week, and often students are allowed to choose their words from any sources: school reading, recreational reading, the Internet, TV, conversations, popular songs, or anyplace else they come across an interesting and important word.
- Tell students to bring in their words to class and tell where they found them, what they think they mean, and why they are important for the class to know. Also bring one word yourself.
- Once words are submitted, use discussion and perhaps the dictionary to clarify their meanings, and have students record the words and definitions in a vocabulary journal.
- During the week, work with the words in various ways using discussion, semantic mapping, semantic feature analysis, and other interactive techniques.

FIGURE 4.11. Concept Map Focusing on the Earth's Surface and Events that Change It

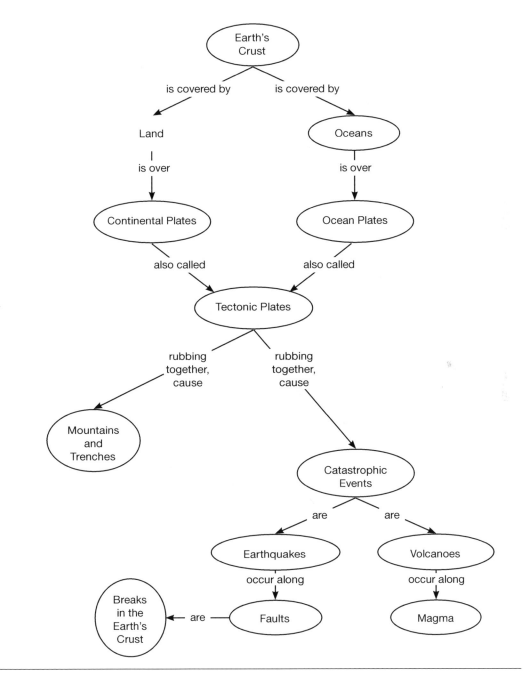

t the end of the week, evaluate students on their ability to explain the words' meanings and to use them in sentences.

While these steps describe the form the Vocabulary Self-Collection technique typically takes, like other instructional techniques, it can be modified to fit you and your class. For example, it can be used for any length of time and need not follow a weekly schedule, and it works well when the sources of words are limited to the content materials students are currently studying.

Robust Instruction

Robust Instruction is a powerful procedure that has been developed and investigated in a series of studies by Beck and her colleagues (Beck, Perfetti, & McKeown, 1982; McKeown, Beck, Omanson, & Perfetti, 1983; McKeown, Beck, Omanson, & Pople, 1984) and described in detail in Beck et al. (2002, 2008). Robust Instruction is designed to give students deep and lasting understanding of word meanings and is particularly appropriate and effective when used with interesting and somewhat intriguing words such as *banter, retort, glum, berate,* and *impatient.* Recent research with ELLs uses these techniques with some additional scaffolding and produced quite positive results (August, Artzi, Barr, & Massoud, in preparation). Here is a version that can be used in a number of situations. For the sake of simplicity, this example deals with a single word—*ambitious.* Often, however, Robust Instruction is used to teach a set of words over a period of a week or so.

- Begin with a student-friendly definition: ambitious—Ambitious means really wanting to succeed at something
- Arrange for students to work with the word several times. One encounter with a word is unlikely to leave students with a rich and lasting understanding of its meaning.
- Provide the word in more than one context so that students' understanding is not limited to one situation. The several contexts need not come at the same time, nor do they need to use the same morphological form of the word.
  - » Susan's ambition to become an Olympic high jumper was so strong that she was willing to practice 6 hours a day.
  - » Jiang had never been an ambitious person, and after his accident he did little other than watch television.
- Engage students in activities in which they need to deal with various facets of the word's meaning and investigate relationships between the target word and other words.
  - » Would you like to have a really ambitious person as a friend? Why or why not?
  - » Which of the following better demonstrates ambition to win a marathon? (1) A person who runs each day, increasing the distance and speed over time. (2) A person who runs once a week for a few minutes.

» How likely is it that an *ambitious* person would be *lethargic*? How likely is it that an *ambitious* person would be *energetic*? Explain your answers.
- Have students create uses for the word.
  » Tell me about a friend whom you see as very *ambitious*. What are some of the things she does that show how *ambitious* she is?
- Encourage students to use the word outside of class.
  » Come to class tomorrow prepared to talk about someone who appears to be *ambitious*. This could be a stranger you happen to notice outside of class, someone in your family, someone you read about, or someone you see on TV.

Quite obviously, Robust Instruction will create deep and lasting understanding of words. Equally obviously, Robust Instruction takes a great deal of time, certainly more time than you can spend on most words you teach. You will need to decide just which words merit its use.

REPETITION AND REVIEW

No matter how well we initially teach a word, it is much more likely that students will internalize and remember the word if they see it again and, better yet, actively work with it in a review. Sometimes review can be very brief and simply embedded in class discussion. For example, noting that the word *catastrophic*, which you have previously taught, appears again in the selection students are reading, you might say something like, "You might have noticed that the word *catastrophic*, which we learned several weeks ago, comes up again in today's chapter. Again, a *catastrophic* event is a really serious event, something that would produce widespread damage, like a hurricane might."

At other times, repetition will involve specific procedures. Here are three time-efficient procedures for reviewing words students have already been taught, plus suggestions for helping students incorporate newly learned words into their writing, another form of review.

Anything Goes

With Anything Goes (Richek, 2005), you begin by prominently displaying the words to be reviewed where everyone in the class can see them and explaining to students that occasionally you are going to point to some of the words displayed and ask questions about them. For ELLs, it is helpful to include a picture of the word or first-language translation of the word. Often you'll post a particular set of words for a week, but you can certainly put them up for a longer or shorter period. Once the words are posted, you can ask students to do any of the following:

- Define the word.
- Give two of its meanings.

- Use it in a sentence.
- Give an example of the thing named or described by the word.
- Say where you would find the word or the thing named or described by the word.
- Explain the difference between two of the words, or between one of the words on the list and some other word.
- Give the past tense, plural, or *-ing* form of a base word.
- Give the roots of words with prefixes or suffixes.
- Give prefixed or suffixed forms of root words.

Note that you certainly don't use all of these with any one word. You'll typically use two or three of them with each word—whatever seems enough. Suppose the list for intermediate-level ELLs included 10 words, among which were *melody, agenda,* and *mention.* You might ask students to define *melody,* give an example of a melody, and say where they might hear a melody. Then you might ask them to use *agenda* in a sentence, tell you where they are likely to find an agenda, and say the plural of *agenda.* After that, you might ask them to use the word *mention* in a sentence, tell you something that they might mention to a friend, and explain the difference between "mentioning" something and "discussing" something.

Once you have worked with Anything Goes enough that you think most of your students understand the way it works, you may want to post the list of prompts on the board, discuss them, and invite students to sometimes do the prompting. If you do this, you can save class time by sending the list home with students and asking them to prepare prompts for two or three of the words. Of course, you can always make generating prompts group work. The time the groups spend generating prompts is likely to be well spent, although this will increase the time spent on the review significantly.

Connect Two

With Connect Two (Blachowicz, 1986; Richek, 2005), you give students two columns of perhaps 10 words each and ask students to identify similarities or other relationships between a word in Column One and a word in Column Two. Here are some words that Richek has used to illustrate the procedure.

Column One	Column Two
bayonet	hoarse
disgrace	exuberant
muffled	cunning
exposed	pondered
insignificant	ruefully
splendid	courier
roll	musket
magazine	incense
ravine	restrain

Children may at first come up with relationships that are superficial, such as that *bayonet* and *cunning* have the same number of letters. That is fine to start with, but what you want to encourage is children searching for meaningful relationships that require deep processing. Modeling can be useful here as it so frequently is, so you may want to explain that you are looking for deeper relationships and model a few of those. You might, for example, note that *muffled* and *hoarse* have to do with sound, that a person is not likely to be *exuberant* about being *disgraced*, and that a *bayonet* might be attached to a *musket*. Soon, children will begin finding meaningful relationships, and the thought processes they engage in while doing so will help them remember the words and deepen their understanding of them.

Word Wizard

Word Wizard (Beck et al., 1982) was developed some years ago and is now widely used. It is almost too simple. You give students a list of the words they are reviewing and ask them to find the words used outside of class. When students find a word, they record the context in which it was used and report their findings in class, earning a point for each instance they report. In their work, which was with 4th-graders, Beck and her colleagues went all out to make Word Wizard a big deal. They first advertised the notion by creating and distributing leaflets titled "You Can Be a Word Wizard." One part of the leaflet, which included engaging graphics, described what a Word Wizard was and the various levels of word wizardry students could achieve and earn points for finding the words they were learning in class outside of school. These included Word Wildcat, Word Whirlwind, Word Winner, Word Worker, and Word Watcher, along with the ultimate level, Word Wizard. Another part of the leaflet explained how points are earned:

> If you hear a word—on TV, on the radio, on the street, or at home [today, of course, we would add on a video, a CD, your iPod, or the Internet]—you can earn one point. Just tell your teacher where you heard or saw the word and how it was used. (Beck et al., 2002, p. 119)

On the back of the leaflet, students were reminded to look for their name on the Word Wizard chart. The Word Wizard chart was a large and colorful chart with students' names and space for tallying their sightings of words. In class, students' sightings were heartily celebrated, and much was made of their efforts displayed on the chart. All in all, the activity was really well received by the students and engendered a lot of interest in vocabulary. In fact, Beck and her colleagues comment that the children "went absolutely wild with bringing in the words." And the procedure isn't just for challenging words like those Beck and her colleagues used. Richek reported success with the procedure when a primary-grade ELL teacher used it to reinforce common words like *bed*, *table*, and *television*.

Incorporating Vocabulary into Students' Writing

Writing offers still another opportunity for review. Most of the procedures we have discussed in this chapter are designed primarily to build students' oral and reading vocabularies. These are important tasks, but it also makes sense to give some attention to building students' writing vocabularies. One method to accomplish this is to provide opportunities for students to write about words in conjunction with discussion and reading. Opportunities for writing include copying the words (for young children), defining the words, using them in sentences, making affective responses to them, comparing them to one another and to other concepts, and keeping a written record of work with them. You can also select a subset of words that you have taught or have students select a subset of the words and encourage them to incorporate the words into longer writing assignments that are ongoing in your classroom.

For ELLs, providing models of what you expect prior to having students produce their own writing and providing sentence frames to help scaffold the writing can be very helpful. For example, if you want students to write the answer to a question that has been posed orally, such as, "What is one exceptional thing that happened to you last year?", you might provide the sentence frame, One exceptional thing that happened to me last year was _____.

A FINAL WORD

Although teaching individual words is only one part of a comprehensive vocabulary program for ELLs, it is a very important part. It is also a relatively complex part in terms of both planning and delivering the instruction. Planning involves recognizing the part that teaching individual words plays in ELLs' overall vocabulary development, considering the levels of word knowledge you want students to achieve, and selecting vocabulary to teach. Instruction involves identifying the word-learning task or tasks represented by the words you are teaching, choosing an appropriate method of instruction, and of course creating and providing that instruction. Our goal in the chapter has been to provide you with the information you need to do all of this and do it well.

CHAPTER 5

Teaching Word-Learning Strategies

For every word known by a child who is able to apply morphology and context, an additional one to three words should be understandable.

> William Nagy and Richard Anderson,
> Vocabulary Researchers

Teaching students word-learning strategies—strategies such as using word parts and cognates to unlock the meanings of words they don't know—is tremendously important for English language learners. With tens of thousands of words to learn and the need to attain vocabularies the size of those of their native English-speaking peers, anything we can do to help ELLs become more proficient independent word learners is an absolute necessity. Fortunately, we can indeed help ELLs sharpen their skills at learning words on their own.

In this chapter, we discuss seven ways in which we can help ELLs become increasingly competent at doing so. These are using word parts and context clues to unlock the meaning of unknown words, drawing on cognate knowledge to recognize words that are familiar in a first language but not in a second, using the dictionary, recognizing and dealing with multiword units, developing strategies for dealing with unknown words, and adopting a personal approach to building their vocabularies. One thing to constantly keep in mind when teaching strategies to ELLs is that it is essential to couple strategy instruction with methods that make the content the strategy is applied to comprehensible. To help accomplish this, the scaffolding techniques described in this and previous chapters can be applied. Figure 5.1 provides a list of many of the scaffolding techniques that are particularly helpful for ELLs.

Before describing instruction to build students' competence in each of these important areas, we will first describe a very powerful general model for teaching strategies and then describe some preliminary instruction that needs to take place before instruction on individual strategies.

A POWERFUL MODEL FOR TEACHING STRATEGIES

A substantial body of theory and research has supported two approaches to teaching strategies—"direct explanation of strategies" (Duke & Pearson, 2002; Duke, Pearson, Strachan, & Billman, 2011) and "transactional strategies instruction"

FIGURE 5.1. ESL Scaffolding Techniques Described Thus Far

Using students' first language to preteach vocabulary, preview an upcoming reading, provide background information prior to their reading in English, or describe an upcoming task or assignment

Using students' first language in reviewing newly taught or particularly challenging material

Using video clips, visuals, gestures, word cards, graphic organizers, concept maps, and models of the task to be done

Using bilingual dictionaries and glossaries

Using student-friendly definitions and explanations, and using newly taught words in a variety of contexts

For younger students, providing students with opportunities to act out word meanings

Pointing out cognates when they occur

Partnering ELLs with strong native speakers or weaker ELLs with stronger ones

Providing opportunities for teacher-student interaction and instructional conversations that permit some discussion in the students' first language

Providing repeated exposures and reviews of newly taught words, concepts, and skills

---

(Graves, Ruda, Sales, & Baumann, 2012; Pressley, Harris, & Marks, 1992). The approach used for much of the instruction described in this chapter, "balanced strategies instruction" (Graves et al., 2012; Sales & Graves, 2009c), combines these two approaches and modifies them in several ways. Balanced strategies instruction is initially more deliberate and carefully planned than transactional instruction but later on includes more review, rehearsal, integration, and constructivist activities than direct explanation. Additionally, balanced strategies instruction includes more direct attention to motivation and engagement than is often included in direct explanation. Finally, in keeping with the approach to strategy instruction described by Paris, Lipson, and Wixson (1983), with balanced strategies instruction, students are given declarative, procedural, and conditional knowledge. That is, they receive detailed knowledge about the strategies, they learn how to actually use them, and they learn when to use them.

This method is ideal for ELLs because the strategies can be applied to text that students have come to understand through English-as-a-second-language (ESL) scaffolding methods and they include a lot of modeling with practice. Here are the basic components of balanced strategies instruction, with some special provisions for ELLs added.

- Motivate students to use the strategy, explaining and discussing its value.
- Generally avoid simply giving students information; instead, try to give them opportunities to construct knowledge.
- Provide a description of the strategy and information on when, where, and how it should be used.
- Use ESL scaffolding techniques with the relevant portion of text to ensure that it is comprehensible for ELLs.

- Model use of the strategy for students on this portion of text.
- Continue using ESL scaffolding techniques, and when you reach the next portion of text that lends itself to the target strategy, give students opportunities to work in pairs to apply the strategy.
- Ask several pairs of students to share the responses they have arrived at as a result of applying the strategy.
- Discuss with students how the strategy is working for them, what they think of it thus far, and when and how they can use it in the future.
- Guide and support students as they use the strategy over time. Use the gradual release of responsibility model, at first providing a lot of support and later providing less and less.
- Make certain students use the newly learned strategy in various authentic tasks.
- Once students have learned one strategy, teach another strategy using the same methods.
- Have students apply the strategies they have mastered in previous lessons during successive lessons.
- Help students integrate their use of the strategies. In many situations, students will employ a set of strategies, not a single strategy.
- Review all the strategies taught and further discuss students' understanding of them and responses to them from time to time.

We follow this model in our suggestions for teaching students strategies for working with prefixes, context, and the dictionary. Then, to provide a range of options, we suggest other approaches to teaching the other word-learning strategies discussed in the chapter.

PRELIMINARY INSTRUCTION ON WORD-LEARNING STRATEGIES

Assuming that students have not had previous instruction on word-learning strategies or need to review their understanding, there are two preliminary matters to attend to. First, teach the meaning of *strategies*. We suggest that you use a constructive process to do so. You might, for example, ask students to suppose there is a jar of cookies high on the shelf out of their reach and ask which strategies they could use to get the jar. Student can volunteer ideas like *Get a stepstool or ladder, Climb a chair,* or *Ask someone tall to get the jar.* Have the class discuss these, and then ask for other situations in which people might use strategies. Students might respond with situations like *When they are playing card games or board games, When coaches describe strategies to use in games like football and basketball,* and *When they use strategies like "pick out the key terms" when solving math word problems.* Next, move to a discussion of strategies students might use when trying to figure out the meaning of an unknown word they run across while reading, and tell them that the class will be working on a variety of strategies for doing so in the upcoming weeks.

Second, teach the meaning of *inferences*, describing them as educated guesses. You might do so by first having students guess the meaning of some compound words by considering the meanings of the root words that comprise them, and then telling students that what they have been doing is making *inferences*, "educated guesses." Next, tell the students that whenever they work with word-learning strategies, they will be making inferences. Word-learning strategies, you should note, seldom tell us exactly what a word means; instead, they allow us to make educated guesses about what a word means.

USING WORD PARTS

Using word parts to infer the meanings of unknown words is a very powerful approach and an excellent set of strategies to begin with. As Nagy, Anderson, Schommer, Scott, and Stallman (1989) have noted, "more than 60% of the new words that readers encounter have relatively transparent morphological structure—that is, they can be broken down into parts." Once words are broken into parts, students can use their knowledge of word parts to attempt to infer their meanings—if, of course, they understand the root words and word parts and how they function. Here, we consider three types of word parts: prefixes, suffixes, and non-English roots.

Teaching Prefixes

As you plan prefix instruction, several matters deserve careful consideration: which prefixes to teach, when to teach them, and in which order to teach them. White, Sowell, and Yanagihara (1989) have identified the most frequent prefixes, and this is an excellent list to work from. These prefixes are shown in Figure 5.2. As can be seen, these 20 prefixes are used in approximately 3,000 words. Learning them thus provides students with a tremendous resource. Regarding the matter of when to begin teach prefixes, in keeping with the CCSS we suggest informal instruction on the most common prefixes beginning in kindergarten and more formal and substantial instruction beginning at about grade 3, the time at which students begin to encounter a significant number of prefixed words in their reading (White, Power, & White, 1989). If possible, ELLs should learn the prefixes at the same time as native English speakers, but you need to be extra-careful to ensure that students understand the meaning of the root words. Finally, with regard to the order in which to teach prefixes, it makes sense to teach the most frequent ones first, although there is no need to follow a rigid sequence. All 20 or so prefixes, and of course a strategy for using prefixes to infer the meanings of unknown words, can be taught in a single year. Alternately, about six of them can be taught each year over a 3-year period. Below, we first describe some informal instruction on the most frequent prefixes to be used in kindergarten through grade 2. Then we describe the first 3 days of a unit on teaching prefixes designed for students in grades 3, 4, and 5 modeled on a federally funded program titled *Word Learning Strategies* (Graves, Sales, & Ruda, 2012).

FIGURE 5.2. Twenty Most Frequent Prefixes

Prefix	Number of Words with the Prefix
un-	782
re-	401
in-, im-, ir-, il-, "not"	313
dis-	216
en-, em-	132
non-	126
in-, im-, "in or into"	105
over- "too much"	98
mis-	83
sub-	80
pre-	79
inter-	77
fore-	76
de-	71
trans-	47
super-	43
semi-	39
anti-	33
mid-	33
under-	25
TOTAL	2,859

Modified from White, Sowell, & Yanagihara (1989).

Informal Instruction for Kindergarten Through Grade 2

For young ELLs, it is useful to provide a very simple definition of what a prefix is and use actions or pictures to model how a prefix changes the meaning of a word. Begin by showing the prefix *in-* (meaning "not") and briefly explain its meaning. Write the word *direct* so it is visible to all children. Act out *direct*, perhaps by walking a straight line between two points, and then act out *indirect*, perhaps by meandering from one point to another, and have a child come to the board and add *in-* to the word *direct* to make it *indirect*. Give other children a chance to act out meanings for the unprefixed and prefixed forms of other words, with their classmates adding the prefix *in-*. Make sure to have children say the words before and after they change forms. As further practice, guide students in completing a worksheet like that shown in Figure 5.3. As can be seen, it lists the prefix *in-* and its meaning at the top of the page. The first column then shows an unprefixed word and a drawing illustrating the meaning of the word, the second shows the prefix plus the base word and a drawing illustrating the meaning of the prefixed form of the word, and the third provides a space for children to write the meaning of the prefixed form of the word. This sequence is then repeated with the prefix *in-* and two other base words. Additionally, to reinforce the meanings of unprefixed and prefixed forms, you can say each form and have children draw and label pictures that correspond to each form.

FIGURE 5.3. Prefix Worksheet

A prefix comes at the beginning of a word to make a new word. Print the new word formed by the prefix on the line.

The prefix **in-** means not.

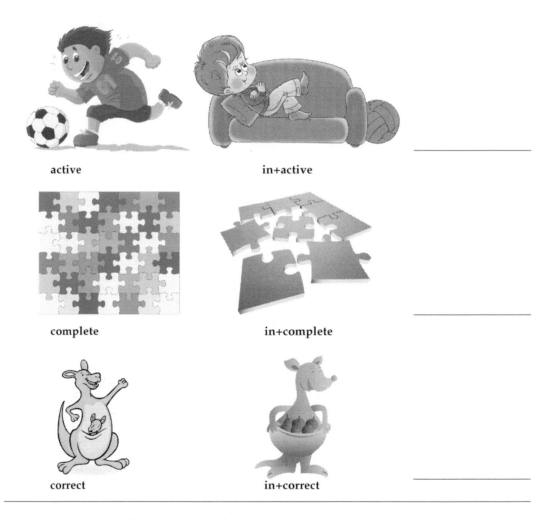

active   in+active

_____

complete   in+complete

_____

correct   in+correct

_____

Overview of the Unit for Students in Grades 3–5

If taught for half an hour a day, a unit to teach six prefixes and a strategy for using prefixes to unlock the meanings of novel words might last 10 days or so. If less time were devoted to the program each day, the unit would of course require more days of instruction. The unit includes the components of balanced strategies instruction listed above, and each day follows a similar, although flexible, structure designed to make it useable, interesting, and effective for both students and teachers.

Lesson 1. In Lesson 1, introduce the concept of prefixes; note that prefixes change the meaning of the word to which they are attached; teach the prefixes *un-* and *dis-*, meaning "not" and "do the opposite of"; and note that we can infer the meaning of a word by combining the meaning of its parts. Before beginning the lesson, ensure that students are familiar with the vocabulary you are using by preteaching the meanings of the root words that will be used in the lesson—in our example *safe, known, load, under,* and *uncle*—providing students with an English definition and if possible a definition in their native language and a picture depicting each word.

Begin by telling students that they will be studying root words, or small words that are inside of larger words. The roots or small words have their own meaning. Explain that the root for the word *unsafe* is *safe.* Tell students that they will also study prefixes, which are word parts that are attached to the beginnings of root words and that change the meaning of the word to which they are attached. Ask students what they think the prefix is in the word *unsafe.* Ask them what the word *safe* means and what the word *unsafe* means and then what they think the prefix *un-* might mean. Also, explain to students that learning about prefixes and how they work is important because this can help them learn the meanings of new words, a very important part of becoming proficient in English.

Next, drawing a large box on the board or using a projection device, write several words beginning with the prefixed *un-* (for example, *unsafe, unknown, unhurt,* and *unload*) inside the box, and write several words beginning with the letters "un" that are not prefixed words (for example, *under* and *uncle*) outside the box. Then, ask students to figure out how the words inside the box and outside the box differ, and lead them to the conclusion that the words inside the box have smaller words inside of them and the words outside the box do not. Finally, tell students that they will be making inferences about the meanings of the larger words by considering the meanings of the smaller word (the root word) and the prefix.

After this, use the words beginning with *un-* that you have assembled as examples to make the following points, not simply lecturing but asking students for examples and insights and drawing them into the discussion:

- A root word is the small word inside a larger word that can stand on its own; for example, *safe* is the root word in *unsafe.*
- A prefix is a group of letters that goes in front of a root; for example, *un-* is the prefix in *unsafe.*
- Prefixes change the meaning of the word to which they are attached; for example, *safe* and *unsafe* have different meanings.
- Prefixes do not appear by themselves; for example, *un-* does not appear by itself.
- Sometimes what looks like a prefix isn't one; for example, in the word *uncle,* the letters "un" are not a prefix.

Note that while we give a single example illustrating each point here, you will want to give several examples and elicit examples from the students.

FIGURE 5.4. Initial Activity Sheet on the Prefix *Un-*

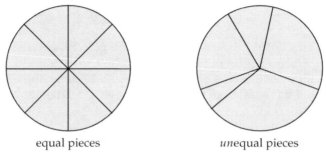

equal pieces   *un*equal pieces

This is a picture of two pies.

The first pie has equal pieces; the pieces are the same size.

The second pie has **unequal** pieces; the pieces are *not* the same size.

For number 1, circle the answer that best completes the sentence.

1.   When a knight is afraid, he is scared.

If a knight is unafraid, that means
a.   the knight is scared.

b.   the knight is not scared.

For number 2, read the sentence. Then use your knowledge of the prefix -*un* to tell the meaning of the word in bold.

2.   The girl made an **unwise** choice.

If wise means "smart," **unwise** means *[not wise, not smart]*.

For number 3, write the answer in the space provided.

3.   What does -*un* mean?   [not, the opposite of]

Next, you and the class as a whole complete an activity sheet on the prefix *un-* like that shown in Figure 5.4. In doing so, explain the activity; teach the meanings of the root words to which the prefixes are attached as shown in the figure, ensuring that the meanings are comprehensible to ELLs in your classroom; read Question 1 aloud and elicit the answer from the students; have a student read Questions 2 and 3 and elicit answers to these questions from other students; and remind students that the reason they are learning prefixes is to help them infer the meanings of unknown words.

After this, have students work in pairs, partnering strong native English speakers with ELLs to complete an activity sheet similar to the one shown in Figure 5.4 but that deals with the prefix *dis-*, using procedures similar to those we just described. This time, however, have the pairs complete Questions 2 and 3 on their own. Thus, students progress from an activity in which they work only with your assistance to one in which they work some with each other. Alternately, here and elsewhere, it may be necessary to create a small group of students with very lim-

FIGURE 5.5. Basic Facts About Prefixes Poster

Basic Facts About Prefixes

A prefix is a group of letters that goes in front of a base word.

Example: The prefix *-un* can go in front of the word *equal* to make the word *unequal.*

Prefixes change the meaning of the word to which they are attached.

Example: When you add the prefix *-un* to the word *equal* (meaning: the same) to make the word *unequal*, it changes the meaning of the word to not equal, or not the same. Prefixes do not appear by themselves.

Example: The prefix *-un* has to be attached to another word; you can't use it on its own.

Sometimes, something that looks like a prefix isn't one.

Example: Seeing the letters "un" at the beginning of a word doesn't always mean that the word starts with the prefix *-un.* The word *under,* for instance, begins with the letters "un" but this isn't the prefix *-un;* you can figure this out if you know that "der" is not a word.

---

ited English proficiency and work with them on this activity, reading the sentences aloud.

Finally, work with the class as a whole to correct the *dis-* activity sheet, doing everything possible to ensure that students know the correct answers and understand why they are the correct answers.

Lesson 2. In Lesson 2, teach the meanings of the prefixes *re-* (meaning "again"), *mis-* (meaning "wrong," "bad," or "badly"), and *over-* (meaning "too much" or "above"), using student activity sheets like the one used to teach the prefix *un-.* Also, review the fact that students can infer the meaning of an unknown word if they know the meaning of the root word and the prefix.

First, review the basic facts about prefixes using a poster like that shown in Figure 5.5. In doing so, have students read the first fact and ask the class to name the two prefixes they studied in Lesson 1, have them read the second fact and ask a student to give an example of a prefixed word and explain how the meaning changes when a prefix is added, remind them that prefixes are not words themselves, and ask a student to explain the fact that sometimes what looks like a prefix isn't one.

Next, ask students to get into their groups or pairs from Lesson 1 and assign the groups to work with one of the three prefixes they are studying this day: *re-,* *mis-,* or *over-.* Then, give each group an activity sheet similar to the one shown in Figure 5.4 and have the group complete it, telling the students that they will be reporting back to the class so that they can learn from each other. It is helpful to make a children's dictionary and/or bilingual children's dictionary available for ELLs as they work on this activity so that they can look up the meanings of unfamiliar roots they encounter.

After this, bring the class back together, have one of the *re-* groups give the meaning of *re-,* have another *re-* group confirm the meaning, and have yet another *re-* group explain how they figured out the meaning of *re-*. Write that meaning on the board. Then, repeat this process with the *mis-* group and with the *over-* group.

Next, have students work independently or in pairs (pairing less English-proficient with more English-proficient students) to complete another activity sheet on *re-*, *mis-*, and *over-*. This activity sheet should require them to review the meaning of each prefix and give each student some practice using each prefix to infer the meaning of a novel word. Model the first item if it differs in format from previous items, and be sure the students get enough practice as a class before requiring them to work independently.

Finally, tell the students that they will check the activity sheet they just completed during the next lesson, and ask them to go on a word hunt for homework. They should be on the lookout for words beginning with the prefixes they have studied thus far (*un-*, *dis- re-*, *mis-*, and *over-*) when reading in the various subjects they study in school and in any reading they do outside of school, and they should come to class with a list of at least 10 words, two words for each prefix. It is helpful to create a prefix log like that shown in Figure 5.6 that students can use to record the words they find on their hunt. As can be seen, next to each prefix are spaces where students can record the prefixed word they found, the word's meaning in English, its meaning in their first language, an English sentence using the word, a sentence using the word in their first language, and a drawing representing the word.

Lesson 3. In Lesson 3, review the meanings of *un-*, *dis- re-*, *mis-*, and *over-*; provide lots of examples of words with these prefixes; and give students multiple opportunities to use prefixes and root words to infer the meanings of prefixed words.

First, have students correct the activity sheet they worked on in the previous lesson, the one on *re-*, *mis-*, and *over-*.

Next, have them share the prefixed words they found for *un-*, *dis- re-*, *mis-*, and *over-*, and go through the prefix log discussing each prefix, its meaning in English, its meaning in their native language if possible, and the sample sentences students recorded.

Finally, have students complete a short quiz that requires them to recognize some of the basic facts about prefixes, identify the meanings of the five prefixes they have studied, and infer the meanings of several prefixed words. Make sure that the instructions are comprehensible to the ELLs and that the root words are words your ELLs are likely to know prior to the quiz. As soon as possible, correct these quizzes, return them to the students, and go over the correct responses.

The Remaining Lessons in the Unit. Thus far, we have described the first three lessons on prefixes. As we have noted, your initial work on prefixes is likely to contain another half-dozen or so lessons. In these, continue to use the balanced strategies approach described in this chapter. During these lessons, students should acquire the additional prefixes *pre-* (meaning "before"), *fore-* (meaning "in front of," "before," or "earlier"), and *in-*, *im-*, and *non-* (meaning "not"). Motivate, teach, model, guide, and scaffold students; gradually turn increasing responsibility over to students to work as a whole class, in small groups or pairs, and indi-

FIGURE 5.6. Prefix Log

Directions: Fill in this log by writing the words you find, their meaning in English, their meaning in your first language, a sentence in English using the word, and a sentence in your first language. Then draw a picture of the word. The first one is done for you.

Prefix	Prefixed Word	Meaning in English	Meaning in Your First Language	Sentence in English	Sentence in Your First Language	Picture
un-	unhappy	not happy	infeliz	The boy was unhappy because he lost his lunch.	El chico era infeliz porque perdió su almuerzo.	☹
un-						
dis-						
dis-						
re-						
re-						
mis-						
mis-						
over-						
over-						

vidually; and review, assess, and provide students with plenty of feedback. A very important new topic that is introduced in these lessons is the Word Parts Strategy, a series of steps students will use when they come to an unknown word that can possibly be divided into parts. Students will use it not only in their work with prefixes but also with their work with other word parts such as suffixes. A poster displaying these five steps is shown in Figure 5.7. At some point in learning this strategy, you may want to scaffold students' efforts by having them use a dictionary along with the strategy; however, the long-term goal is for them to be able to use the Word Part Strategy without the aid of dictionary. Note that students will need to spend a good deal of time learning and practicing the steps of the Word Parts Strategy. Finally, these lessons should become more authentic and lead toward students transferring their use of prefixes and the prefix strategy in stories (instead of simply in sentences) and in longer, authentic texts.

In concluding this discussion of a unit on teaching prefixes, we want to again mention one component of our balanced strategies instruction model—motivation. In work on prefixes or any other word-learning strategy, keep the importance of motivation firmly in mind and go out of your way to motivate students. In the *Word Learning Strategies* program, for example, the curriculum is built around the theme of superheroes, and each strategy is represented by a superhero. Enfracta, the superhero shown in Figure 5.8, is the word parts specialist, and relies on her strength,

FIGURE 5.7. Word Parts Strategy Poster

Word Parts Strategy

1. Decide if you can break the unknown word into meaningful word parts.

    Example: *redo*

    Word: redo ⟶ re-   +   do

    Meaning: do again ⟶ again +   do

    Decision: Yes! The word can be broken into meaningful parts.

    Counter-example: *regular*

    Word: regular ⟶ re-   +   gular

    Meaning: normal, usual ⟶ again +   ???

    Decision: No, the word cannot be broken into smaller meaningful parts because even though *re-* is meaningful, "gular" is not.

2. Refer to your prefix glossary and a dictionary if necessary.

3. Underline the word root and bracket the other word parts.

    Example: *reread*

    reread ⟶ [re] *read*

4. Figure out the meanings of the parts to infer the meaning of the unknown word.

    Example: *reread*

    Word: reread ⟶ re-   +   read

    Meaning of the word parts: again +   read

    Therefore, *reread* means "read again."

5. Try out your inference to see if it makes sense.

---

the use of gadgets, and the assistance of robotic characters in breaking words into parts. In providing this example, we are not of course suggesting that instruction in word-learning strategies needs to include superheroes. We are, however, very strongly suggesting that doing everything possible to keep students interested and involved in the learning is vital.

Teaching Suffixes

In considering how to teach suffixes, it is important to distinguish two types of suffixes—inflectional suffixes and derivational suffixes. Inflectional suffixes (typically called *inflections*) have grammatical functions (for example, *-ed* indicating the past tense), while derivational suffixes often have abstract and difficult-to-explain meanings and change the word's part of speech (for example, *-ence*, indicating "the state of being"). We will consider first the matter of inflections. While native Eng-

FIGURE 5.8. Enfracta, the Word Parts Superhero

lish speakers already have a tacit understanding of the grammatical functions of inflections, many ELLs do not. For example, they may not know that -*ed* indicates the past tense. Fortunately, the number of inflections is quite limited. Below is a list of them:

-s	3rd person singular, present tense
-ed	past tense
-ing	progressive aspect
-en, -ed	past participle
-s	plural (nouns)
-'s	possessive
-er	comparative
-est	superlative

Figure 5.9, Introduction to Action Words and Suffixes, provides an example of how to teach students about inflections. In keeping with the CCSS, we suggest beginning this work in kindergarten. In teaching inflections, it is important to first explain the general grammatical concept before explaining the use of a particular inflection, something we illustrate at the top of Figure 5.9. After you introduce an inflection, students should have opportunities to practice with it as a group, in pairs, and eventually on their own. Reviewing student work is also important. Finally, inflections might be grouped together for instruction by type—those relat-

FIGURE 5.9. Introduction to Action Words and Suffixes

An action word is a word that shows action. An action word often tells what someone or something is doing. Let's look at these action words—*nap, play,* and *dig.* What does each word mean?

Now let's look at these sentences that use the action words. Read them with me.

1.   The cat naps on the mat.
2.   Sam plays in the van.
3.   The pig digs in the sand.

What is the action word in each sentence? What letter comes at the end of the action word? This letter is called a suffix.

Now look at these sentences. Some action verbs tell about actions that are hard to see.

1.   Dawn hears the song.
2.   Ben knows the story.
3.   David likes the puppy.

Who can come up and underline the action word in each sentence and circle the suffix?

Teacher Note: Point out that there is one person or animal performing the action and that the action takes place in the present or right now. When one person is performing the action and the action takes place in the present, the suffix *s* appears at the end of the action word. Practice more examples if you feel they are necessary.

---

ed to verbs, possessives, and comparatives and superlatives. After students have mastered one inflection, teach another and then give them practice working with more than one inflection at a time. With students in grades 2 and above, you can reinforce their awareness of inflections by having them find and underline inflections they have learned in material they are reading in class and then discuss the meanings of the inflection and the inflected word as a group. You can also ask students to work with a partner to make up their own sentences using particular inflections.

Now consider the matter of derivational suffixes. Because the meanings of many derivational suffixes are abstract and difficult to explain, attempting to teach their meanings may be confusing for elementary students whether they are native speakers or ELLs. It seems wise, therefore, to proceed in keeping with the advice that Thorndike (1941) gave over 60 years ago and that White, Sowell, and Yanagihara (1989) more recently endorsed for native English speakers: Some derivational suffixes might be taught to ELLs at opportune times when words containing those suffixes come up in the material students are reading. See Figure 5.10 for a sample of common derivational suffixes. Additionally, for students literate in Spanish, it may be helpful to teach students that some derivational suffixes in English regularly correspond to suffixes in Spanish (for example, *-able* corresponds to *-able, -ity* to *-idad, -ing* to *-a* or *-endo,* and *-ly* to *-mente*). Figure 5.11 lists some English deri-

FIGURE 5.10. Common Derivational Suffixes

Part of Speech	Suffix	Example(s)
Noun	-er/-or	consumer, container, sailor
Noun	-ess	princess
Noun	-hood	childhood, neighborhood
Noun	-ian	magician
Noun	-ity	possibility, reality, security
Noun	-ment	movement, excitement, statement
Noun	-tion/-sion	action, expression, discussion
Noun	-ness	sickness, kindness, happiness
Noun	-ship	friendship, relationship
Verb	-ate	decorate
Verb	-en	awaken
Verb	-ify	identify
Verb	-ize	realize
Adjective	-able	suitable, valuable, comfortable
Adjective	-al	musical, medical, mechanical
Adjective	-ary	primary, imaginary
Adjective	-ful	successful, dreadful, colorful
Adjective	-ish	foolish
Adjective	-y	dusty, icy, noisy
Adverb	-ly	sadly, eagerly, safely
Adverb	-ward	southward, upward, backward
Adverb	-wise	clockwise

vational suffixes that regularly correspond to Spanish suffixes. In teaching derivational suffixes, we recommend using the balanced strategies instruction approach we have described.

Teaching Non-English Roots

Non-English roots include, for example, *anthro*, meaning "man," appearing in such words as *anthropology, misanthrope,* and *philanthropy.* There are many non-English roots, individual roots are not used in nearly as many words as common prefixes and suffixes, they are often variously spelled and thus difficult to identify, and the relationship between the original meaning of the root and the current meaning of the English words in which it is used varies depending on the particular English word. For these reasons, we recommend teaching a mini-lesson on root words at the beginning of the year for students in grade 4, the grade specified in the CCSS, and if certain roots come up repeatedly in the material students are reading—as might be the case in a science class—then teach these roots as they appear. Figure 5.12 gives an example of how you might teach word roots to intermediate or advanced ELLs and how the part of speech of the root changes depending on the suffix that is added to it. Before beginning the lesson, explain what a root is and how suffixes can change a word from one part of speech to another. After that, have the class as a whole fill in several missing suffixes and words that can be

FIGURE 5.11. Derivational Suffixes in English that Regularly Correspond to Suffixes in Spanish

English Suffix	Spanish Suffix	English Example	Spanish Example
-able	-able	reasonable	razonable
-acy	-acia	democracy	democracia
-aire	-ario	millionaire	millonario
-ance	-ancia	admittance	admitancia
-ancy	-ancia	infancy	infancia
-ation	-ación	nation	nación
-ence	-encia	independence	independencia
-ent	-ente	patient	paciente
-fy	-ficar	identify	identificar
-ible	-able	responsible	responsable
-ic	-ico/a	arctic	ártico
-ice	-icia/o	justice	justicia
-id	-ido	placid	plácido
-ile	-il	automobile	automóvil
-ism	-ismo	organism	organismo
-ity	-idad	quantity	candidad
-or	-(i)or	superior	superior
-ory	-orio/a	history	historia
-tude	-tud	attitude	actitud
-ute	-uto	absolute	absoluto

FIGURE 5.12. Teaching Roots to Intermediate and Advanced ELLs

Some Non-English Word Roots

Instructions: Use the information in the chart to figure out the missing words and suffixes.

Sentences

1. *Gravity* causes the ball to fall to the ground. The *gravitational* pull of the Sun keeps the Earth in orbit.

2. A *parasite* lives in the dog's stomach. The relationship between the dog and the round-worm is *parasitic*.

3. I *illuminate* the room with a candle. Now I can see the bed in the *illuminated* room.

composed by combining a root with a suffix, and then have student pairs complete the chart. At each stage, review responses with students and make corrections as necessary.

USING CONTEXT CLUES

Using context clues to infer the meanings of unknown words is another very important word-learning strategy. Although beginning ELLs are not likely to learn a lot of words from context, as ELLs become increasingly competent in their English, learning from context becomes more important. Eventually, as is the case with native English speakers, ELLs will learn most of their words from context, although in many cases they will use context in conjunction with other strategies such as the use of word parts, cognates, and the dictionary. Thus, if we can increase students' proficiency in learning from context even a small amount, we will greatly increase the number of words they learn. It is therefore vital that we provide students with rich, robust, and effective instruction on using context clues. As with instruction on word parts and in keeping with the CCSS, we suggest informal instruction beginning in kindergarten and more formal and substantial instruction beginning about grade 3. The informal instruction is described just below, and the more formal instruction follows. As was the case with the more formal prefix instruction we described, the more formal context instruction we describe here is modeled on that developed for the *Word Learning Strategies* program (Graves, Sales, & Ruda, 2012).

Informal Instruction for Kindergarten through Grade 2

For young children, you can model using context clues by playing the following game. Tell students that context clues are clues that help us figure out what something is or what a word means. Then tell them that they are going to play a game. You are thinking of an object in the classroom and you are going to give them context clues to help them try to figure out what the mystery object is. Give students a set of increasingly revealing clues, and write down the clues as they are given so all students can see them. When they have enough information, they can try to guess what it is. Next tell students they can use one type of clue, context clues—the information that surrounds a word in text—to help them figure out the meaning of a word they might not know. Write sentences with nonsense words and revealing context clues on the board, and see if students can come up with a plausible meaning for the nonsense words (there will probably be a variety of possible responses). Finally, create short passages that provide enough context clues for students to figure out the meaning for real words that they might not know, have students offer possible meanings, and have them describe the clues that helped them figure out the meanings.

Overview of a Unit for Students in Grades 3–5

As is the case with word parts, with context it is important to decide just what to teach, when to teach it, and how to sequence instruction. It is also important to consider how much instruction to provide. We suggest teaching a strategy for using context to infer the meanings of unknown words and several specific types of context clues plus "general" context clues. We also suggest that formal instruction in context begin at about grade 3. And we suggest that instruction proceed from work with more revealing context clues to less revealing ones. With respect to how much instruction to provide, we believe that an initial unit of about 10 20- to 30-minute lessons taught 3 days a week would be a good start. If less time

FIGURE 5.13. Overview of a Unit on Context Clues

Lesson 1	Lesson 2	Lesson 3	Lesson 4	Lesson 5
Motivation and introduction to using context to infer meaning using a set of slides	Introduction to using context clues to infer word meanings and to the context strategy	Using the context clue strategy with definition and synonym clues	Using the context clue strategy with contrast clues	Using the context clue strategy with antonym clues

Lesson 6	Lesson 7	Lesson 8	Lesson 9	Lesson 10
Practice using the context clue strategy with all of the clue types taught thus far	Using the context clue strategy with general clues	Using the context clue strategy with general clues (cont.)	Practice using the context clue strategy with all of the clue types taught thus far	Using the context clue strategy along with the other word-learning strategies taught thus far

were devoted to the program each day, it would of course require more days of instruction. The unit we describe here includes the components of balanced strategies instruction described earlier in this chapter, and each day follows a similar, although flexible, structure designed to make it useable, interesting, and effective for both students and teachers. A sample schedule is shown in Figure 5.13. In what follows, we describe the first 3 days of instruction in some detail and then much more briefly describe the rest of the unit.

Lesson 1. Because learning to use context clues is a challenging task, introduce the unit with a substantial motivational activity designed to both gain students' interest and enable them to get a feel for using context to make inferences. In this example, students make inferences from picture clues.

Begin by telling students that over the next few weeks the class is going to be working on using context clues to figure out the meanings of unknown words they come across while reading. Note further that using clues to figure out things they don't know is something they do all the time and are good at. Show students a series of slides that are increasingly stronger clues to a place students can identify. Here, we illustrate the approach using Hawaii as the mystery place. If your students are not likely to be familiar with Hawaii, pick a place they are likely to be familiar with.

Suppose you had 10 slides. The first might be of two students about the age of those in your class gazing outward and asking "Where are we?" The second might be of the ocean, the third a large cruise ship, the fourth a large airliner, the fifth a tropical flower, the sixth some palm trees, the seventh a hula dancer, the eighth an aloha shirt, the ninth the beach at Waikiki without any identifiable background, and the tenth the beach at Waikiki with Diamond Head in the background. Your goal is to show students that (1) they can make inferences from context (in this case pictures), (2) in order to do so they may have to slow down, go backward and forward in the context, and consider it several times, and (3) some context is more revealing than others.

In order to do this, go through the slides several times, have students jot down the clues they come up with as you go, and have them discuss the clues, but tell them not to shout out the answer until you ask for it. Begin by going through the first four slides very quickly, not giving students a chance to study or discuss them. Next, you might go back through these four, this time giving students time to study them, jot down their thoughts, and discuss them. After this, go through the remaining slides except the last one similarly, repeating them and going back and forth as seems appropriate and perhaps responding to students' request to go back and forth or look at a particular slide again. At some point, reveal the last slide (the one with Waikiki and Diamond Head), take students' inferences, and reveal that the secret place is indeed Hawaii. Finally, discuss with the students what this activity revealed—that pictures can serve as clues to a place, that some pictures are more revealing than others, and that to use a set of pictures as clues, they may have to look at them several times and go back and forth among them as they do so. If making inferences from the pictures seems too difficult for some of your ELLs, you can scaffold their efforts by providing verbal prompts to accompany the pictures. For example, with the second picture, the one of the ocean, you could tell students that they will need to cross an ocean to get to the destination. And with the third picture, the one of the cruise ship, you could tell them that people sometimes get there on a cruise ship.

Conclude the lesson by telling students that in the next lesson on context clues, you will consider how the words and sentences that surround an unknown word can serve as clues to that word's meaning.

Lesson 2. In the second lesson, you transition from looking at picture clues to looking at clues to unknown words in text, note that clues can come before or after an unknown word, and introduce the context clue strategy.

Remind students that in the last lesson they used picture clues to figure out an unknown location, and that today they will work with written clues to figure out unknown words. Show a sentence like the one below with a word deleted and some strong clues to the word.

Julie's favorite <u>zoo animal</u> is the _____. She thinks its <u>stripes</u> make it even more beautiful than <u>other large cats.</u>

Talk through the example with the class, underlining the clues (those already underlined in the example), and point out that the clues can come before or after the unknown word. Make sure that all students know the meanings of the underlined words. Then tell the students that the words and sentences around an unknown word are called "context" and explain that the clues to the unknown word are called "context clues."

At this point, put up a context strategy poster like the one shown in Figure 5.14, talk through the strategy with students, and tell them that the poster will stay up throughout their work on context clues and that both you and they can use it as a reminder of how the strategy works.

As the last activity of the lesson, display a short and relatively simple paragraph with the words likely to be unknown are underlined like that shown in Figure 5.15 on the board or a projection device so that all students can see it, read it aloud, and think aloud as you use the context strategy to infer the meanings of

FIGURE 5.14. The Context Strategy Poster

The Context Strategy

1.   Pause when you find an unknown word.

2.   Read the surrounding words and
     sentences looking for context clues.

3.   Use the clues to infer the meaning of the unknown word.
4.   Try out your inference to see if it makes sense.

FIGURE 5.15. Using the Context Strategy—Victoria's Birthday Party

> Victoria's birthday was coming up, and she was excited about planning her party. She wanted to have a lavish event, with a <u>fancy</u> cake, <u>beautiful</u> decorations, <u>lots</u> of <u>delicious</u> drinks and snacks, and <u>fun</u> party favors for her friends. The one thing she was adamant about was that the cake would have purple flowers—purple was her favorite color, and she loved flowers. She <u>knew</u> that a cake with purple flowers was the one thing she <u>really wanted</u>!
>
> When the day of the party came, all her friends were there and everyone had a wonderful time. The best part of the day, though, wasn't the decorations or the cake or the favors. It was when her friends told her how much they cared about her—it was a poignant moment, and Victoria <u>almost cried</u>, she was <u>so happy</u>! The day turned out even more perfect than she thought!

likely unknown words, in this case *lavish, adamant,* and *poignant*. As with the previous activity, make sure all students know the meanings of the words in the paragraph that are not the target words students are trying to figure out. Once students understand the paragraph, it is a good idea to underline the context clues while you are engaged in the think-aloud, which we have done in Figure 5.15.

Lesson 3. In the third lesson, you work with the context strategy with the two most revealing sorts of context clues: definition clues and synonym clues.

Remind students that in the last lesson they worked with the context strategy and review previous work by asking volunteers to respond to three questions:

1.   What is context? (the words and sentences around an unknown word)
2.   What is a strategy? (a plan for achieving a goal)
3.   What is the goal of the context strategy? (to infer the meaning of unknown words met while reading)

FIGURE 5.16. Definition and Synonym Clues

	Clue Types	
Definition	The author defines the un-known word.	Stellaluna's wings are delicate. They are easy to break. Stellaluna thinks that landing is complicated; she thinks it's hard to do. The family lives opposite, or across from, Aunt Ida.
Synonym	The author uses a word that means about the same as the unknown word.	The proper way for bats to sleep is hanging by their feet—it is the right way for bats to sleep. Stellaluna says that lately, or recently, she has been flying in the daytime. Stellaluna saw a most peculiar face; the face looked strange to her.

Direct students' attention to the Context Strategy Poster that you introduced during the last lesson and tell them that today they will be working with two types of context clues: definition clues and synonym clues. Put a definition of each type and short passages that include each of the types on the board or a projection device, go over the definitions, and guide students as they identify the clues in the passages and infer the meaning of the unknown words. Figure 5.16 shows a definition of each type and a sample passage for each.

Create several passages with unknown words and definition clues and make a handout. Remember that the passages need to be readily understandable by all students and contain few if any unknown words except for the target words. After you have guided students through the sample passages shown in Figure 5.16, tell them that they will work in pairs finding the definition and synonym clues to unknown words in some other passages, distribute these passages, and perhaps work through one more example with students. Then, monitor the pairs as they do their work, offering assistance to those who seem to need it.

As the final activity of the lesson, correct students' work as a whole-class activity, letting students volunteer answers and encouraging and responding to questions.

The Remaining Lessons. As shown in Figure 5.13, in Lessons 4, 5, and 6, the class uses the context strategy with contrast clues, with antonym clues, and then with all four of the clue types taught thus far. Then, in Lessons 7 and 8, they work with general context clues. This is the most challenging type of clue to work with and the type of clue students will find most frequently in authentic text. General clues are usually hints to the meanings of unknown words; they are not nearly as easy to recognize as definitions and synonyms; and frequently they reveal only partial word meanings. Finally, in Lesson 9, students work on all five clue types they have learned—definition, synonym, contrast, antonym, and general clues—and in Lesson 10 they combine use of the context strategy with the use of other word-learning strategies they have been taught.

There are also several important features of the instruction that Figure 5.13 cannot show: Increasingly, the students talk more and you talk less, the students do more of the work, they take more responsibility for the strategy, and they increasingly self-monitor and self-regulate their use of the strategy. At the same time, you are always there to support students' efforts, providing encouragement, scaffolding, and feedback as needed. Additionally, you want to be sure that students use the context strategy with expository text as well as with narrative text, use the strategy with authentic texts that they read both in and out of class, and make plans for using the strategy in the future.

USING COGNATES

Cognates are words that have similar spellings, similar meaning, and sometimes similar pronunciations across two languages. Holmes and Guerra Ramos (1995) consider cognates to be crucially important, noting that cognates account for from a third to as much as a half of the active vocabulary of an educated person. Although, as we have noted, native English-speaking 12th-graders probably have *total* vocabularies of something like 50,000 words, their *active* vocabularies are considerably smaller than this. Nash (1997) estimates that adults' active vocabulary ranges from 10,000 to 15,000 words, and thus cognates could account for somewhere between 5,000 and 7,500 frequently used words.

Teaching Spanish-speaking children to take advantage of their cognate knowledge is a particularly powerful tool because many English words that are cognates with Spanish are high-frequency Spanish words, but low-frequency English words. Thus, students are likely to know the words in Spanish (concept and label) but lack the English label. Moreover, many of the words that are cognates are words that have importance and utility; they are characteristic of mature language users and appear frequently across a variety of domains; and they have instructional potential because they are words that can be worked with in a variety of ways so that students can build rich representations of them and their connections to other words and concepts. Examples include (*singular/singular, event/evento,* and *portion/porción*).

Research supports the commonsense notion that students are more likely to recognize cognate pairs that sound alike and are spelled alike (for example, *amorous-amoroso*). In addition, students' levels of first-language literacy and first-language knowledge of a word's meaning influence the ease of recognizing cognates.

Cognate strategy instruction generally helps students draw on their first-language knowledge by (1) briefly explaining what cognates are, (2) giving students an opportunity to find cognates in authentic text, and (3) helping students realize that while cognates are similar in sound, spelling, and meaning, there is a range in how similar cognates are on these attributes (August, Carlo, Dressler, & Snow, 2005). See Figures 5.17 and 5.18 for an example of methods that can be used to introduce students to cognates and give them opportunities to apply this knowledge to finding cognates in texts they are reading.

USING THE DICTIONARY

Teaching students to use the dictionary is a much smaller task than teaching the use of word parts, context clues, or cognates. Nevertheless, it is definitely to ELLs'

FIGURE 5.17. Cognate Strategy Instruction: Introduction to Cognates

Directions:

Look at the word *televisión* in Spanish and *television* in English. What do you notice? Cognates are words that mean more or less the same thing in English and Spanish, sound alike, and look alike.

What is the English word for *problema*? Are *problema* and *problem* cognates? Why or why not?

What English word means *pie*? Are *pie* and *foot* cognates? Why or why not?

Let's work as a class to come up with some other cognates and false cognates. I'll write them in the chart.

Spanish Word	English Word	Real Cognate?
televisión	television	Yes No
problema		Yes No
pie		Yes No
		Yes No
		Yes No
		Yes No
		Yes No

FIGURE 5.18. Cognate Strategy Instruction: Rainforest Cognate Hunt

Directions:
- Listen and follow along as I read the first sentence in "About the Amazon."
- What cognate is in the first sentence?
- Now work with a partner to find cognates in the rest of the passage.
- With your partner, complete the chart using the cognates you find in the passage.

About the Amazon

The Amazon rainforest is important. It has a lot of materials, food, and medicine that we use. It is always hot. There are millions of plants and trees and many different animals.

English Word	Spanish Word	Letters that are not the same
important	importante	
	materiales	
medicine		
	usar	
	millones	
plants		
	diferentes	
animals		

advantage to become effective and efficient in using this tool. As Miller and Gildea (1987) have convincingly demonstrated, students, even native English speakers, frequently have difficulty using the dictionary to define unknown words. For example, after finding the phrase "eat out" in the definition of *erode,* one student showed her confusion in using the definition by composing the sentence "Our family erodes a lot." Obviously, this student found the dictionary definition considerably less than helpful. Perhaps this should not be surprising. While students sometimes receive instruction in alphabetizing, in using guide words, and in using pronunciation keys, the instruction usually does not go much beyond this, and such instruction is not sufficient for teaching students to effectively work with a tool that they will use throughout their schooling and that most adults continue to use almost daily.

The starting point in helping ELLs become effective and efficient dictionary users is getting them the right type of dictionaries. There are many dictionaries that have been designed for ELLs that highlight core vocabulary; provide labeled illustrations; and help with grammar, usage, spelling, and pronunciation. Many include more example sentences than traditional dictionaries. Some have downloads for computers and even smartphones and tablets. Our favorites include the *Collins COBUILD New Student Dictionary* (2005), written for users who speak English as a second language, and the online Wordsmyth beginner's and children's dictionaries (http://www.wordsmyth.net/), both of which contain fewer words and have simpler definitions than the advanced Wordsmyth dictionary. The *Word by Word Basic Picture Dictionary-International* (Molinsky & Bliss, 2006) is specifically designed for absolute beginners, and Scholastic and Macmillan also publish good children's dictionaries.

There is also an abundance of bilingual dictionaries that are very helpful for students literate in their first language. One widely used bilingual dictionary is the *Longman Diccionario Inglés Básico* (2004), which has translations from Spanish to English and English to Spanish. To the extent that the words are high-frequency and can be found in children's dictionaries, it is best to direct students to these dictionaries because the language used to describe the target words is more comprehensible. One very important thing for ELLs to learn when using either English dictionaries or bilingual dictionaries is that many English words have more than one meaning and that they will need to take extra care in finding the meaning that is appropriate for the context in which the unknown word appears.

Once students have appropriate dictionaries, the instruction parallels that for word parts and context, although it is not nearly as lengthy as that instruction. According to the CCSS, instruction in using glossaries and simple dictionaries should begin at about grade 2. As is the case with teaching the use of other word-learning strategies, motivation; an explanation of what they are going to be working on; and the use of guidelines, modeling, and the gradual release of responsibility provide a powerful approach. Perhaps a week or so before the instruction begins, you could post this question on the board: "What book appears in every classroom, every library, and many people's homes, and is available in many forms on the Internet?" On the first day of instruction, take students' responses in writing, tally them, and report the results. In all probability, most students will answer the question correctly, and you can congratulate them. Whether or not most answer correctly, note that the answer is "the dictionary," and stress that it is a very important book and online source indeed. Tell students that you are going to be working on using an English dictionary to find the meanings of unknown words they encounter in text or in speech, or using a bilingual dictionary to look up the English equivalents for words they know in their first language. Tell them that spending some time learning to use the dictionary is worthwhile, and that using the dictionary sometimes isn't as simple as it seems. Next, create some guidelines like those shown below. Introduce these a few at a time, posting them as you introduce them and leaving them up throughout your instruction on the dictionary and longer if wall space permits.

- Reread the sentence that contains the word you want to define.
- Use the dictionary to find the target word. If you are using an English dictionary, the definition will be in English; if you are using a dictionary that translates words from English to your first language, when you look up the English word, you will find definitions in your first language.
- When reading a definition, be sure to read all of it, not just part of it.
- Remember that many words have more than one meaning.
- Be sure to check all the definitions the dictionary gives for a word, not just one of them.
- Decide which definition makes sense in the passage in which you found the word.
- Often, the dictionary works best when you already have some idea of a word's meaning. This makes the dictionary particularly useful for checking on a word you want to use in your writing. When writing, you may check the meaning of an English word you think you might want to use or look up the English word for a word you know in your first language but not in English.
- If you want to remember the word, you might try the following:
  » Write the word and its definition in a personal glossary.
  » Write another sentence that uses the word.

Don't have students memorize these guidelines, but talk through them, amplifying on them as necessary. For example, you should probably add to the third guideline by telling students that if they find that they still know nothing about an important word after checking the dictionary, they will probably want to ask someone about its meaning. Similarly, you might want to add to the last guideline by noting that one of the most frequent uses of the dictionary, whether for reading or for writing, is to confirm, clarify, or refute the meaning they have arrived at using context or a meaning they are only somewhat confident of.

Additionally, if students are using traditional dictionaries instead of online ones, you may want to give them practice in alphabetizing and using guide words, and you may want to teach them how to use the pronunciation key for the particular dictionary they have. Alternately, if students are using online dictionaries, be sure they know how to use the search and pronunciation features the sites provide.

The remainder of the procedure continues to parallel that used with word parts and context. Do some modeling to demonstrate how you would look up the meaning of an unknown word in English or the English equivalent for a word they know in their first language but not in English. Think aloud, sharing your thinking with students as you come across the unknown word in a text. Show students how you find a word, find the definition that seems to fit, consider all of that definition, and then mentally check to see if the meaning you choose makes sense in the context in which the unknown word occurred. Gradually let students take over the procedure and model it for you and for one another. Encourage them to use the procedure when they come across unknown or vaguely known words in context. Finally, from time to time, give them opportunities to model their thinking as they use the dictionary so that you can check their proficiency, and give them feedback and further instruction as needed.

In addition to learning this general approach to using a dictionary, students need to learn some things about the particular dictionary they use—what the entries for individual words contain and how they are arranged, what aids to its use the dictionary provides, and what features beyond the basic word list the dictionary includes. Much of the important information appears in the front matter of the dictionaries themselves, but it is very seldom read, and simply asking students to read it is hardly sufficient instruction. Thus, explicit instruction in how to use specific dictionaries is usually useful.

RECOGNIZING AND DEALING WITH MULTIWORD UNITS

In addition to knowledge of individual words, vocabulary knowledge involves knowledge of multiword units. Recent work by Simpson-Vlach and Ellis (2010) provides a useful list of multiword units that appear in oral and written academic English. These words were selected because they cohere as a unit, they appear frequently, and experienced ESL teachers rated them as worth teaching. There is a core list of academic units, with separate lists for oral and written units. The units have been sorted into functional groupings. Examples of multiword units that appear in each group include referential expressions (*is based on, the concept of, with respect to*), stance expressions (*assumed to be, you need to*), discourse-organizing functions (*first of all, what I mean*), and discourse markers (*as well as, at the same time*). Compound nouns (*interior designer*) and phrasal verbs (*run into* meaning "meet") are other types of multiword units. For teaching multiword units, we recommend the various procedures for teaching individual words described in Chapter 4. Additionally, students can be taught about the existence of multiword units and prepared to look them up if they pose problems for comprehension. Both Wordsmyth (http://www.wordsmyth.net/) and other online dictionaries such as Simple Vocab (http://www.simplevocab.com/home.html) provide definitions for many multiword units.

DEVELOPING STRATEGIES FOR DEALING WITH UNKNOWN WORDS

In addition to learning to use context cues, word parts, cognates, various types of dictionaries, and multiword units, students will profit from having some plans for what to do when they encounter an unknown word as they are reading, listening, or want to use a word when speaking that they have in their first language but not their second. Our advice is to give them a definite strategy for each situation, discuss the strategy with them, let them try it out, and then discuss how it works and how they might modify it to fit their specific needs. Here are the steps for one strategy each for reading, one for listening, and one for speaking:

Reading

1. Recognize that an unknown word has occurred.
2. Attempt to sound out the word and see if you come up with a word you know.
3. Decide whether you need to understand it to understand the passage.
4. Attempt to infer the meaning of the word using your word parts, context, or cognate skills.
5. Turn to a dictionary, glossary, or another person for the meaning.

Listening

1. Recognize that an unknown word has occurred.
2. Decide whether you need to understand it to understand the conversation.
3. Attempt to infer the meaning of the word using some of the word-learning strategies you have been taught, for example, using context clues and cognate knowledge.
4. If you can't figure out the word, turn to the speaker or another person and ask him or her what the word means. Or use a handheld electronic dictionary for the meaning or first-language equivalent.
5. If you have a portable notebook (hard copy or electronic version), note the English word and its first-language equivalent.

Speaking

1. Recognize that you need to use a word that you don't know.
2. Figure out a way to get your meaning across using the words you already know in your second language, in this case English. You can also try pointing and gesturing. You might also try using a bilingual dictionary to find the English equivalent or see if the word you know in your first language might be a cognate and try that.
3. If possible, record the word and its definition (in English or your first language) and review at other times.
4. Add it to your lexicon.

The initial instruction for each of these could be completed in a half-hour or so. Then students should use the strategy for a few days. After that, it is appropriate to discuss how it worked for students and to bring up the matter of modifying the strategy so that it best fits their needs. Finally, from time to time, briefly review the strategy and ask students how their approaches to dealing with unknown words they encounter are working and what suggestions they may have to share with the class.

ADOPTING A PERSONAL APPROACH TO BUILDING VOCABULARY

As we have already noted, because of the size of the vocabulary-learning task ELLs face, it's important to promote a rich variety of approaches to learning words. One of them is to have students individually commit themselves to an approach that they will use independently. Many approaches can be beneficial. What is important is that students consciously recognize that building their vocabularies is important and make some sort of personal commitment to learning words. Listed here are some alternatives, a list you can add to as you work with students and elicit their suggestions.

- Make a commitment to learn at least a few English words a day, from almost any source.
- Identify a particular prefix or suffix, and learn and use words containing that word part over a period of a week or a month or so, probably compiling a list of those words.
- Decide to become a real sleuth at using context and agree to learn at least two or three new words each week from context and to record both the words learned and the context from which they were learned.
- Decide to become a real sleuth at using cognates and agree to identify and record two or three cognates each week.
- Become a master at using the dictionary. Get ahold of a paper or online dictionary that you really like, become really familiar with it, and frequently use it. Of course, the dictionary can be used along with any of these other approaches.

The basic approach is to post these guidelines someplace where students can readily see them and discuss them with students. In doing so, be particularly attentive to drawing out student suggestions. Then, in closing the discussion, attempt to secure a vocabulary-learning commitment from each student. Initially, you might ask for a month's commitment. During the month, check periodically to see how students' approaches are working and give them feedback and encouragement. Then, at the end of the month, hold another discussion on the matter. At that time, try to decide whether individual students should continue with the approach to independent word learning they have been using or perhaps try another approach. As you are doing this, it is probably worth considering that students having an approach is probably more important that what exactly that approach is.

WHEN SHOULD THE STRATEGIES BE TAUGHT TO ELLs?

Obviously, teaching all of the strategies described in this chapter is not the responsibility of a single teacher or something that can be done in a single year. Exactly what is taught when and who is responsible for the instruction will differ from school to school and will depend on what instruction students have had in the past. Here, however, are some suggestions. During the primary-grade years, short and informal mini-lessons followed by practice in the context of reading, listening to text read aloud, or discussion should be sufficient. The one procedure that needs to be taught formally during the primary grades is suffix removal, which is actually a decoding procedure.

As indicated in the CCSS, grades 3 through 5 are when most of the more formal instruction should begin. We suggest that you give significant attention to using cognates, word parts, and context in these grades. With all three of these strategies, instruction should extend across more than one grade level, probably across all three of these grades. Teaching students to use the dictionary and related reference tools, deal with multiword units, develop a strategy for dealing with unknown words, and develop a personal approach to building vocabulary are much shorter endeavors. These can be taught whenever you deem students need them. Regardless of when the strategies are initially taught, they need to be reviewed, students need to be reminded about them, and students need to be prompted to use them in the years following initial instruction, not just during the elementary grades but also in the secondary grades, and not just in reading and language arts classes but in all content-area classes.

If all of the strategies are taught well in grades 1 to 5, then the main tasks left for grades 6 to 12 are reviewing, prompting, and encouraging. In the best of all worlds, this would not be left to chance. That is, reviewing certain word-learning strategies at certain times would be specified in the curriculum. Of course, for ELLs who have entered schools where English is the language of instruction in the later grades and who have not been taught these strategies, word-learning instruction is likely to extend into the upper grades. One target of instruction that becomes increasingly important in the upper grades is that of Latin and Greek roots. When a Latin or Greek root shows itself to be useful in a particularly content area—science, history, and so on—it should probably be taught. Also, if any of the strategies have not been taught well in the earlier grades, then they need to be taught well in the secondary grades. Many ELLs may need substantial instruction in word-learning strategies in the secondary grades.

A FINAL WORD

The purpose of this chapter has been to describe several approaches to teaching word-learning strategies and then to give detailed procedures for teaching students seven powerful strategies: using word parts, employing context clues to unlock the meaning of unknown words, drawing on cognate knowledge to recognize words that are familiar in a first language but not in a second, using the dictionary, recognizing and dealing with multiword units, developing a strategy for dealing with unknown words, and adopting a personal approach to building their vocabularies.

It is vital to realize that the instruction on word-learning strategies we have described in this chapter, substantial as some of that has been, is only the first step in assisting students to become competent and confident users of these important strategies. In the weeks, months, and years after the initial instruction, students need lots of independent practice, feedback, brief reviews and mini-lessons, more advanced lessons, opportunities to use the strategies, reminders to use them, and motivation to do so. It is only with such a long-term effort that students will fully learn the strategies, internalize them, and make them a part of their ongoing approach to building their vocabularies. ELLs' vocabularies will continue to grow throughout their years of schooling and even after they have completed school, and independent word learning will be the vehicle for most of that growth.

CHAPTER 6

Promoting Word Consciousness

Word consciousness—and especially understanding the power of word choice—is essential for sustained vocabulary growth. Words are the currency of written language. Learning new words is an investment, and students will make the required investment to the extent that they believe that the investment is worthwhile.

Judith Scott and William Nagy,
Vocabulary Scholars

Words are indeed the "currency of written language," as Scott and Nagy (2004) so nicely put it. Moreover, as Scott and Nagy also note, students are likely to make the required investment needed to learn vocabulary only if they believe that the investment is worthwhile. Making such an investment is especially critical for English language learners because the sheer number of words they need to learn will require that they learn most of these on their own. Thus, one of the major long-term goals of vocabulary instruction for ELLs is to help them to gain a deep appreciation of words and to value them, a goal that has been termed *word consciousness*. Simply stated, word consciousness refers to *awareness of* and *interest in* words and their meanings. As noted by Anderson and Nagy (1992), word consciousness involves both a cognitive and an affective stance toward words. Word consciousness integrates metacognition about words, motivation to learn words, and deep and lasting interest in words. Of particular relevance to ELLs is the role of metacognition (or thinking about thinking). Some work suggests that, compared to their native English-speaking counterparts, ELLs have an advantage in the development of metacognitive skills, as they already have a template in place about the fundamental principles of language structure in their first language (Bialystock, 2001). At the same time, and as with all students, if ELLs do not feel competent and if they have high levels of anxiety, they may not be motivated and interested in learning new words.

ELLs who are word-conscious are aware of the words around them—those they read and hear and those they write and speak. This awareness involves an appreciation of the power of words, an understanding of why certain words are used instead of others, and a sense of the words that could be used in place of those selected by a writer or speaker. It also involves, as Scott and Nagy (2004) emphasize, recognition of the communicative power of words, of the differences between spoken and written language, and of the particular importance of word choice in written language. And it involves an interest in learning and using new words and becoming more skillful and precise in word usage.

The process of acquiring vocabulary is complex, and for many ELLs acquiring the rich store of words that will help them succeed in and beyond school is a challenge. With tens of thousands of words to learn and with most of this word learning taking place incidentally as they are reading and listening, a positive disposition toward words is crucial to ELLs' success in expanding the breadth and depth of their word knowledge. Word consciousness exists at many levels of complexity and sophistication, and thus can and should be fostered among beginning, intermediate, and advanced ELLs.

Two additional factors further argue for the importance of word consciousness. First, there is the growing realization that for all learners motivation and affect are every bit as important to learning as cognition (Malloy, Marinak, & Gambrell, 2010; Pressley et al., 2003a, 2003b; Wigfield & Eccles, 2002). Word consciousness is the motivational and affective component of the multifaceted vocabulary program described in this book. Second, there is increasing evidence that lack of vocabulary is a key factor underlying school failure (Adams, 2010–2011; Becker, 1977; Biemiller, 2004; Chall, Jacobs, & Baldwin, 1990; Hart & Risley, 1995), particularly for ELLs (García, 1991; Mancilla-Martinez & Lesaux, 2010, 2011; Mancilla-Martinez, Pan, & Banu Vagh, 2011). Kindling students' interest and engagement with words is thus a vital part of helping ELLs develop rich and powerful vocabularies. The National Research Council (2004) sums up the cost of disengagement for students from less advantaged backgrounds, a category that includes many ELLs, particularly well: "When students from advantaged backgrounds become disengaged, they may learn less than they could, but they usually get by or they get second chances; most eventually graduate and move on to other opportunities. In contrast, when students from disadvantaged . . . backgrounds become disengaged, they . . . face severely limited opportunities." Gersten (1996) further points out that the regimen in many schools may both hinder ELLs' cognitive development and undermine their motivation to learn.

In the remainder of this chapter, we discuss a number of specific approaches to fostering word consciousness in *all* students, with particular attention to the needs of ELLs, and in a variety of contexts—in reading, in writing, and in discussion. They include Creating a Word-Rich Environment, Recognizing and Promoting Adept Diction, Promoting Word Play, Fostering Word Consciousness Through Writing, Involving Students in Original Investigations, and Teaching Students About Words (Graves & Watts-Taffe, 2008). In general, the approaches are arranged from those that are less formal and less time-consuming to those that are more formal, more time-consuming, and more demanding on the learner, although this is not a hard-and-fast progression. Ultimately, the goal is for word consciousness activities to become a seamless, enjoyable, and regular part of the school day.

CREATING A WORD-RICH ENVIRONMENT

All students can benefit from being in classrooms that are filled with words, and this is especially true for ELLs. Because ELLs have had less exposure to the English language than their native English-speaking peers, they need to hear words being used, they need opportunities to say words themselves, they need to see words in

FIGURE 6.1. Sensory Web for *Anger*

Looks Like
shattered glass on the pavement
a hurricane making landfall

Smells Like
hot burning coals
a huge forest fire racing toward you

Feels Like
a cold wind gripping you all over
you've been in a fist fight

ANGER

Tastes Like
dry sand burning in the desert
chili peppers

Sounds Like
fingernails on a blackboard
raccoons screeching in the dark

print, they need to read them, and they need to write them as often as possible. Fortunately, there are many ways to create a classroom environment that is inundated with spoken and written language.

Let's begin with the classroom library. Having a well-stocked library is essential. It is also essential that this library include books for beginning, intermediate, and advanced ELLs. Additionally, it is critical that a variety of genres are represented, and that these genres are available at various reading levels. Many classrooms include more fiction than nonfiction books, especially in the primary grades (Duke, 2000). As noted in the Common Core State Standards, ELLs, like all children, need to read both fiction and nonfiction, and they need to read nonfiction expository texts (text not organized as narratives) as well as nonfiction narrative texts (texts that are organized as stories, such as biographies). It is also important to include texts that deal with the cultures of the ELLs in your classroom. It is important that your classroom library include more than books; magazines, newspapers, and pamphlets are also needed. And we would include books in ELLs' native languages, books that are available in both English and your ELLs' native languages, and bilingual books (books that include both English and another language, usually on facing pages). For example, Language Lizard (http://www.languagelizard.com/) provides award-winning bilingual and multicultural children's books that are appropriate for use across all age and grade levels. The International Children's Digital Library (http://en.childrenslibrary.org/) is a great online resource for PreK–8 teachers who want access to books that represent numerous cultures and that are written in multiple languages. Daphne Muse's *The New Press Guide to Multicultural Resources for Young Readers* (1997) contains an annotated bibliography of multicultural literature likely to engage ELLs. McClure and Kristo's *Books That Invite Talk, Wonder, and Play* (1996) is a great resource for K–8 teachers who want to learn how to select books of all genres that are rich in language, and this resource is available online by Googling ED398530. For newer lists, we recommend the International Reading Association's Children's Choices, Teachers' Choices, and Young Adult Choices. These annual lists include many of the best books published each year and are available at www.reading.org/Resources/Booklists.aspx from 1998 through the present.

Now let's move to the classroom's physical space in general. Word walls are one popular means of displaying words to promote word consciousness. It is essential, however, that word walls be truly functional; they should not just be décor. This means that word walls must be frequently used and well maintained. While there is no right or wrong way to create and use a word wall, the most important criterion is that it be useful. For instance, one teacher might find that a word wall on transitional words is most useful to her class, while another might focus on science vocabulary. Or one teacher might supply the words for the wall himself, while another has students supply them. For ELLs, some effective strategies for the wall include defining the words in students' native languages, including basic terms alongside more sophisticated choices, providing images representing the words, and including cognates when appropriate.

A word-rich classroom will also have a dedicated area devoted to words—word card files, word play and riddle books, dictionaries, thesauri, and word games that represent a wide range of readability levels and are appropriate for students with various levels of proficiency. In other words, careful attention is needed to ensure that the students can access the material available for them for independent work and that opportunities for pair or small-group work are encouraged. This special area might be named The Word Station, Lexicon Lounge, or even the Vocabulary Sanctuary. Alternately, it is probably a good idea to have your students name it. Such a dedicated space will go a long way toward providing a strong foundation for the development of word consciousness. Your involvement in ensuring that students actively engage with their word-rich environment on a consistent basis and in meaningful ways will be of utmost importance. This is especially true for students with smaller vocabularies, a category in which ELLs are overrepresented. We next describe specific ways for you and your students to engage with the words in their environment.

RECOGNIZING AND PROMOTING ADEPT DICTION

Recognizing skillful diction in the texts students are reading and constantly encouraging students to employ adept diction in their own speech and writing are starting points in building word consciousness. Depending on students' native languages and levels of English proficiency, there are specific English sounds that may be problematic for ELLs to pronounce (for more details, see Kress, 2008). Thus, ELLs may feel especially hesitant to speak up in class if they are overly focused on "correct" pronunciation at the expense of using language. It is important to recognize that all speech is accented and that accent is not an indicator of knowledge of a language (American Association for Applied Linguistics, 2011).

Also, keep in mind that modeling is critical. Specifically, it is vital to model both enthusiasm for and proficiency in adept word usage. Consider the difference between asking a student to close the door because it is *not quite closed* and asking him to close the door because it is *ajar,* the difference between describing the color in a student's painting as *greenish-yellow* as opposed to *chartreuse,* or the difference between describing Dwight Howard as an *excellent* athlete or a *consummate* athlete. When students hear unfamiliar words used to describe concepts they are familiar with and care about, they become curious about the world of words. In addition, they learn—from experience—that word choice possibilities are immense and varied. As their "word worlds" open up, so, too, do the wider worlds in which they live.

Because books are a particularly rich source of interesting and sophisticated words, read-alouds, particularly repeated read-alouds, represent an excellent means of promoting adept diction. It is essential that care is taken in the selection of pieces to be read aloud. Repeated readings of a text (3 or 4 times a week) give students opportunities to become familiar with the text and its context, as well as to focus on a small set of words in the text. As Watts-Taffe (2006) points out, some ways for discussing such words include:

- Explaining the meaning of the new word (or having other students explain it).
- Extending the meaning of the word by providing examples.
- Engaging students with the word by helping them to make connections with their own experiences.

For ELLs in particular, visual, auditory, and tactile aids are great ways to further their word and overall conceptual knowledge (Samway & Taylor, 2008). For example, you might extend the meaning of the word *avalanche* by presenting a still or video of an avalanche and an audio track of an actual avalanche. Further, purposeful partnering in which pairs of readers are selected based on specific strengths and weaknesses (Klingner & Vaughn, 1996), along with books on tape (Blum, Koskinen, Tennant, Parker, Straub, & Curry, 1995) or some other electronic medium, provide ELLs with opportunities to experience authors' skillful use of words.

Aside from talking about the new words found in read-alouds and providing lots of opportunities for students to listen to and practice using language, an essential activity is to recognize and discuss the adept word choices authors have made. Scott and her colleagues (1996) have studied vocabulary as a vehicle for connecting reading and writing. Within the context of literature discussion groups, they assign one student the role of word hunter (also referred to as word wizard), whose job it is to look for particularly interesting uses of language in the literature read by the group. This student might, for example, draw the group's attention to Sharon Creech's use of the word *lunatic* in *Walk Two Moons* (1996) to describe a mysterious stranger. Why doesn't the author use *mentally ill* or *weirdo*? How does the author's word choice relate to the character who first uses the word to describe the mysterious fellow? Such discussions can lead students to more thoughtful word choices in their own speech and in their own writing. Of course, depending on the proficiency levels of the ELLs in your classroom, additional scaffolding might be necessary. In this case, before a student can discuss alternative word choices, you need to ensure that he understands the target word *lunatic*, something you might do by referring to its Spanish cognate, *lunático*.

Another way to encourage adept diction in students' writing and speaking is to scaffold their use of new words. With your guidance, they might construct sensory webs for words likely to be useful in their writing or for words they have read and would like to understand more fully. The lines leading from the word itself outward provide places for students to fill in what the word smells like, tastes like, looks like, sounds like, and feels like. Scott and her colleagues (1996), for example, report that one of the 6th-graders they worked with wrote that anger smells like "hot burning coals," looks like "shattered glass on the pavement," tastes like "dry sand burning in the desert," sounds like "fingernails screeching on the black-board," and feels like "a cold wind gripping you all over." Figure 6.1 shows this student's responses along with some additional ones.

A related technique used by Scott and her colleagues to help students expand the word choices used in their writing is to have them brainstorm words related to a key word. For the word *anxious*, one student came up with the related words *shaky, fidgeting, worried, apprehensive, nervous,* and *impatient.* Spanish-speaking ELLs can also consider cognates if there are some; in this case, *ansioso, nervioso,* and *impaciente* are worth considering.

Another opportunity to recognize and promote adept diction is to use the tried-and-true word-of-the-day approach. Allocating time each day to examine a new word can be effective with ELLs of all ages and proficiency levels. The word can be teacher-selected or student-selected and might be chosen from books, magazine articles, or newspapers, or from heard contexts such as appropriate television programs, discussions, and other teachers. It often works well to begin with teacher-selected words and to present the word and its meaning, including both definitional and contextual information, an explanation of why it was selected, and examples of how it relates to the lives of one or more members of the class. As we have noted, adding relevant pictures, cognates, gestures, concrete objects, and drama increases students' enthusiasm and understanding and can be especially beneficial for ELLs. Further, providing time for students' questions and comments allows for the type of deep processing necessary for effective word learning.

PROMOTING WORD PLAY

It is always important to teach and reinforce the notion that words convey meaning. But words do much more than convey meaning. Words and phrases can simultaneously feel good on the tongue, sound good to the ear, and incite a riot of laughter in the belly. Verbal phenomena such as homophones and homographs, idioms, clichés, and puns offer myriad opportunities for investigating language. Students get real pleasure out of words that sound alike, words that look alike, and words that sound nothing like what they mean. At the same time, word play can be challenging for many ELLs, as, for example, they may only know a single meaning for a word and thus have difficulty understanding when a word represents an alternative meaning (e.g., *kid* as in child vs. *kid* as in the baby goat), or they may be confused when non-literal meanings are used (e.g., *hit the roof*). It is important to keep in mind that some languages have more words with multiple meanings than others. For example, compared to English, Japanese has many words with multiple meanings, while Spanish has fewer. This means that it will not be as straightforward as simply using students' first language to teach about multiple word meanings. Instead, explicit explanations that words and phrases can carry different meanings depending on the context in which they are used will be imperative. For instance, you can focus on two sentences in which the word *fair* is used, such as "it was a *fair* decision" and "we enjoyed the rides at the *fair*," and discuss their different meanings with the class, pointing out that it is used as an adjective in the first sentence and as a noun in the second. Once students have had practice with multiple word meanings, they can work in small groups, discussing pairs of sentences that use the same word but that represent different meanings based on the context, words like *will*, *run*, and *mean*.

For ELLs, as for all students, it needs to be emphasized that word play is not a frill. As Blachowicz and Fisher (2004) explain, it is an activity firmly grounded in sound pedagogy and in research:

- Word play calls on students to reflect metacognitively on words, word parts, and context.
- Word play requires students to be active learners and capitalizes on possibilities for the social construction of meaning.
- Word play develops domains of word meaning and relatedness as it engages students in practice and rehearsal of words. (p. 219)

At the same time, as we have pointed out with many facets of ELLs working with vocabulary, they will often need scaffolding when dealing with word play.

Homophones and Homographs

Homophones present many opportunities for enjoyment and learning. Children delight in images such as those of a "towed toad," a "sail sale," or a "Sunday sundae." One activity that many children enjoy is drawing such homophone pairs, and one approach that has proven useful is to have students fold a piece of drawing paper into quadrants so they can write homophone pairs in the boxes on the left side of the paper and draw corresponding pictures in the boxes on the right side of the paper. Games such as Homophone Bingo and Homophone Concentration offer additional possibilities for experimenting with homophones.

Some words, of course, not only sound alike, but are spelled alike—and still have more than one meaning. In fact, as we have already noted, a large proportion of English words have more than one meaning. These homographs allow for a variety of games, including the following one, modified from a game in Lederer's *Get Thee to a Punnery* (1988), a word play book for adults. In each of the lines below, students insert a word that means the same as the word or phrase at either end; the number of blanks indicates the number of letters in the missing word.

1. summit __ __ __   spinning toy
2. hole __ __ __ fruit stone
3   nation __ __ __ __ __ __ rural area

It is possible and sometimes necessary to scaffold this and similar open-ended tasks by making them multiple-choice items. For number 1, for example, you could provide the alternatives *boy*, *top*, and *net*. Having students complete such puzzles can be fun and entertaining, but having them create such items can be even more valuable. When creating such items is within students' reach, creating them can provide an active, creative, and rewarding learning experience.

Idioms, Clichés, and Puns

Children are often fascinated by idioms such as "A bird in the hand is worth two in the bush" and "Don't count your chickens until they're hatched." Representing as they do the language of particular groups, idioms reflect particular periods of time, particular regions of the country, and particular cultures. Children can enjoy drawing or dramatizing the literal meanings of idioms such as "Don't look a gift horse in the mouth," "Roll with the punches," and "food for thought" and contrasting them with their figurative meanings. Recognize that idioms can present a particular challenge for ELLs, and be on the lookout for idioms and clarify their meaning. You may want to explain that idioms are phrases that do not mean exactly what the words say. In doing so, begin with simple and frequent examples such as "piece of cake." You might write the sentence "the puzzle was a *piece of cake*" and explain that this does not mean the puzzle was made out of cake. Showing a picture of a puzzle made of out cake will help students understand that the idiom should not be interpreted literally. You can then explain that *piece of cake* is an expression used when something is very easy because eating a piece of cake is easy and enjoyable. Once students are comfortable with simple and frequent expressions, you can proceed to more complex expressions that may require more background knowledge for interpretation (for example, *A leopard can't change his spots*). The *Longman American Idioms Dictionary* (1999) provides a listing of over 4,000 of them, and idiomdictionary.com lists over 5,000.

Clichés are often thought of as being unimaginative and trite. But in fact they are examples of language use that has endured over time, expressing familiar sentiments and wisdom that are timeless. They are at once phrases that many are familiar with and expressions of shared human experience, making them accessible and important forms of language for students to experience. You can kindle students' word awareness by being "down to earth" with them, warning them about "jumping out of the frying pan into the fire," and repeatedly playing around with phrases such as "until the cows come home."

Like clichés, puns are memorable and often quite clever. Advertisers often use them in songs and jingles, noted authors make use of them, and newspapers frequently employ them in headlines. In *Romeo and Juliet,* for example, the dying Mercutio can't resist a pun as he exclaims, "Look for me tomorrow, and you will find me a grave man." The day after the Minnesota Vikings' star kicker muffed a short field goal that led to the team's ouster from the playoffs, the *Minneapolis Star-Tribune* ran the headline "Kicked Out!" And even the prestigious *New York Times* employs them occasionally, as seen in the line, "Balloons have become a high flying business and sell at inflated prices."

Word Play Books

A wide array of books lend themselves to raising word consciousness and to learning a host of interesting facts about words. Books are available for every age and many levels, and they deal with many aspects of words. There are alphabet books, books that include extensive word play, books in which words play a central role, books about word play, books filled with word games, books about the history of words, books of proverbs, books about slang, and books about nearly any other aspect of words you could think of. There are far more word and word play books than we can possibly describe here. The medium-size public library one of us uses lists over 150 books under the term "words," and a search on Amazon.com using the term "word books for children" lists over 250,000 items. Since we cannot consider all of these, here we list one book in each of several categories to suggest the range of books available, but we encourage you to check your local library, your local bookstore, and the Web for many more titles.

Two wonderful alphabet books are Graeme Base's *Animalia* (1996) and Judith Viorst's *The Alphabet from Z to A (with Much Confusion on the Way)* (1997). Each combines clever illustrations with inviting text and appeals to both beginning and more sophisticated readers. As with any book, attention to word meanings is essential. However, the key focus when using alphabet books is on solidifying sound-symbol correspondence, ensuring that the words represent common sounds. An excellent example is a book like *Animalia*, in which you will find "crafty crimson cats carefully catching crusty crayfish" representing the letter "C."

Two books that highlight the richness of language are Fred Gwynne's *The King Who Rained* (1970) and Louis Sachar's *Holes* (1998), which won the 1999 Newbery Medal. The first revolves around words with multiple meanings, and the second is filled with interesting words, some of which provide clues to the central puzzle of the novel, and others of which, like Stanley Yelnats, the palindrome name of the protagonist, are simply fun.

Two books whose plots center around words and language are Andrew Clements's *Frindle* (1998) and Roni Schotter's *The Boy Who Loved Words* (2006). Clements's novel tells the story of Nick, who invents the word *frindle*, convinces kids in his school to use it instead of the word *pen*, and watches as his word spreads to the city, the nation, the world, and even the dictionary. This book is also available in Spanish and Chinese. Schotter's picture book tells the story of Selig, a boy who is passionate about words, collects them endlessly, and decides that his life's work is to share his wealth of words with others. *The School Library Journal* calls this book, "An inspiring choice for young wordsmiths and anyone who cherishes the variety and vitality of language."

Two word play books we particularly like are Lederer's *Pun and Games* (1996), which would be appropriate for intermediate and advanced ELLs in middle school or high school, and *Get Thee to a Punnery* (1988), which you as a teacher could use to get ideas. *Pun and Games* includes, as recorded in the subtitle, "jokes, riddles, daffynitions, tairy fales, rhymes, and more word play for kids," while *Get Thee to a Punnery* contains lots of puns but also some challenging word games. Additionally, Blachowicz and Fisher's "Keep the 'Fun' in Fundamental" (2004) provides dozens of word-play activities as well as sources for still more activities.

Still another very useful sort of books is bilingual books. These books contain the text in English and in another language, usually on facing pages. Some of these books are for ELLs just beginning to read English. The books in the My First Bilingual Book–Numbers series by Milet Publishers present the numbers 1–10 and illustrations in English on one side of the page and, for example, Chinese (2011a), German (2010a), Japanese (2011b), Korean (2011c), Polish (2010b), Somali (2011d), and Vietnamese (2011e) on the other side of the page. Other bilingual books are for beginning or intermediate-level ELLs. *Talking with Mother Earth/Hablando con Madre Tierra* (2006), written by Jorge Argueta and illustrated by Lucia Angela Perez, for example, is an illustrated book of poems exploring a Pipil Nahus Indian boy's connection to Mother Earth and how that connection heals the wounds of racism.

Finally, two books about words and language appropriate for teachers are Greenman's *Words That Make a Difference—And How to Use Them in a Masterly Way* (2001), and Pinker's *The Language Instinct: How the Mind Creates Language* (2000). Almost all of *Words That Make a Difference* is exactly what a vocabulary book is not supposed to be—an alphabetical list of words and their definitions. But two things save it from being a bad book and instead make it a very good one. Accompanying each word and definition is a short passage from the *New York Times* in which a writer used the word in a clever, memorable, and appropriate way. Additionally, the words are at just the right level of difficulty for advanced ELLs—ones that they have probably heard but don't use because they are not quite sure of them. *The Language Instinct,* on the other hand, is very much what a book about language directed at a general audience ought to be. In it, Pinker, an eminent MIT linguist, gives his theories about the nature, origin, and development of language. Although not all agree with Pinker, the book is definitely interesting, exciting, accessible, and filled with ideas to share with students. *Publishers Weekly* called it "a beautiful hymn to the infinite creative potential of language."

FOSTERING WORD CONSCIOUSNESS THROUGH WRITING

We begin this section by providing a very brief rationale for focusing on writing to enhance students' vocabulary knowledge in general and to foster word consciousness specifically. Work with monolingual English speakers suggests that limited vocabulary knowledge contributes to dependence on repetitive uses of the same words and thus to under-elaboration of thoughts and ideas in writing (Moats, Foorman, & Taylor, 2006). And, of course, writers' familiarity with the writing topic is related to their writing performance (Saddler & Graham, 2007), meaning that background knowledge plays a central role in the quality of students' writing. Given that ELLs tend to have more limited vocabularies than their native English-speaking peers, their writing can be expected to be impeded. Despite the logic connecting word knowledge and writing quality, the nature of this relationship has seldom been studied, particularly among ELLs. Two approaches that have been used with monolingual speakers but are relevant to ELLs are those of Beck and McKeown and of Duin, and one line of work that deals specifically with ELLs and writing has recently been described by one of us (Mancilla-Martinez, 2010).

In Chapter 4, we described how Beck and McKeown's Robust Instruction can be used to teach individual words. Here, we discuss Beck and McKeown's approach (Beck, Perfetti, & McKeown, 1982; McKeown & Beck, 2004) and a version of that approach created by Duin (Duin & Graves, 1987, 1988) that can foster students' use of richer vocabulary in their writing. The first step in either approach is to select a small set of words that are semantically related. One set used by Beck and McKeown—*rival, hermit, novice, virtuoso, accomplice, miser, tyrant,* and *philanthropist*—contains words that refer to *people.* A set used by Duin—*advocate, capability, tether, criteria, module, envision, configuration,* and *quest*—contains words that can be used in talking about *space exploration.*

The next step, the central part of the instruction, is to have students work extensively and intensively with the words, spending perhaps half an hour a day over a period of a week or so with them and engaging in a dozen or so diverse activities with them—really getting to know them, discovering their shades of meaning and the various ways in which they can be used, and realizing what interesting companions words can be. Beck and McKeown's activities, for example, included asking students to respond to words like *virtuoso* and *miser* with thumbs up or thumbs down to signify approval or disapproval; asking which of three actions an *accomplice* would be most likely to engage in—robbing a bank by himself, stealing some candy, or driving a getaway car; and asking such questions as, "Could a *virtuoso* be a *rival*? Could a *virtuoso* be a *novice*? and Could a *philanthropist* be a *miser?*" Duin's activities included asking students to discuss how *feasible* space travel might soon be, asking them how a space station could *accommodate* people with disabilities, and having them write brief essays called "Space Shorts" in which they used the words in dealing with such topics as the foods that might be available in space.

The third step, which was used only in Duin's instruction, is to have students write more extensive essays using as many of the taught words as possible, playing with them and exploring their possibilities. Duin's students appeared to really enjoy this activity. As one of their teachers observed, "Students who were asked to write often and use the words in written class work showed great involvement in their writing." The students also showed that they could indeed use the new words adroitly. One student, for example, noted that "the space program would be more *feasible* if we sent more than just astronauts and satellites into space" and then suggested that designers should "change the whole *configuration* of the space shuttle so that it could *accommodate* more people."

Finally, we would add a fourth step—that of directly discussing with students the word choices they make, why they make those choices, and how adroit use of words makes our speech and writing more precise, more memorable, and more interesting. Note that when either Beck and McKeown's or Duin's instruction is used for the purpose of fostering word consciousness, the main goal is to get students involved with and excited about words rather than to teach a small set of words. Using these clever and intriguing approaches several times a year should be a substantial contribution to reaching this goal.

Focusing specifically on ELLs, one of us (Mancilla-Martinez, 2010) conducted a study on the effectiveness of the Word Generation vocabulary program, which we describe in some detail in Chapter 7, on 5th-grade ELLs' writing. Word Generation was designed to build students' academic vocabulary by targeting five high-utility words each week to be learned in the context of brief passages outlining controversies under debate in the United States (for example, abilities of women in math and science). Although no writing instruction was provided, each Friday students composed a short piece based on the controversial topic. As was the case with Duin's instruction, incorporating a weekly writing component provided students with the opportunity to explore the use of newly taught vocabulary in their writing, which is critical to cultivate deeper learning of the words. Results showed that students indeed used the target words in their writing, including using previously taught words. Furthermore, the combination of vocabulary instruction (including other aspects of the intervention such as weekly debates, which fostered increased language use) and of having students write on a weekly basis likely contributed to the improvement in their writing. Importantly, the gains were not simply the result of increased essay length, as students did not produce longer essays over time. This work suggests that ELLs' writing improved because they were writing on a consistent basis and because they had accumulated a store of new words that could make their writing more precise and effective. That is, awareness of words appeared to improve students' writing, even without explicit writing instruction. At the end of the study, students were asked to comment on the vocabulary program. Surprisingly, given the lack of writing instruction, they overwhelmingly cited the benefits of vocabulary instruction on their writing. For example, one student wrote that Word Generation helped her because "It got me familiar to new words and my writing got better." Another wrote, "Before I only used simple and boring words. Now I'm a better writer because my writing has Word Generation words and it makes it more interesting." It seems clear that raising students' awareness of words can go a long way in improving their word knowledge and in encouraging them to use it in their writing.

INVOLVING STUDENTS IN ORIGINAL INVESTIGATIONS

The activities described in the previous sections call students' attention to words in various ways—some of which are more deliberate than others. This section addresses the role of still more systematic efforts—research conducted by students themselves—in the development of word consciousness. Such original investigations centered on vocabulary provide a wealth of opportunities for increasing word consciousness. An array of options for investigations exists, some focused on text, some on speech, and some on interviews of language users. The possibilities include:

- The words or word parts students have learned
- The vocabulary used in certain situations (e.g., playground vs. classroom) or by certain professions (e.g., medical doctors vs. sports broadcasters)
- The vocabulary used by certain individuals (e.g., very young children vs. teenagers)

- Oral vs. written vocabulary (e.g., repetition vs. conciseness)
- How vocabulary changes over time (e.g., use of "text me")
- Terms of address by different people in different settings (e.g., Doctor, Professor, Mister)

Investigations focusing on written text are particularly doable because the data sources are readily available. You might, for example, have beginning ELLs who have learned the most frequent English words search through a page or so of a text they are reading and record the number of times that the 10 most frequent English words—*the, of, and, to, a, in, is, that, it,* and *was*—are used. If they check the number of times these 10 words came up against the total number of words on the page, they'll find that these 10 words make up about 25% of the total, a finding that we believe they will find encouraging. Similarly, you might have slightly more advanced ELLs tally the number of inflections—say, *-s, -ed,* and *-ing*—occurring on a page of text they are reading. What they will find is that these inflections occur a lot—perhaps in 5% of the words—and the point you would want to make here is that learning these inflections is very important.

Another option, this one more appropriate for intermediate and advanced ELLs, is to investigate the vocabulary used in various texts. For example, students might compare the typical number of words in articles in *USA Today* and the *New York Times*. As part of such a study, they could use some metric of word difficulty to examine the differential difficulty of the vocabulary in the two papers, perhaps sampling 100 words of text and tallying words beyond the first 4,000 most frequent words, a list available at thefirst4000words.com. Such a study could lead to fruitful discussions of why those differences exist, as well as a discussion of the reading process and text features associated with lower and higher levels of text difficulty.

Investigations of spoken language are somewhat more difficult because the language must be recorded before it can be analyzed. One source of spoken language that is readily accessible, however, is television. Intermediate-level ELLs might enjoy analyzing the vocabulary used in cartoons, looking perhaps for colorful adjectives used by the characters. Similarly, advanced ELLs might enjoy comparing the terminology used in police dramas, medical series, news broadcasts, and other types of programs. More demanding tasks might involve recording language use in natural settings. Students could work in small groups to study vocabulary use within particular contexts such as the school cafeteria, the gym during basketball practice, or the doctor's office. Students with very young siblings might record 5 to 10 minutes or so of talk a week over a period of a month and draw some conclusions about the contents of their younger siblings' vocabularies and any changes in that content over time.

Another possibility is for students to investigate usage variation across geographic areas. You of course will need to point out possible usages to investigate. One of us, a Californian transplanted to Minnesota, found two regionalisms particularly interesting. Minnesotans use *rubber binders* to hold things together. Is their use restricted to Minnesota? Wisconsin students look for a *bubbler* if they're thirsty. What do Californians, New Yorkers, or Floridians drink from? E-mail offers a convenient way for two or more schools to collaborate and ask these and other questions about word usage. Somewhat similarly, students might investigate the use of slang among English learners with different language backgrounds, for example, students whose first language is Spanish and those whose first language is Vietnamese.

TEACHING STUDENTS ABOUT WORDS

Most of the activities we have discussed thus far encourage students to become aware of words, manipulate them, appreciate them, and play with them in ways that do not involve explicit instruction. In this final section of the chapter, we consider some knowledge about words that teachers should definitely have and the possibility of explicitly instructing students on some of these concepts. The section draws heavily on work by Nagy and Scott (2000) in which they discuss the complexity of word knowledge and the role of metalinguistic awareness in learning words.

The Complexity of Word Knowledge

According to Nagy and Scott (2000), if we are to understand the processes underlying students' vocabulary growth—and, we would add, if we are to effectively assist that growth—we must recognize at least five aspects of the complexity of word knowledge. These five aspects are incrementality, multidimensionality, polysemy, interrelatedness, and heterogeneity. More recently, Scott and Nagy (2004) have added a sixth aspect, understanding the role of definitions, context, and word parts in vocabulary learning.

Incrementality. Word learning is incremental; that is, it proceeds in a series of steps. As Clark (1993) has pointed out, the meanings young children initially assign to words are incomplete, but over time these meanings become increasingly refined until they eventually approximate those of adults. *Dog*, for example, may at first refer to any small animal—dogs, cats, hamsters, squirrels—and only later be applied exclusively to dogs. ELLs of all ages take a similar course in learning many of the words they eventually master. Dale (1965) attempted to capture this incremental nature of word learning by proposing four levels of word knowledge: (1) never having seen it before, (2) knowing there is such a word, but not knowing what it means, (3) having a vague and context-bound meaning for the word, and (4) knowing and remembering it. Dale's fourth level could be further broken down—into, for example, having a full and precise meaning versus having a general meaning, or using the word in writing versus only recognizing it when reading. However levels of word knowledge are defined, it is clear that reaching high levels is no mean task. McKeown, Beck, Omanson, and Pople (1984) found that even 40 high-quality instructional encounters with words was insufficient for students to fully master the words. This has important implications for ELLs, as they generally have had fewer opportunities to hear and use English compared to their native English-speaking peers. It is also clear that high levels of word knowledge are needed to effect reading comprehension (Nagy, 1988; Stahl & Fairbanks, 1986).

Multidimensionality. The second aspect of word knowledge, being multidimensional, is in some ways a qualification of the first. Although it is useful to think of levels of word knowledge, in actuality there is no single dimension along which differences in word knowledge can be considered. As we pointed out in Chapter 2, Calfee and Drum (1986) note that knowing a word involves "depth of meaning; precise usage; facile access . . . ; the ability to articulate one's understanding; flexibility in the application of the knowledge of the word; the appreciation of metaphor, analogy, word play; the ability to recognize a synonym, to define, to use a word expressively." To this we would add a central theme of this chapter, namely that word knowledge has both a cognitive and an affective component.

Polysemy. The third aspect of words, polysemy, refers to the fact that many words have multiple meanings, a potential problem area, especially for ELLs. Polysemy is more frequent than it is often thought to be; a lot of words have multiple meanings, and the more frequent a word is the more likely it is to have two or more meanings. Additionally, it is worth recognizing that the multiple meanings of words range from cases in which the meanings are completely unrelated (the *bank* of a river versus the *bank* where you cash checks) to cases in which the differences are so subtle that it is difficult to decide whether or not they are indeed different meanings (*giving* Mary $10 versus *giving* Mary a kiss). Moreover, words virtually always gain some meaning from the context in which they are found, with the result that meanings are infinitely nuanced.

Interrelatedness. The fourth aspect of words to note is their interrelatedness: A learner's knowledge of one word is linked to his knowledge of other words. Here, conceptual knowledge is very relevant, and ensuring that ELLs have ample opportunities to discuss the ways in which words are interrelated is particularly crucial, as they may already have the conceptual knowledge in their native language. To use Nagy and Scott's example, "How well a person knows the meaning of *whale* depends in part on his or her understanding of *mammal*. A person who already knows the words *hot, cold,* and *cool* has already acquired some of the components of the word *warm*, even if the word *warm* has not yet been encountered."

Heterogeneity. The fifth aspect of words to be concerned with is their heterogeneity: What it means to know a word is dependent on the type of word in question. To again use Nagy and Scott's example, "knowing function words such as *the* or *if* is quite different from knowing terms such as *hypotenuse* or *ion*." But it is not just different words that require different sorts of knowing. Different word users require different sorts of word knowledge. As a potential purchaser of a diamond engagement ring, a young man is certainly better served if he has some knowledge of diamonds. As a seller of diamond rings and possibly a large-scale purchaser of diamonds, a jeweler needs and typically has considerably more knowledge of diamonds than his customers. And as the artisan and artist who shapes a beautiful stone from an unremarkable piece of rock, a diamond cutter must have both richer and quite different knowledge than the jeweler.

Definitions, Context, and Word Parts. This last aspect of words that Scott and Nagy consider includes topics that we have discussed in detail in Chapter 5 as part of teaching students word-learning strategies. The point that Scott and Nagy make about the need for students to understand word-learning strategies is that in addition to knowing *how to use* word-learning strategies, students need to know some things *about* word-learning strategies. Most notably, students need to understand when to use these strategies, when not to use them, and the strengths and limitations of each of them. Definitions, for example, are useful for checking on the meaning of a word you think you know or for getting some general idea of a word's meaning. They are not so useful and certainly not sufficient for learning rich and precise word meanings. Somewhat differently, it is useful for students to understand that many English words come from Latin and Greek roots and that they may share cognates with their native languages. Cognate instruction can be particularly beneficial for Spanish-speaking ELLs after the primary grades because a substantial number of English academic words are cognates of more common Spanish words (Lubliner & Hiebert, 2011). For instance, *acquire* and *demonstrate* are part of the academic register in English, whereas *adquirir* and *demostrar* are everyday words in Spanish. Thus, Spanish-speaking ELLs can use their knowledge of *adquirir* and *demostrar* as aids to learning *acquire* and *demonstrate*.

The Role of Metalinguistic Awareness in Word Learning

What sorts of metalinguistic awareness of words and word learning are important to teachers and to students? The question with respect to teachers can be easily answered. Everything in this section of the chapter, everything in Nagy and Scott's chapters (Nagy & Scott, 2000; Scott & Nagy, 2004), and a good deal of the information contained in the references to this chapter and to Nagy and Scott's chapter is important for teachers. Understanding incrementality, multidimensionality, polysemy, interrelatedness, and heterogeneity cannot help but be valuable to you as you work with students. In addition to information on these topics, Andrews' *Language Exploration and Awareness* (2006) offers a number of insights about words and about other aspects of language that teachers who work with ELLs should find useful. Similarly, Nagy (2007) provides an extremely convincing argument for the importance of metalinguistic awareness for vocabulary learning, underscoring the *need* to explicitly promote word consciousness.

The answer with respect to students is not as easily arrived at. While some metalinguistic awareness about words and word learning can certainly be valuable to students, just what students need to learn and how they can best learn it are matters yet to be decided. It seems likely, however, that much of our attempts to build metalinguistic awareness should be embedded in students' ongoing work with words and be brought to conscious attention as appropriate opportunities arise.

Here, we offer three specific examples. Polysemy can be appropriately dealt with when students are being instructed in using dictionaries or when they are actually using them to look up word meanings. As we have noted, one of the principles students should follow when looking up definitions is to choose the definition that fits the context in which they find the word, and this means recognizing that words have different meanings that are both shaped and revealed by context. Incrementality can be appropriately dealt with when students are learning to use context to unlock word meanings. Something that students learning to use context clues to identify word meanings need to recognize is that a single instance of a word in context is likely to reveal only a small increment of a word's meaning, but that each additional instance of the word in context is likely to reveal another increment. Finally, interrelatedness can be appropriately dealt with when students are learning new concepts (or labels for concepts in a new language, as is often the case for ELLs), particularly when they are learning concepts in a relatively unfamiliar domain. Students who are studying literary elements of narratives, for example, will need to learn the meanings of *rising action, falling action,* and *plot* as part of learning the meaning of *climax*; and the context of their doing so provides an excellent opportunity for introducing the notion of the interrelatedness of words.

Additionally, students will learn a lot about words as part of engaging in many of the informal learning experiences described throughout this chapter. The adept diction that professional writers use is possible because there are so many different words available to choose from. Much word play—puns, for example—works because words have multiple meanings. And intensive instruction is necessary because word learning is an incremental process. These and other insights about words can be briefly pointed out as students are involved in these various activities.

As these considerations of teaching students about words demonstrate, some approaches to word consciousness are fairly complex and academic, and such approaches certainly have a place. Nonetheless, we need to remember that one definite purpose of word consciousness work is to foster students' enthusiasm about words, a fact illustrated in Figure 6.2.

A FINAL WORD

The purpose of this chapter has been to define and elaborate on the concept of word consciousness, to argue for the importance of word consciousness as a deliberate goal of vocabulary instruction for ELLs, and to suggest some approaches to fostering word consciousness. The student who is word-conscious knows a lot of words, and he knows them well. Equally importantly, he is interested in words, and he gains enjoyment and satisfaction from using them well and from seeing or hearing them used well by others. He finds words intriguing, recognizes adroit word usage when he encounters it, uses words adroitly himself, is on the lookout for new and precise words, and is responsive to the nuances of word meanings. He is also cognizant of the power of words and realizes that they can be used to foster clarity and understanding or to obscure and obfuscate matters. Given the size and complexity of the task of learning tens of thousands of words, developing students' word consciousness so that they have both the will and the skill to improve their vocabularies is hugely important, especially for ELLs. However, despite the importance and complexity of the vocabulary-learning task, it makes good sense to keep most efforts to foster word consciousness light and lowkey. Whenever possible, word consciousness activities should encourage a playfulness like that shown in these snippets of word play we recently came across.

FIGURE 6.2. Give Me a Big W!

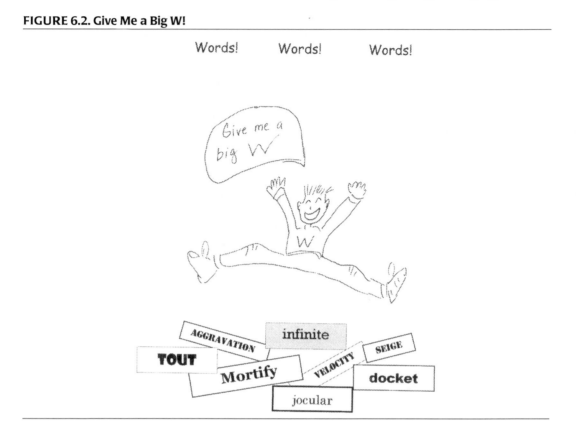

If ignorance is bliss, why aren't more people happy?
Why is the man who invests all your money called a broker?
When cheese gets its picture taken, what does it say?

Or like that shown by these winners of the *Washington Post*'s annual contest in coming up with alternate meanings for words:

flabbergasted—appalled over how much weight you have gained.
lymph—to walk with a lisp.

CHAPTER 7

Empirically Validated Vocabulary Programs for English Language Learners

We think it is time to move beyond the study of individual mechanisms and ask whether evidence-based vocabulary instruction and curriculum packages can be developed that will make a difference in real classrooms.

Michael Pressley, Laurel Disney, & Kendra Anderson,
Reading Researchers

As we have emphasized throughout this book, vocabulary learning is a huge task, especially for English language learners. Fortunately, there are many ways to help ELLs succeed at this task. One important way is to devote considerable instructional attention to vocabulary instruction starting in the primary grades and continuing throughout schooling. In this chapter, we highlight four vocabulary programs that have been implemented and found effective for ELLs. Together, the programs span the PreK years through the middle grades. All of them incorporate research-based principles of vocabulary learning, with specific attention to the needs of ELLs. For example, both the Vocabulary Improvement and Oral Language Enrichment Through Stories (VIOLETS) and the Quality English and Science Teaching (QuEST) programs use many scaffolding techniques proven to be effective with ELLs, the Acquisition of Vocabulary in English (AVE) program focuses on Spanish-English cognates to facilitate ELLs' word learning, and Word Generation (WG) includes a writing component to help ELLs cultivate deeper learning of the words. In short, the vocabulary programs described in this chapter include purposeful activities that provide students with authentic contexts to learn and use newly taught words.

THE VOCABULARY IMPROVEMENT AND ORAL LANGUAGE ENRICHMENT THROUGH STORIES (VIOLETS) PROGRAM

Overview

The VIOLETS program is an early childhood language program that promotes the development of key and basic vocabulary through the use of children's literature.

"Key vocabulary" refers to words that appear frequently in a wide variety of texts, words for which students already have concepts represented by the words but that serve as more precise and complex synonyms for their more familiar version of the word (for example, *lovely* for *pretty*). These are also words that students can work with in a variety of ways so that they can build rich representations of them and establish connections to other words and concepts. "Basic words" refers to words that are generally more concrete than key words and are part of a category such as foods or vehicles. In the program, these categories are aligned PreK and kindergarten standards. The curriculum uses as a starting point 12 Big Books, chosen on the basis of their quality, their appeal to young children, and the extent to which their content aligns with state (in this case, the Maryland Model for School Readiness) and national PreK standards. In the program, a specified number of carefully selected words and idiomatic expressions that occur in the stories are taught before, during, and after story reading. In addition, paraphrasing and questioning techniques are employed during reading to further develop students' oral language proficiency, build children's background knowledge, and develop and reinforce conceptual knowledge structures appropriate to this age group. The program builds on effective practices used with native English-speaking children, but uses many of the scaffolding techniques described in previous chapters—using hand gestures, body language, pictures, and objects to accompany speech; providing a model of a task or response before requiring students to undertake it; previewing material prior to questioning students; and providing repeated exposures to words, concepts, and skills. Additional components of the program include the presentation of "core knowledge" themes that tie the book to state and/or national standards, and a language awareness component in which pre-reading skills and concepts of print are introduced.

A 15-week randomized evaluation of VIOLETS with pre-kindergarten 4-year-old children indicated that there were large and significant gains for both key words and basic words between the pretest and posttest and that both native English-speaking students and ELLs showed overall gains in their vocabulary knowledge (August & Barr, 2010).

Program Components

For most books, each unit consists of four lessons (taught Days 1–4) and a fifth lesson taught on Day 5. During the first four lessons in each unit, children listen to a fiction or nonfiction book with content aligned with state and national standards in the domains of Physical Development, Language and Literacy, Social and Emotional Development, Mathematical Thinking, Scientific Thinking, Social Studies, and the Arts. During the fifth lesson, children learn a function word or phrase and engage in a language-awareness activity. The units for three books consist of seven rather than five lessons because the books are longer. In these units, the children listen to a book during the first six lessons, and during the seventh lesson they learn a function word or phrase and engage in a language-awareness activity.

Introduce core knowledge theme. On Day 1, the first activity introduces the core knowledge theme that the read-aloud will present. As noted, these themes are drawn from state and national PreK standards. While listening to Russell Hoban's *Bread and Jam for Frances* (1986), for example, the relevant standard relates to physical development and health: *The student is expected to identify types of foods that help the body grow such as healthy breakfast foods and snacks.*

Preteach key words. On Days 1–4, the second activity is "Preteach Key Words." To teach key words, the teacher uses picture cards that are labeled to indicate the story and day of the unit (for example, *Bread and Jam*, Day 1) for which they are used. Each picture card shows one picture that exemplifies a single key word. The text for each picture is on the opposite side of the card to make it easy for the teacher to read it while showing the picture to students. The teaching procedures for each key word follow the same pattern: teacher providing a child- friendly definition of the target word; teacher and students repeating the target word three times; teacher providing a description of how the picture demonstrates the meaning of the word; teacher saying the name and sound of the first letter of the word; teacher modeling of the word used in a new context; students coming up with their own sentences using the word; and students deciding if examples are or are not related to the word in some way.

Concepts of Print. On Day 1, students sing a song that reminds them that a book has a front and back cover and that we read from left to right.

Story Recall. Beginning on Day 2 and extending through Day 4, the portion of the story read on the previous day is reviewed. This activity is designed both to remind the children what has happened in the story thus far and to provide them with practice in retelling the main events of a story in the order they occurred.

Interactive Reading. During Days 1–4, the teacher reads a quarter of the week's text. In addition to employing interactive reading techniques that entail paraphrasing and questioning, the teacher shows the book to the students while reading, points to elements of the picture, and demonstrates word meanings with whatever actions are possible to help make the text meaning clear. Figure 7.1 shows a sample interactive reading lesson. Although the lesson provides some paraphrasing and questions, teachers are encouraged to paraphrase any portions of the text they think might be unclear and ask students additional questions to help them process the text.

Closing Activity. Days 1–4 end with a closing activity intended to allow the children to relate the story to their own experiences or to allow them to experience some aspect of the story through movement in role-plays called Act-Out Word Meanings. Act-Out Word Meanings are scenarios crafted to allow children to more fully visualize the word meanings and to move around the classroom without causing too much disruption. Two key words from the lesson are combined into a short "scenario" that is read to the children. As the children listen, they have the

FIGURE 7.1 VIOLETS Interactive Reading Lesson

Passage 1:

Look at Chrysanthemum's miserable face [point to Chrysanthemum]. *(Picture)*

Let's make a face like that. *(Gesture)*

How do we feel? We feel miserable! *(Previewing prior to open-ended questioning, below)*

Let's say that together: We feel miserable! We feel miserable! *(Choral repetition)*

Why does Chrysanthemum feel so miserable? *[Anticipated response: Because the children keep making fun of her name.] (Oral language and knowledge structure development: causes)*

Passage 2:

Here is the new baby [point to Chrysanthemum]. *(Picture)*

Her parents are so happy. They said she was perfect, absolutely perfect.

Let's say that together: Absolutely perfect! *(Choral repetition)*

The little baby is perfect; that means she is just right. She is as good as she could be. *(Defining vocabulary in context)*

Chrysanthemum's parents loved their new baby. She was absolutely perfect. *(Summary)*

Passage 3:

Poor Chrysanthemum wilted again. Wilted is what a flower does when it needs water. It droops like this [demonstrate wilting]. *(Dramatization)*

Show me what you would look like if you were wilting. *(Dramatization)*

FIGURE 7.2. VIOLETS Act-Out Meaning Lesson

Act-Out Meaning

Lovely + Practice

Let's pretend its summer and we are outside. It's a lovely day. The sun is shining and it feels so warm. Let's all say that together: It's a lovely day! [Pause for the children to repeat.] Let's pretend that we have just learned to hop on one foot, and now we want to practice; we want to get better. [Demonstrate hopping on one foot and encourage the children to do the same.] Let's all say, "We are practicing hopping on one foot."

---

opportunity to act out part of the scenario and repeat sentences that use the key words. Figure 7.2 shows a sample Act-Out Word Meanings lesson.

Building Word Meaning. On Day 5, a Function Words and Phrases activity focuses on idioms and other expressions. First, the target word or phrase is defined in English and presented as it appeared in the context of the read-aloud. Then children are invited to explore the word or expression and deepen their understanding of it through dialogues with the teacher.

As with the key words, the teacher uses picture cards. Each of these shows a picture that exemplifies a single function word. As with some other cards, the text for each picture is on the opposite side of the card to make it easy for the teacher to read the text while showing the picture to students. The teaching procedures for each function word follow the same general pattern as with key words.

Language Awareness Activity. This Day 5 activity is designed to develop children's phonological and phonemic awareness, and introduce them to concepts of print and pre-reading skills. The specific topics covered in a unit arise from the reading selection. For example, in *Bread and Jam for Frances*, several songs and rhymes appeared and lent themselves to the topic of rhyme.

Extension Activities. There are also several extension activities. The first activity is completed on the same day as the corresponding read-aloud section, but at another time. In the first of these, the Basic Word Activity, the teacher uses the text that accompanies basic word images to talk about the basic word meanings. Figure 7.3 shows some basic word picture cards like those used in VIOLETS. The following procedure is used to teach these words:

- Show students the picture.
- Use the text on the opposite side of the card to describe the image. Make sure to point to relevant elements of the image as you describe the word.
- Ask students a question that relates to the picture or have them act out the word's meaning.
- Have students repeat each word twice.
- Once the daily basic words have been instructed, review all the basic words that have been taught during the week and include some words instructed during previous weeks.

During the second activity, the teacher briefly reviews basic words selected from the current and previous lessons by flashing the words, saying the word, and then having students say the word. During the second flash, students say the words on their own. At the end of the week, several games are suggested to help students further review both key and basic words learned in the current and previous units. If teachers have other ideas for games to reinforce word meaning, they can replace the suggested games with their own.

ACQUISITION OF VOCABULARY IN ENGLISH (AVE)

Overview

The AVE program is a primary-grade program for Spanish-speaking ELLs with the goal of promoting the development of academic vocabulary that appears frequently in grade-level text. The curriculum consists of five daily lessons per week delivered over 8 weeks. Each 40-minute lesson is composed of two segments. The first segment focuses on content words such as *impression, survive,* and *delicate;* the second segment focuses on connectives such as *because, meanwhile,* and

FIGURE 7.3. Basic Word Picture Cards Like Those in VIOLETS

| happy | curious | safe |

Teacher Talk	Chrysanthemum was very happy on the first day of school. Now, we will talk more about feeling happy, and about other feelings we can have.
Teacher Talk	*Happy* This is a picture of happy. If you are happy, you are pleased and glad. This family is very happy or pleased because they are outside together. Show me a happy face. Say "happy" with me two times.
Teacher Talk	*Curious* This is a picture of curious. If you are curious, you are excited to learn. This girl is curious or excited to learn about insects in the grass. What kinds of things do you think a curious kitten might do? Say "curious:" with me two times.
Teacher Talk	*Safe* This is a picture of safe. When you are safe, you are not in danger. The girl is safe when she wears a helmet. The girl is not in danger. What are some rules we follow to stay safe at school? Say "safe" with me two times.

if. Professional development is provided prior to the intervention, and teachers are mentored on a regular basis. The program uses two basic methods of instruction—direct instruction and paraphrasing in context. Direct instruction consists of the introduction of vocabulary in the context of authentic children's literature; clear, student-friendly definitions and explanations; questions and prompts to help students think critically about word meanings; examples of how words are used in other contexts; visual aids illustrating the meaning of words in authentic contexts other than the book in which the word was introduced; encouragement for students to pronounce, spell, and write about words; opportunities for students to compare and contrast words; and repetition and reinforcement. With the paraphrase method, students listen to and read simple definitions of target words. They also engage in reinforcement activities in which the target words and simple definitions are presented in songs and writing activities. Four types of vocabulary words are taught: abstract noncognates (for example, *pride, profit*), abstract cognates (for example, *impression, attitude*), concrete non-cognates (for example, *motionless, fierce*), and concrete cognates (for example, *delicate, singular*).

An 8-week experimental study found that 2nd-grade ELLs from elementary schools with high concentrations of poverty made statistically significant gains on all types of words in the directly instructed and paraphrased conditions, but not when they were simply exposed to the words. In addition, there were small to moderate gains on word-decoding and word-knowledge subtests of a standardized measure of reading (August, 2011).

Program Components

There are two daily segments. The first focuses on content words and the second on connectives. Each segment follows an established pattern that consists of pre-teaching individual words, interactive reading, and reinforcement. On the last day of each week, both types of words are reviewed.

Work with content words. During the teaching of individual content words, teachers preteach directly instructed content words with picture cards and procedures like that shown in Figure 7.4. Starting on the second day of the unit, teachers use a picture walk to review the previous day's reading. Following the picture walk, pairs of students use book images to guide their retellings of the story thus far. Teachers then read the next quarter of the book. After reading each page, the teacher summarizes the text, presenting paraphrased definitions of target words and using prompts to engage students in conversation about the text. The prompts and conversations help reinforce key vocabulary and develop students' oral language proficiency and comprehension. Figure 7.5 shows an example of interactive reading.

Teachers use reinforcement activities to strengthen students' knowledge of content words and include additional work with picture cards, glossaries, and writing. They also reinforce directly instructed words by asking students to determine whether the words are used appropriately when presented in other contexts, through pocket chart picture sorts in which students select images and labels that belong together, and by completing student glossaries. Finally, they reinforce paraphrased words through singing songs and writing sentences that contain the target words and their definitions.

Weekly review activities provide additional reinforcement of content vocabulary instructed in prior lessons. Previously instructed words are spiraled through the curriculum four times, with two events consisting of oral reinforcement and two events consisting of written reinforcement.

Work with connectives. As noted above, the connectives component also consists of daily teaching of individual words, interactive activities, and reinforcement activities. During the daily teaching of individual words, teachers introduce the words with picture cards. There are three types of picture cards designed to advance students from receptive to active use of the connectives in various contexts. An introductory picture card explains the meaning of the word in English and Spanish; a book-based picture card places the connective in the context of the story, where students use it to make connections between two pictures in the story; and a transfer picture card asks students to use the connective to make connections

FIGURE 7.4. AVE Content Word Picture Card

A word we are going to learn is *impression*. If something makes an impression on you, it influences you in some way, and you do not forget it.

Impression en español es *impresión*. Si algo te causa una impresión, te influye en una manera, y no lo olvidas.

Impression and *impresión* are cognates. They sound alike and have the same meaning.

Whole-class response: Let's all say *impression* three times. Let's look at a picture that helps us understand the word *impression*. The children have never seen eggs laid by a hen. Seeing the eggs made an impression on the children.

Model: The giraffe at the zoo made an impression on me. His neck was so long and he was so tall. I could not forget about him.

Call on one or two students: Think about a trip you took to the zoo or aquarium. What animal made an impression on you? Why? Use this phrase in your answer: "... made an impression on me ..."

Point to the letters in *impression*: Let's all spell the word *impression*. What do the letters say? As we read, I want you to listen for the word *impression*. If you hear it, touch your nose!

---

between two pictures unrelated to the story. Figure 7.6 shows the two types of connective picture cards.

During interactive activities, teachers lead students through a series of active endeavors, such as kinesthetic games, songs, and plays, aimed at furthering students' experience with the word while providing the necessary support needed to learn it. Figure 7.7 shows two interactive connectives activities, a song and a mini-play.

Reinforcement activities are used to strengthen students' knowledge of the connective and include additional writing activities that progress in difficulty as the week advances. The week begins with a connect-the-pictures activity in which students use the target connective to connect two pictures in the story text. Next, students use a chart to write structured sentences with the target connectives. The week concludes with a cloze passage that is a letter to a character in the story. Figure 7.8 shows a connectives reinforcement activity in which students work with structured sentences.

Review activities provide additional oral and written reinforcement of previously instructed connectives. In these, the teacher reviews the connectives with activities such as kinesthetic games, plays, songs, and cloze exercises.

FIGURE 7.5. AVE Interactive Reading

PAGE SUMMARY

After reading the page, point to the picture on page 8: Jo makes fun of Chrysanthemum's name because it is long. She tells her that her name *scarcely* fits on her nametag. That means Chrysanthemum's name doesn't fit on her nametag very well. Rita laughs at Chrysanthemum as Chrysanthemum *applies* her nametag. That means that Rita laughs at Chrysanthemum as she puts on her nametag. Chrysanthemum feels terrible.

- Summary with paraphrased vocabulary definitions and clarifications

Page prompt:

Jo asked Chrysanthemum if she was aware that her name is so long.
Remember, to be *aware* means to know something.
Partner talk: What do you think Chrysanthemum might be aware of now? Start your sentence with: "Chrysanthemum might be aware that . . ."
[Anticipated response: Her name is different. Other children don't like her name. She won't have a good time in school.]

- Prompt utilizing vocabulary word

Closing prompts

Partner talk: Imagine that the good luck charms work. If they work, what do you think school would be like for Chrysanthemum today?
[Anticipated response: It would be better. Nobody would make fun of her and she would be happy.]
Partner talk: When you feel bad, what are some things you do to feel better?
[Responses will vary.]

- Prompt connected to students' background

Standard:

Social Studies 2.13C: Students are expected to identify ordinary people who exemplify good citizenship.
Model: People who are good citizens are kind and accepting of people who are different.
Partner talk: How did Mrs. Twinkle show good citizenship? In what ways could Victoria have been a better citizen? [Responses will vary.]

- Prompt connected to weekly state content standard

WORD GENERATION (WG)

Overview

WG is designed to build middle-grade students' academic vocabulary by engaging them in working with words in several content areas. The program centers on the weekly presentation of five high-utility, high-functional, and cross-disciplinary words delivered over 20 weeks. The words appear in the context of brief passages

FIGURE 7.6. AVE Connective Picture Cards

Sometimes two different things are going on at the same time. *Point to the picture as you talk about it.* In this picture, a girl is pouring water on plants. *Meanwhile,* her father is cutting the grass.

Repeat after me: The girl is pouring water on the plants. *Meanwhile,* her father is cutting the grass.

The word *meanwhile* means "at the same time."

En español, la palabra *meanwhile* quiere decir "al mismo tiempo."

Whole-class response: What does *meanwhile* mean? [At the same time]

Repeat after me: meanwhile, meanwhile, meanwhile.

Sometimes it makes sense to connect sentences with *meanwhile* and sometimes it makes more sense to use *because.* These are two pictures of girls in a baseball game.

Point to the picture on the left: This picture shows a girl up at bat.

Point to the picture on the right: This picture shows other girls sitting on a bench.

Whole-class response: Are these two things happening at the same time? [Yes.]

Call on one student: When two things happen at the same time, what connecting word do we use, *because* or *meanwhile?* [Meanwhile]

Call on one student: Who can put the two sentences together with the word *meanwhile?* [The girl is up at bat. *Meanwhile,* her team is sitting on the bench.]

Repeat after me: The girl is up at bat. *Meanwhile,* her team is sitting on the bench.

---

outlining controversies currently under debate in the United States and likely to be of interest to middle school students. A few examples of controversial topics and the corresponding topic-specific target words are shown in Figure 7.9. WG aims to make writing an integral part of the vocabulary program. Thus, at the end of each week, students write a short piece based on the controversial topic they have discussed during the week. This provides yet another means of allowing students to express their thoughts and opinions. For ELLs in particular, writing can serve as a nonthreatening way for students to express their views and helps cultivate deeper learning of the words.

A 24-week quasi-experimental study showed that 5th-graders from Spanish-speaking homes, most of whom were formerly classified as limited English proficient, who received the Word Generation program went from knowing about 65%

FIGURE 7.7. AVE Interactive Activities

- ☐ *The Instead Song* is about the word *instead*.
- ☐ *Instead* means "in place of."
- ☐ First, we will read the words to the song two times.
- ☐ Then, we will sing the words two times.
- ☐ Read the words as you sing along.
- ☐ When you are finished singing, I will ask you some questions about the song.

The Instead Song

We wanted a nice little dog
we could keep.
We wanted a nice little dog.
"Instead" means in place of.
Instead of a dog,
we got a blue parakeet.

Song Questions
1. What does *instead* mean?
2. Finish this sentence using the word *instead*: "I wanted a kitten. Instead of a kitten, I got a . . ."

A Mini-Play

Students choral read parts of the play. Half the students read one part and half the students read the other part. Each week the play progresses in difficulty.

Example:

Big Anthony:	This pot will cook ***until*** it is filled up with pasta.
Townsperson:	Ha, ha, ha.
Big Anthony:	You will see. Cook, pasta pot! Cook ***until*** I say "stop!"
Townsperson:	Look—Big Anthony did it! The pot is filled up with pasta!
Big Anthony:	Stop, pasta pot, stop!
Townsperson:	Hey, Big Anthony got the pot to cook, ***although*** now it will not stop!
Big Anthony:	Stop, stop, STOP!
Townsperson:	Hey, Big Anthony, stop the pot! Help! Help! Help!
Big Anthony:	It boils and boils ***although*** I am telling it to stop!
Towsperson:	Help! Help! Help! We need Strega Nona!
Big Anthony:	Look! Here she comes!
Big Anthony and Townsperson:	Strega Nona, come fast!

FIGURE 7.8. AVE Connectives Reinforcement Activity

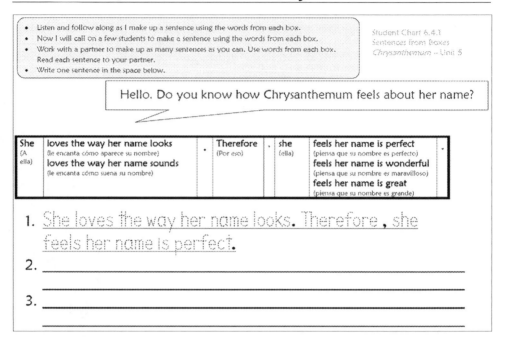

FIGURE 7.9. WG Sample Controversial Topics and Target Words

Controversial Topics	Target Words
What is the purpose of school?	Analyze Factor Function Interpret Structure
Cloning: Threat or Opportunity?	Design Feature Impact Potential Transfer
Censorship: Who Should Decide What Kids Read?	Access Civil Despite Integrate Promote
Asthma: More Than a Medical Problem?	Phenomenon Priority Transmission Intervention Suspended
What Should Be Done to Prevent Teens from Dropping Out of School?	Convince Enormous Integrity Persistent Reluctant

of the target words at pretest to knowing about 83% at posttest, while students who did not receive the program went from knowing 65% of the target words at pretest to knowing about 68% at posttest. Additionally, an analysis of students' essays revealed that students actively used the target words in their writing, and their overall writing quality improved (Mancilla-Martinez, 2010). Another study of Word Generation (Snow, Lawrence, & White, 2009) found similar results.

Program Components

The WG materials include a teacher's guide that explains the structure of the program and the rationale behind it, a set of paragraphs about controversial topics selected to connect to real-world issues and to students' lives, brief instructional activities associated with weekly topics and target words, and supporting materials to help teachers implement the program. It is designed to be used for about 15 minutes a day, 5 days a week, for 20 weeks. Each week begins with the introduction of the passage and target words and ends with an open-response writing activity. The Tuesday–Thursday activities vary from week to week, as these are the days on which the teacher selects from an array of activities to discuss the target vocabulary in the content areas (science, math, and social studies). Including the target words in the content areas is not designed with the goal of teaching content-area knowledge per se; rather, the focus is on exposing students to the weekly target vocabulary in different contexts. Below we give a brief description of the activities for each day of the 5-day cycle.

Monday: Introduce the controversial topic and establish word meanings. On Monday, the teacher introduces the controversial topic of the week along with the target vocabulary. Before reading the weekly passage with the class, she shows the five weekly target words on large index cards to the class, one at a time, asking if students know what the words mean. If any of the students indicate that they know the meaning of a target word, the teacher asks for a definition and then provides the definition included in the teacher's manual. This serves as a way for the teacher to gauge students' knowledge of the words. She then tells the class that they will be discussing their thoughts on, for example, whether schools should sell junk food. She also directly tells the class that they will be focusing on five words, which are underlined in the passage. Figure 7.10 shows a typical student passage with the target vocabulary underlined.

Tuesday: Establish a science version of the definitions. The science activities are designed to help students understand that words often have multiple meanings, depending on the context in which they are used. When applicable, the teacher discusses the target words in reference to scientific concepts. For instance, the target word *transfer* is a concept with many applications in science. Thus, she might discuss energy *transfer* as an important idea in physics, or she might explain that using a battery to light bulbs involves the *transfer* of chemical energy to electrical energy. Most often, however, students complete cloze paragraphs in which many of the five target words need to be filled in to complete the sentences dealing with a science topic, or they engage in analyzing data in fictional micro-experiments.

FIGURE 7.10. WG Student Passage

Word Generation: Week 1 Student Materials

Name_____ Date_____

What is the purpose of school?

Why do we go to school? Some people think the primary goal of education is giving knowledge to students. They feel there is specific information that all kids should know. For instance, they want kids to know what happened in the Revolutionary War and how the food chain works. Others <u>interpret</u> the main role of school as one of preparing students to earn a living. They are most concerned about students learning particular skills, such as reading, writing, and arithmetic. Some argue tht schools should introduce a set of shared values, including liberty and justice. They believe this will help students understand the <u>structure</u> of our democratic government. While each of the three branches of government has a different <u>function</u>, they work together to make sure we all enjoy certain freedoms and live by the same rules. Some think schools should teach students to critically <u>analyze</u> what they see, hear, and read. They want students to be able to think carefully about different perspectives, respect and challenge other viewpoints, and form their own opinions about issues that affect them. Although many people say that they want kids to be able to think for themselves, students do not always have the freedom to do so in the classroom. What do you think the function of school is? What do you consider the most important <u>factors</u> in providing a good education? Which ingredients are essential in your recipe for a good school?

Wednesday: Math word problems. Whenever possible, the teacher establishes mathematical meanings of the target words. For example, she might explain that the target word *factor* can refer to one of two or more numbers that can be multiplied to make another number, that it can refer to an independent variable in statistics, or that it can refer to one of two or more integers that can be exactly divided into another integer (for example, What are the 4 *factors* of 6?). The consistent math activity, however, is the "problem of the day," which includes at least two of the five target words in a word problem that resembles the type of word problems students are likely to encounter on state or standardized tests. Figure 7.11 shows a math problem of the day.

Thursday: Debate. The most typical social studies activity is a weekly whole-class debate. During the debate, students take a stance on the controversial topic they are learning about, and present their view to a group holding an opposing view. When time permits, students rebut the opposing group's argument. Many of the scaffolding techniques used by the teacher during the debate are ones chosen to be especially helpful to ELLs. For example, she might repeat a student's statement with the purpose of checking back with her for clearer interpretation of their position (revoicing), or she might give students who are less inclined to join whole-group discussions the opportunity to talk with a partner to ensure that all students are on the same page (partner talk).

FIGURE 7.11. WG Math Problem of the Day

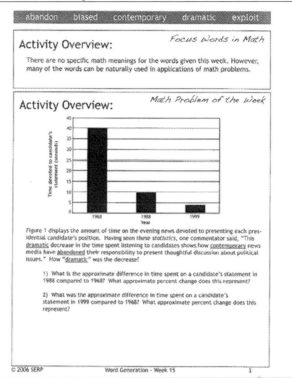

Friday: Persuasive writing. On this last day of the cycle, students take a stand by writing a short persuasive essay about the controversial topic they have been learning about and discussing all week. Students are encouraged to use the five weekly target WG words, as well as previously learned target words, in their essays. This component provides yet another means of allowing students to express their thoughts and opinions. Additionally, writing gives students one more opportunity to explore the newly taught words, which is critical to cultivating deeper learning of the words.

A very detailed description of the WG program, a teacher's guide, a sample weekly lesson, and all the materials necessary for implementing the program are available at http://wordgeneration.org/index.html.

THE QUALITY ENGLISH AND SCIENCE TEACHING (QuEST) PROJECT

Overview

QuEST is a middle-grades science program that explicitly develops both academic and discipline language in ELLs and their native English-speaking classmates. An overriding principle in program development was to make instruction effective for both ELLs and English-proficient students because these two groups of students are often placed in the same classrooms in the middle grades. Additionally, because discipline-specific vocabulary knowledge depends on students' ability to acquire conceptual knowledge related to the domain, in this case science, QuEST also involves developing science knowledge through formal science instruction. As with the other programs described in this chapter, the instruction is aligned with district and state standards and uses district resources such as the district's science textbook. QuEST draws on the research based on high-quality science instruction for students as well as the role of English-language proficiency, learning in a second language, and knowledge acquired in the first language (in this case Spanish) to tailor the interventions to meet the language and literacy needs of ELLs.

A 9-week randomized trial showed that at posttest, both middle school ELLs and their English-speaking classmates who were involved in the QuEST intervention showed statistically significant improvement in both science knowledge and vocabulary over those who had not received it (August, Branum-Martin, Cardenas-Hagan, & Francis, 2009). The findings highlight the importance of combining good science teaching with scaffolding, and a focus on language development is an effective method for helping ELLs in science classrooms.

Program Components

As noted, QuEST was designed to develop the science knowledge and academic language of ELLs and their native English-speaking classmates. The program built on a curriculum already established in a district that used published textbooks and workbooks, as well as district-developed labs that were aligned with the textbook content. The program consists of two components that are not part of the district's curriculum: instructional materials following the principles of the 5E model of science instruction, and professional development to help teachers in using the instructional materials. The 5E model, a highly rated inquiry approach to teaching science to monolingual English speakers, was developed by the Biological Science Curriculum Study (BSCS), a nonprofit corporation dedicated to improving students' understanding of science and technology by developing exemplary curricular materials, supporting their widespread and effective use, providing professional development, and conducting research and evaluation studies. The 5E model consists of activities designed to help students engage, explore, explain, extend, and evaluate. The QuEST curriculum also calls for direct instruction of both general and discipline-specific vocabulary. Definitions of target words are provided in students' first and second languages, and students are taught to draw on cognate knowledge.

The program requires teachers to use a variety of scaffolding techniques shown to foster ELLs' understanding of academic content. For example, teachers use visuals, including illustrations of vocabulary concepts and graphic organizers. Teachers also preview the experiments to ensure that students understand the goals and procedures. They engage students in instructional conversations during science tasks and while reading the textbook to help ensure comprehension.

FIGURE 7.12. QuEST Student Glossary

Vocabulary Word	Cognate?	Definition	Question	Picture	My Understanding: drawing, examples, or notes
English:		An energy pyramid is a diagram that shows the amount of biomass at each part of the food chain.	An energy pyramid shows that an ecosystem requires more _____ than consumers.	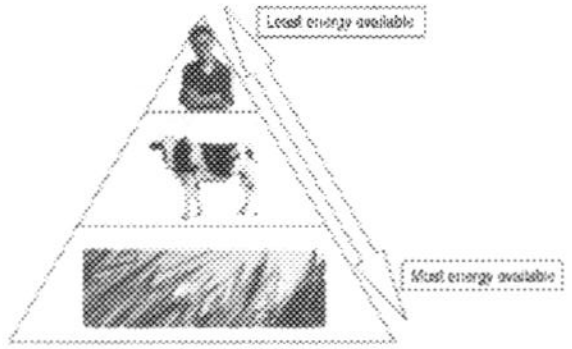	
Español:		Una pirámide energética es un diagrama que muestra cuántos organismos hay en cada una de las partes de la cadena alimenticia.			
English:		Producers are organisms at the beginning of the food chain that make their own food, usually through the process of photosynthesis.	Name some producers that live in the ecosystem near your house or school. _____ _____		
Español:		Productores son las plantas y vegetales que se encuentran al comienzo de la cadena alimentaria y que fabrican su propia comida por medio de la fotosíntesis.			

Figure 7.13 QuEST Concept Map

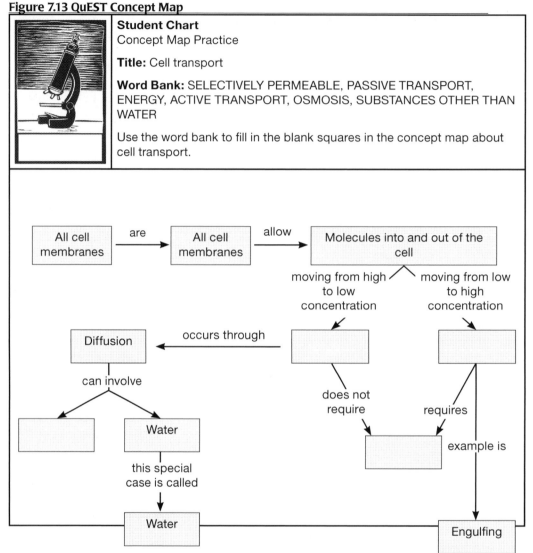

Instructional conversations are discussions "geared toward creating opportunities for students' conceptual and linguistic development. They focus on an idea or a student's idea. The teacher encourages expression of students' own ideas, builds upon information students provide and experiences they have had, and guides students to increasingly sophisticated levels of understanding" (Goldenberg, 1991). Thus, instructional conversations support development of students' conceptual knowledge and oral proficiency. Teachers encourage students with very limited English proficiency to respond in their first language and then interpret or have a classmate interpret their responses in English.

For example, in a lesson on the concept of osmosis, the teacher has the students engage in an introductory activity in which they observe the process of osmosis with a tea bag and water. For each activity, students are given a chart containing instructions and space where they can record relevant information and answer related questions. In this activity, the students use charts to record observations after 30 seconds, 1 minute, and 1 minute and 30 seconds. At the end of the lesson, students review the concepts by completing a student glossary like that shown in Figure 7.12. At the end of each week, students have an opportunity to synthesize what they have learned by completing a concept map that relates the concepts of diffusion and osmosis to the more general concept of cell transport. A sample concept map is shown in Figure 7.13.

A FINAL WORD

Given the importance of vocabulary to success in reading and the fact that many English language learners have vocabularies significantly smaller than those of their native English-speaking classmates, it is vital that long-term, sustained efforts—beginning in preschool and continuing throughout the school years—be developed and implemented. In this chapter, we have described four sustained programs for developing vocabulary in ELLs—a preschool program, a primary-grade program, and two middle school programs. In the programs we have described, we have highlighted the importance of developing various sorts of vocabulary, including basic vocabulary, general academic vocabulary, and domain-specific academic vocabulary. It is important to recognize that although these programs are based on effective practice with native English-speaking students, many adjustments have been made to accommodate to the fact that ELLs are acquiring both academic content and a second language at the same time. The adjustments used in these programs include using hand gestures, body language, pictures, and objects to accompany speech; providing a model of a task or response before requiring students to undertake it; previewing material prior to questioning students; providing repeated exposures to words, concepts, and skills; and using approaches such as revoicing, partner talk, and instructional conversations. Additionally, we have demonstrated how to capitalize on students' first-language strengths and provided specific, concrete examples of the methods and materials used in these programs to help them come alive and encourage their use in the tens of thousands of classrooms that include English language learners.

Children's Literature Cited

Argueta, J. (2006). *Talking to Mother Earth/Hablando con Madre Tierra*. Toronto: Groundwood Books.

Base, G. (1996). *Animalia*. New York: Puffin.

Beals, K. (2007). *Earthworms underground*. Nashua, NH: Delta Education.

Clements, A. (1998). *Frindle*. New York: Aladdin Paperbacks.

Creech, S. (1996). *Walk two moons*. New York: HarperCollins.

Giblin, J. C. (1997). *Charles Lindbergh: A human hero*. New York: Clarion Books.

Gwynne, F. (1970). *The king who rained*. New York: Simon & Schuster Books for Young Readers.

Hoban, R. (1986). *Bread and jam for Frances*. New York: HarperCollins.

Milet Publishing. (2010a). *My first bilingual book—numbers (English-German)*. West Sussex, UK: Author.

Milet Publishing. (2010b). *My first bilingual book—numbers (English-Polish)*. West Sussex, UK: Author.

Milet Publishing. (2011a). *My first bilingual book—numbers (English-Chinese)*. West Sussex, UK: Author.

Milet Publishing. (2011b). *My first bilingual book—numbers (English-Japanese)*. West Sussex, UK: Author.

Milet Publishing. (2011c). *My first bilingual book—numbers (English-Korean)*. West Sussex, UK: Author.

Milet Publishing. (2011d). *My first bilingual book—numbers (English-Somali)*. West Sussex, UK: Author.

Milet Publishing. (2011e). *My first bilingual book—numbers (English-Vietnamese)*. West Sussex, UK: Author.

Sachar, L. (1998). *Holes*. New York: Farrar, Straus and Giroux.

Schotter, R. (2006). *The boy who loved words*. New York: Schwartz and Wade Books.

Viorst, J. (1972). *Alexander and the terrible, horrible, no good, very bad day*. New York: Aladdin Books.

Viorst, J. (1997). *The alphabet from Z to A (with much confusion on the way)*. New York: Aladdin.

References

Adams, M. J. (1990). *Beginning to read: Thinking and learning about print.* Cambridge, MA: MIT Press.

Adams, M. J. (2010–2011). Advancing our students' language and literacy: The challenge of complex test. *American Educator, 34*(4), 3–11, 53.

American Association for Applied Linguistics. (2011). *AAAL resolution against discrimination on the basis of accented speech.* Retrieved from http://www.aaal.org/displaycommon.cfm?an=1&subarticlenbr=15#Resolution_against_Discrimination_on_the_Basis_of_Accented_Speech

American Heritage Dictionary. (4th ed.). (2001). Boston: Houghton Mifflin.

Anderson, R. C. (1996). Research foundations to support wide reading. In V. Greaney (Ed.), *Promoting reading in developing countries* (pp. 55–77). New York: International Reading Association.

Anderson, R. C., Hiebert, E. F., Scott, J. E., & Wilkinson, I. A. G. (1985). *Becoming a nation of readers.* Washington, DC: National Academy of Education.

Anderson, R. C., & Nagy, W. E. (1992, Winter). The vocabulary conundrum. *American Educator, 14*–18, 44–47.

Anderson, R. C., Wilson, P. T., & Fielding, L. G. (1988). Growth in reading and how children spend their time outside of school. *Reading Research Quarterly, 23,* 285–303.

Andrews, L. (2006). *Language exploration and awareness: A resource book for teachers* (3rd ed.). Mahwah, NJ: Erlbaum.

Anglin, J. M. (1993a). Knowing versus learning words. *Monographs of the Society for Research in Child Development, 58,* 176–186.

Anglin, J. M. (1993b). Vocabulary development: A morphological analysis. *Monographs of the Society for Research in Child Development, 58.*

Applebee, A. N., Langer, J. A., Nystrand, M., & Gamoran, A. (2003). Discussion based approaches to developing understanding: Classroom instruction and student performance in middle and high school English. *American Educational Research Journal, 40,* 685–730.

Artzi, L., Kenyon, D., August, D., Barr, C., Massoud, L., & Dressler, C. (in preparation). *Development of a task type used in an assessment of English vocabulary for young English language learners.*

August, D. (2009). *Developing literacy in Spanish-speaking children: Acquisition of vocabulary in English* (Technical Report 1 Submitted to the National Institute of Child Health and Human Development). Washington, DC: Center for Applied Linguistics.

August, D. (2010). *Developing literacy in Spanish-speaking children: Acquisition of vocabulary in English* (Technical Report 2 Submitted to the National Institute of Child Health and Human Development). Washington, DC: Center for Applied Linguistics.

August, D. (2011). *Developing literacy in Spanish-speaking children: Acquisition of vocabulary in English* (Technical Report 3 Submitted to the National Institute of Child Health and Human Development). Washington, DC: Center for Applied Linguistics.

August, D., Artzi, L., Barr, C., & Massoud, L. (in preparation). *Enriched vocabulary instruction for young Spanish-speaking English language learners.*

August, D., Artzi, L., & Mazrum, J. (2010, August). *Improving science knowledge and academic language in English language learners in the middle grades* [CREATE Brief]. Retrieved from the Center for Applied Linguistics, Center for Research on the Educational Achievement and Teaching of English Language Learners website: http://www.cal.org/create/resources/pubs/academic-language.html

August, D., & Barr, C. (2010). *Effect of VIOLETS on the vocabulary growth of young children* [Tech. Rep. No. 1]. Baltimore, MD: Ready at Five.

August, D., Branum-Martin, L., Cardenas-Hagan, E., & Francis, D. (2009). The impact of an instructional intervention on the science and language learning of middle grade English language learners. *Journal of Research on Educational Effectiveness, 2,* 345–376.

August, D., Carlo, M., Dressler, C., & Snow, C. (2005). The critical role of vocabulary development for English language learners. *Learning Disabilities Research & Practice, 20*(1), 50–57.

August, D., & Gray, J. L. (2010). Developing comprehension in English language learners: Research and promising practices. In K. Ganske & D. Fisher (Eds.), *Comprehension across the curriculum: Perspectives and practices K–12.* New York: Guilford.

August, D., & Shanahan, T. (Eds.). (2006a). *Developing literacy in second-language learners: Report of the National Literacy Panel on Language Minority Children and Youth.* Mahwah, NJ: Erlbaum.

August, D., & Shanahan, T. (2006b). Synthesis: Instruction and professional development. In D. August & T. Shanahan (Eds.), *Developing literacy in second-language learners* (pp. 351–364). Mahwah, NJ: Erlbaum.

August, D., & Shanahan, T. (2008). *Developing reading and writing in second-language learners.* New York: Routledge, in conjunction with the International Reading Association and the Center for Applied Linguistics.

August, D., & Shanahan, T. (2010a). Effective English literacy instruction for English learners. In F. Ong with V. Aguila (Eds.), *Improving education for English learners: Research-based approaches* (pp. 209–237). Sacramento: California Department of Education.

August, D., & Shanahan, T. (2010b). Response to a review and update on *Developing literacy in second-language learners*: Report of the National Literacy Panel on Language Minority Children and Youth. *Journal of Literacy Research, 42,* 341–348.

August, D., & Snow, C. (2007). Developing vocabulary in English-language learners: A review of the experimental research. In B. M. Taylor & J. E. Ysseldyke (Eds.), *Effective instruction for struggling readers, K–6* (pp. 84–105). New York: Teachers College Press.

August, D., & Snow, C. (2008). *Vocabulary instruction and assessment for Spanish speakers.* Research project funded by the National Institute for Child Health and Human Development in the Institute for Education Sciences.

Avila, E., & Sadoski, M. (1996). Exploring new applications of the keyword method to acquire English vocabulary. *Language Learning, 46*(3), 379–395.

Baer, J., Baldi, S., Ayotte, K., & Green, P. (2007). *The reading literacy of U.S. fourth-grade students in an international context: Results from the 2001 and 2006 Progress in International Reading Literacy Study.* Washington, DC: National Center for Education Statistics.

Baumann, J. F. (2005). Vocabulary-comprehension relationships. In B. Maloch, J. V. Hoffman, D. L. Schallert, C. M. Fairbanks, & J. Worthy (Eds.), *Fifty-fourth yearbook of the National Reading Conference* (pp. 117–131). Oak Creek, WI: National Reading Conference.

Baumann, J. F., Blachowicz, C. L. Z., Manyak, P. C., Graves, M. F., & Olejnik, S. (2009). *Development of a multi-faceted, comprehensive, vocabulary instructional program for the upper-elementary grades* (No. R305A090163). Washington, DC: U.S. Department of Education,

Institute of Education Services, National Center for Education Research.

Baumann, J. F., Edwards, E. C., Boland E., Olejnik, S., & Kame'enui, E. J. (2003). Vocabulary tricks: Effects of instruction in morphology and context on fifth grade students' ability to derive and infer word meaning. *American Educational Research Journal, 40,* 447–494.

Baumann, J. F., Edwards, E. C., Font, G., Tereshinski, C. A., Kame'enui, E. J., & Olejnik, S. (2002). Teaching morphemic and contextual analysis to fifth-grade students. *Reading Research Quarterly, 37,* 150–176.

Baumann, J. F., Font, G., Edwards, E. C., & Boland, E. (2005). Strategies for teaching middle-grade students to use word-part and context clues to expand reading vocabulary. In E. Hiebert & M. L. Kamil (Eds.), *Bringing scientific research to practice: Vocabulary* (pp. 179–205). Mahwah, NJ: Erlbaum.

Baumann, J. F., & Kame'enui, E. J. (2004). Vocabulary: The plot of the reading story. In J. F. Baumann & E. J. Kame'enui (Eds.), *Vocabulary instruction: Research to practice* (pp. 3–10). New York: Guilford.

Baumann, J. F., Kame'enui, E. J., & Ash, G. E. (2003). Research on vocabulary instruction: Voltaire redux. In J. Flood, D. Lapp, J. R. Squire, & J. M. Jensen (Eds.), *Handbook on research on teaching the English language arts* (2nd ed., pp. 752–785). Mahwah, NJ: Erlbaum.

Baumann, J. F., Ware, D., & Edwards, E. C. (2007). Bumping into spicy, tasty words that catch your tongue: A formative experiment on vocabulary instruction. *The Reading Teacher, 61,* 108–122.

Beck, I. L., & McKeown, M. G. (1991). Conditions of vocabulary acquisition. In P. D. Pearson (Ed.), *The handbook of reading research, vol. 2* (pp. 789–814). New York: Longman.

Beck, I. L., & McKeown, M. G. (2004). Direct and rich vocabulary instruction. In J. F. Baumann & E. J. Kame'enui (Eds.), *Vocabulary instruction* (pp. 13–27). New York: Guilford.

Beck, I. L., & McKeown, M G. (2006). *Improving comprehension with questioning the author: A fresh and expanded view of a powerful approach.* New York: Scholastic.

Beck, I. L., & McKeown, M. G. (2007). Increasing young children's oral vocabulary repertoires through rich and focused instruction. *Elementary School Journal, 107,* 251–271.

Beck, I. L., McKeown, M. G., & Kucan, L. (2002). *Bringing words to life: Robust vocabulary instruction.* New York: Guilford.

Beck, I. L., McKeown, M. G., & Kucan, L. (2003). Taking delight in words: Using oral language to build young children's vocabularies. *American Educator, 27*(1), 36–39, 41, 45–46.

Beck, I. L., McKeown, M. G., & Kucan, L. (2008). *Creating robust vocabulary: Frequently asked questions and extended examples.* New York: Guilford.

Beck, I. L., McKeown, M. G., Lionni. L., Knowles, S., Cowen-Fletcher, J., Ken Brown, K., et al. (2005). *Text talk: Robust vocabulary instruction.* New York: Scholastic.

Beck, I. L., McKeown, M. G., & Omanson, R. C. (1987). The effects and uses of diverse vocabulary instructional techniques. In M. G. McKeown & M. E. Curtis (Eds.), *The nature of vocabulary acquisition* (pp. 147–163). Hillsdale, NJ: Erlbaum.

Beck, I. L., Perfetti, C. A., & McKeown, M. G. (1982). The effects of long-term vocabulary instruction on lexical access and reading comprehension. *Journal of Educational Psychology, 74,* 506–521.

Becker, W. C. (1977). Teaching reading and language to the disadvantaged—What we have learned from field research. *Harvard Educational Review, 47,* 511–543.

Berninger, V., Nagy, W., Carlisle, J., Thomson, J., Hoffer, D., Abbott, S., Abbott, R., Richards, T., & Aylward, E. (2003). Effective treatment for dyslexics in grades 4–6: Behavioral and brain evidence. In B. Foorman (Ed.), *Preventing and treating reading disabilities: Bringing science to scale* (pp. 381–417). Timonium, MD: York Press.

Bialystock, E. (2001). *Bilingualism in development: Language, literacy, and cognition.* Cambridge, UK: Cambridge University Press.

Biemiller, A. (1999). *Language and reading success*. Cambridge, MA: Brookline Books.

Biemiller, A. (2001, Spring). Teaching vocabulary: Early, direct, and sequential. *American Educator, 25*(1), 24–28, 47.

Biemiller, A. (2004). Teaching vocabulary in the primary grades: Vocabulary instruction needed. In J. F. Baumann & E. J. Kame'enui (Eds.), *Vocabulary instruction: Research to practice* (pp. 28–40). New York: Guilford.

Biemiller, A. (2005). Size and sequence in vocabulary development: Implications for choosing words for primary grade vocabulary instruction. In A. Hiebert & M. Kamil (Eds.), *Teaching and learning vocabulary: Bringing research to practice* (pp. 223–242). Mahwah, NJ: Erlbaum.

Biemiller, A. (2009). *Words worth teaching*. Columbus, OH: SRA/McGraw-Hill.

Biemiller, A., & Boote, C. (2006). An effective method for building meaning vocabulary in primary grades. *Journal of Educational Psychology, 98*, 44–62.

Biemiller, A., & Slonim, N. (2001). Estimating root word and normative vocabulary growth in normative and advanced populations: Evidence for a common sequence of vocabulary acquisition. *Journal of Educational Psychology, 93*, 498–520.

Blachowicz, C. (1986). Making connections: Alternative to the vocabulary notebook. *The Journal of Reading, 29*(7), 643–649.

Blachowicz, C., & Fisher, P. (2000). Vocabulary instruction. In M. L. Kamil, P. B. Mosenthal, P. D. Pearson, & R. Barr (Eds.), *The handbook of reading research, vol. 3* (pp. 503–524). New York: Longman.

Blachowicz, C. L. Z., & Fisher, P. (2004). Keep the "fun" in fundamental: Encouraging words awareness ad incidental word learning in the classroom through word play. In J. F. Baumann & E. J. Kame'enui, (Eds.), *Vocabulary instruction: Research to practice* (pp. 218–237). New York: Guilford.

Blachowicz, C. L. Z., Fisher, P. J. L., Ogle, D., & Watts-Taffe, S. (2006). Vocabulary: Questions from the classroom. *Reading Research Quarterly, 41*, 524–539.

Block, N. F. (2008). *A study of a response to intervention model for urban sixth-grade: Analyzing reading, language, and learning differences in Tier 1 and Tier 2* [Unpublished doctoral dissertation]. Claremont Graduate University and San Diego State University, Claremont and San Diego, California.

Blum, I. R., Koskinen, P. S., Tennant, N., Parker, E. M., Straub, M., & Curry, C. (1995). Using audio taped books to extend classroom literacy instruction into the homes of second language learners. *Journal of Reading Behavior, 27*(4), 535–565.

Bos, C. S., Allen, A. A., & Scanlon, D. (1989). Vocabulary instruction and reading comprehension with bilingual learning disabled students. In S. McCormick & J. Zutell (Eds.), *Cognitive and social perspectives for literacy research and instruction* (pp. 173–178). Chicago: National Reading Conference.

Bravo, M. A., Hiebert, E. H., & Pearson, P. D. (2007). Tapping the linguistic resources of Spanish/English bilinguals: The role of cognates in science. In R. K Wagner, A. Muse, & K. Tannenbaum (Eds.), *Vocabulary development and its implications for reading comprehension* (pp. 140–156). New York: Guilford.

Calderón, M., August, D., Slavin, R., Durán, D., Madden, N., & Cheung, A. (2005). Bringing words to life in classrooms with English language learners. In E. H. Hiebert & M. L. Kamil (Eds.), *Teaching and learning vocabulary: Bringing research to practice*. Mahwah, NJ: Lawrence Erlbaum.

Calfee, R. C., & Drum, P. A. (1986). Research on teaching reading. In M. D. Wittrock (Ed.), *Handbook of research on teaching* (3rd ed., pp. 804–849). New York: Macmillan.

Carlo, M. S. (2007). Best practices for literacy instruction for English-language learners. In L. B. Gambrell, L. M. Morrow, & M. Pressley (Eds.), *Best practices in literacy instruction* (3rd ed., pp. 104–126). New York: Guilford.

Carlo, M. S., August, D., McGlaughlin, B., Snow, C. E., Dressler, C., Lippman, D. N., Lively, T. J., & White, C. E. (2004). Closing the gap: Addressing the vocabulary needs of English-language learners in bilingual and mainstream classes. *Reading Research Quarterly, 39,* 188–215.

Carlo, M. S., August, D., & Snow, C. E. (2005). Sustained vocabulary-learning strategies for English language learners. In E. H. Hiebert & M. Kamil (Eds.), *Teaching and learning vocabulary: Bringing research to practice* (pp. 137–153). Mahwah, NJ: Erlbaum.

Carlyle, J. F. (2007). Fostering morphological processing, vocabulary development, and reading comprehension. In R. K. Wagner, A. E. Muse, & K. R. Tannenbaum (Eds.), *Vocabulary acquisition: Implications for reading comprehension* (pp. 78–103). New York: Guilford,

Carroll, J., Davies, P., & Richman, B. (1971). *The American heritage word frequency book.* Boston, MA: Houghton Mifflin.

CCSS. (2010a). *Common core state standards for English language arts & literacy in history/social studies, science, and technical subjects.* Washington, DC: Council of Chief State School Officers and National Governors Association. Retrieved from http://www.corestandards.org/

CCSS. (2010b). *Common core state standards for English language arts & literacy in history/social studies, science, and technical subjects—Appendix B: Text exemplars and sample performance tasks.* Washington, DC: Council of Chief State School Officers and National Governors Association. Retrieved from www.corestandards.org/assets/Appendix_B.pdf

Chall, J. S., & Dale, E. (1995). *Readability revisited: The new Dale-Chall readability formula.* Cambridge, MA: Brookline Books.

Chall, J. S., Jacobs, V. A., & Baldwin, L. E. (1990). *The reading crisis: Why poor children fall behind.* Cambridge, MA: Harvard University Press.

Chen, H. C., & Leung, Y. S. (1989). Patterns of lexical processing in a nonnative language. *Journal of Experimental Psychology: Learning Memory, and Cognition, 15*(2), 316–325.

Cirino, P. T., Pollard-Durodola, S. D., Foorman, B. R., Carlson, C. D., & Francis, D. J. (2007). Teacher characteristics, classroom instruction, and student literacy and language outcomes in bilingual kindergartners. *The Elementary School Journal, 107*(4), 341–364.

Clark, E. V. (1993). *The lexicon in acquisition.* Cambridge, UK: Cambridge University Press.

Cobo-Lewis, A. B., Pearson, B. A., Eilers, R. E., & Umbel, V. C. (2002). Effects of bilingualism and bilingual education on oral and written Spanish skills: A multifactor study of standardized test outcomes. In D. K. Oller & R. E. Eilers (Eds.), *Language and literacy in bilingual children* (pp. 3–21). Clevedon, UK: Multilingual Matters.

Collins COBUILD new student's dictionary (3rd ed.). (2005). Glasgow, Scotland: HarperCollins.

Collins, M. F. (2004). *ESL preschoolers' English vocabulary acquisition and story comprehension from storybook reading* [Doctoral dissertation]. Available from Dissertations & Theses database (Publication No. AAT 3124816).

Coxhead, A. (2000). A new academic word list. *TESOL Quarterly, 34,* 213–238.

Coyne, M., Kame'enui, E., Simmons, D., & Harn, B. (2004). Beginning reading intervention as inoculation or insulin: First grade reading performance of strong responders to kindergarten intervention. *Journal of Learning Disabilities, 37,* 90–106.

Coyne, M. D., Simmons, D. C., & Kame'enui, E. J. (2004). Vocabulary instruction for young children at risk of experiencing reading difficulties: Teaching word meanings during shared story book reading. In J. F. Baumann & E. J. Kame'enui (Eds.), *Vocabulary instruction: Research to practice* (pp. 3–10). New York: Guilford.

Cronbach, L. J. (1942). An analysis of techniques for diagnostic vocabulary testing. *Journal of Educational Research, 36,* 206–217.

Cummins, J. (2003). Reading and the bilingual student: Fact and friction. In G. G. Garcia (Ed.), *English learners: Reaching the highest level of English literacy* (pp. 2–33). Newark, DE: International Reading Association.

Cunningham, A. E., & Stanovich, K. E. (1998). What reading does for the mind. *American Educator, 22*(1-2), 8–15.

Dale, E. (1965). Vocabulary measurement: Techniques and major findings. *Elementary English, 42*, 82–88.

Dalton, B., Proctor, C. P., Uccelli, P., Mo, E., & Snow, C. E. (2011). Designing for diversity: The role of reading strategies and interactive vocabulary in a digital reading environment for fifth-grade monolingual English and bilingual students. *Journal of Literacy Research, 43*(1), 68–100.

D'Angiulli, D., Siegel, L. S., & Maggi, S. (2004). Literacy instruction, SES, and word-reading achievement in English-language learners and children with English as a first language: A longitudinal study. *Learning Disabilities Research & Practice, 19*, 202–213.

Davison, M. W. (2011). *The first 4,000 words: Vocabulary intervention for struggling readers.* Proposal submitted 6-23-2011 to CDFD # 84.304. Education Research, Development and Dissemination.

De Temple, J., & Snow, C. E. (2003). Learning words from books. In A. van Kleeck, S. A. Stahl, & E. B. Bauer (Eds.), *On reading books to children* (pp. 16–36). Mahwah, NJ: Erlbaum.

Dressler, C., Carlo, M. S., Snow, C. E., August, D., & White, C. E. (2011). Spanish-speaking students' use of cognate knowledge to infer the meaning of English words. *Bilingualism: Language and Cognition, 14*(2), 243–255.

Dressler, C., & Kamil, M. (2006). First- and second-language literacy. In D. August & T. Shanahan (Eds.), *Developing literacy in second-language learners: Report of the National Literacy Panel on Language Minority Children and Youth* (pp. 197–238). Mahwah, NJ: Erlbaum.

Duin, A. H., & Graves, M. F. (1987). The effects of intensive vocabulary instruction on expository writing. *Reading Research Quarterly, 22*, 311–330.

Duin, A. H., & Graves, M .F. (1988). Teaching vocabulary as a writing prompt. *Journal of Reading, 22*, 204–212.

Duke, N. (2000). 3.6 minutes per day: The scarcity of informational texts in first grade. *Reading Research Quarterly, 35*, 202–224.

Duke, N. K., & Pearson, P. D. (2002). Effective practices for developing reading comprehension. In A. E. Farstrup & S. J. Samuels (Eds.), *What research has to say about reading instruction* (3rd ed., pp. 204–242). Newark, DE: International Reading Association.

Duke, N. K., Pearson, P. D., Strachan, S. L., & Billman, A. K. (2011). Essential elements of fostering and teaching reading comprehension. In S. J. Samuels & A. Farstrup (Eds.). *What research has to say about reading instruction* (4th ed., pp. 51–93). Newark, DE: International Reading Association.

Dunn, L. M., & Dunn, D. M. (2007). *Peabody picture vocabulary test* (4th ed.). Minneapolis: Pearson Assessments.

Dupuy, H. J. (1974). *The rationale, development and standardization of a basic word vocabulary test.* Washington, DC: U.S. Government Printing Office (DHEW Publication No. [HRA]74-1334).

Durkin, D. (1981). Reading comprehension instruction in five basal reader series. *Reading Research Quarterly, 16*(4), 515–544.

Duursma, E., Romero-Contreras, S., Szuber, A., Proctor, P., Snow, C., August, D., & Calderón, M. (2007). The role of home literacy and language environment on bilinguals' English and Spanish vocabulary development. *Applied Psycholinguistics, 28*(1), 171–190.

Elley, W. B. (1991). Acquiring literacy in a second language: The effect of book-based programs. *Language Learning, 41*(3), 375–411.

Elley, W. B. (1996). Using book floods to raise literacy levels in developing countries. In V. Greaney (Ed.), *Promoting reading in developing countries* (pp. 148–162). Newark, DE: International Reading Association.

Ellis, R. (1982). The origins of interlanguage. *Applied Linguistics, III*(3), 207–223.

Fehr, C. N, Davison, M. L., Graves, M. F., Sales, G. C., Seipel, B., & Sekhran-Sharma, S.

(2011). The effects of individualized, online vocabulary instruction on picture vocabulary scores: An efficacy study. *Computer Assisted Language Learning, 25,* 87–102.

Filippini, A. L. (2007). *Effects of a vocabulary-added instructional intervention for at-risk English learners: Is efficient reading instruction more effective?* [Doctoral dissertation]. Available from Dissertations & Theses database (Publication No. AAT 3274436).

Folse, K. (2004). *Vocabulary myths: Applying second language research to classroom teaching.* Ann Arbor: University of Michigan Press.

Foorman, B. F., Goldenberg, C., Carlson, C., Saunders, W., & Pollard-Durodola, S. (2004). How teachers allocate time during literacy instruction in primary-grade English language learner classrooms. In P. McCardle & V. Chhabra (Eds.), *The voice of evidence in reading research* (pp. 289–328). Baltimore, MD: Brookes Publishing Co.

Frantzen, D. (2003). Factors affecting how second language Spanish students derive meaning from context. *The Modern Language Journal, 87,* 168–199.

Fukkink, R. G., & de Glopper, K. (1998). Effects of instruction in deriving word meanings from context: A meta-analysis. *Review of Educational Research, 68,* 450–469.

Gamse, B. C., Jacob, R. T., Horst, M., Boulay, B., & Unlu, F. (2008). *Reading first impact study final report* [NCEE 20094038]. Washington, DC: National Center for Education Evaluation and Regional Assistance, Institute of Education Sciences, U.S. Department of Education.

Gandara, P., Rumberger, R., Maxwell-Jolly, J., & Callahan, R. (2003). English learners in California schools: Unequal resources, unequal outcomes. *Education Policy Analysis Archives, 11*(36). Retrieved from http://epaa.asu.edu/epaa/v11n36/

García, G. E. (1991). Factors influencing the English reading test performance of Spanish-speaking Hispanic children. *Reading Research Quarterly, 26,* 371–392.

Genesee, F., Geva, E., Dressler, D., & Kamil, M. (2006). Synthesis: Cross linguistic relationships. In D. August & T. Shanahan (Eds.), *Developing literacy in second-language learners: Report of the National Literacy Panel on Language-Minority Children and Youth* (pp. 523–553). Mahwah, NJ: Erlbaum.

Gersten, R. (1996). Literacy instruction for language-minority students: The transition years. *The Elementary School Journal, 96*(3), 227–244.

Gersten, R., & Baker, S. (2000). What we know about effective instructional practices for English-language learners. *Exceptional Children, 66,* 454–470.

Giambo, D. A., & McKinney, J. D. (2004). The effects of a phonological awareness intervention on the oral English proficiency of Spanish-speaking kindergarten children. *TESOL Quarterly, 38,* 95–117.

Goldenberg, C. (1991). *Instructional conversations and their classroom application* (Educational Practice Report 2). Santa Cruz, CA: The National Center for Research on Cultural Diversity and Second Language Learning.

Goldenberg, C. (1992–1993). Instructional conversations: Promoting comprehension through discussion. *The Reading Teacher, 46,* 316–326.

Goldenberg, C. (2008, Summer). Teaching English language learners: What the research does and does not say. *American Educator, 32*(2), 8–23, 42–44.

Goldenberg, C., & Coleman, R. (2010). *Promoting academic achievement among English learners: A guide to the research.* Thousand Oaks, CA: Corwin.

Gonzalez, J. E., Goetz, E. T., Hall, R. J., Payne, T., Taylor, A. B., Kim, M., & McCormick, A. S. (2011). An evaluation of Early Reading First (ERF) preschool enrichment on language and literacy skills. *Reading & Writing, 24,* 253–284.

Goodwin, A. P., & Ahn, S. (2010). A meta-analysis of morphological interventions: Effects on literacy achievement of children with literacy difficulties. *Annals of Dyslexia, 60,* 183–208.

Goswami, U. (2001). Early phonological development and the acquisition of literacy. In S. B. Neuman & D. K. Dickinson (Eds.), *Handbook of early literacy research* (pp. 111–125). New York: Guilford.

Graves, M. F. (1986). Vocabulary learning and instruction. *Review of Research in Education, 13,* 49–89.

Graves, M. F. (2006). *The vocabulary book.* New York: Teachers College Press.

Graves, M. F. (2009a). *Teaching individual words: One size does not fit all.* New York: Teachers College Press and International Reading Association.

Graves, M. F. (Ed.). (2009b). *Essential readings in vocabulary instruction.* Newark, DE: International Reading Association.

Graves, M. F. & Fitzgerald, J. (2009). Implementing scaffolding reading experiences in diverse classrooms. In J. Coppola & E. Primas (Eds.), *Language, literacy, and learning in multilingual classrooms: Research to practice* (pp. 121–139). Newark, DE: International Reading Association.

Graves, M. F., Ruda, M. A., Sales, G. C., & Baumann, J. E. (2012). Teaching prefixes: Making strong instruction even stronger. In E. B. Kame'enui & J. F. Baumann (Eds.), *Vocabulary instruction: Research to practice* (2nd ed., pp. 95–115). New York: Guilford.

Graves, M. F., Sales, G. C., & Davison, M. (2009, May). *First-fourth grade students' knowledge of the 4,000 most frequent English words.* Research poster presented at the annual meeting of the International Reading Association, Minneapolis.

Graves, M. F., Sales, G. C., & Ruda, M. (2008). *The first 4,000 words.* Minneapolis: Seward Inc. Retrieved from www.thefirst4000words.com.

Graves, M. F., Sales, G. C., & Ruda, M. A. (2012). *Word learning strategies.* Minneapolis: Seward, Inc.

Graves, M. F., & Silverman, R. (2010). Interventions to enhance vocabulary development. In R. Allington & A. McGill-Franzen (Eds.), *Handbook of reading disabilities research* (pp. 315–328). Mahwah, NJ: Erlbaum.

Graves, M. F., & Watts-Taffe, S. W. (2008). For the love of words: Fostering word consciousness in young readers. *The Reading Teacher, 62,* 185–193.

Greenman, R. (2001). *Words that make a difference—and how to use them in a masterly way.* Delray Beach, FL: Levenger.

Gunn, B., Smolkowski, K., Biglan, A., Black, C., & Blair, J. (2005). Fostering the development of reading skill through supplemental instruction: Results for Hispanic and non-Hispanic students. *Journal of Special Education, 39*(2), 66–85.

Guthrie, J. T., & Humenick, N. M. (2004). Motivating students to read: Evidence for classroom practices that increase reading motivation and achievement. In P. McCardle & V. Chhabra (Eds.), *The voice of evidence in reading research* (pp. 213–234). Baltimore, MD: Brookes.

Haggard, M. R. (1986). The vocabulary self-collection strategy: Using student interest and word knowledge to enhance vocabulary growth. *Journal of Reading, 29,* 634–642.

Harris, M. L. (2007). *The effects of strategic morphological analysis instruction on the vocabulary performance of secondary students with and without disabilities* [Unpublished doctoral dissertation]. University of Kansas, Lawrence, KS.

Hart, B., & Risley, T. R. (1995). *Meaningful differences in the everyday experiences of young American children.* Baltimore: P. H. Brookes.

Hart, B., & Risley, T. R. (2003, Spring). The early catastrophe: The 30 million word gap. *American Educator, 27*(1), 4–9.

Hartman, G. W. (1946). Further evidence of the unexpected large size of recognition vocabularies among college students. *Journal of Educational Psychology, 37,* 436–439.

Hayes, D. P., & Ahrens, M. (1988). Vocabulary simplification for children: A special case of "motherese"? *Journal of Child Language, 15,* 395–410.

Heimlich, J. E., & Pittelman, S. D. (1986). *Semantic mapping: Classroom applications.* Newark, DE: International Reading Association.

Henry, M. K., Calfee, R. C., & Avelar-LaSalle, R. (1989). A structural approach to decoding and spelling. In S. McCormick & J. Zutell (Eds.), *Thirty eighth yearbook of the National Reading Conference* (pp. 156–163). Chicago, IL: National Reading Conference.

Hiebert, E. H. (2005). In pursuit of an effective, efficient vocabulary program. In E. H. Hiebert & M. Kamil (Eds.), *Teaching and learning vocabulary: Bringing research to practice* (pp. 243–263). Mahwah, NJ: Erlbaum.

Hiebert, E. H., & Cervetti, G. N. (2012). What differences in narrative and informational texts mean for the learning and instruction of vocabulary. In E. B. Kame'enui & J. F. Baumann (Eds.), *Vocabulary instruction: Research to practice* (2nd ed., pp. 322–344). New York: Guilford.

Hirsch, E. D. (2003, Summer). Reading comprehension requires knowledge—of words and the world. *American Educator, 10*–13, 16–22, 28–29.

Holmes, J., & Guerra Ramos, R. (1995). False friends and reckless guessers: Observing cognate recognition strategies. In T. Huskin, M. Haunes, & J. Coady (Eds.), *Second language reading and vocabulary learning.* Norwood, NJ: Ablex.

Johnson, D. M. (1983). Natural language learning by design: A classroom experiment in social interaction and second language acquisition. *TESOL Quarterly, 17,* 55–68.

Kame'enui, E. J., & Baumann, J. F. (2012). Context for vocabulary instruction. In E. J. Kame'enui & J. F. Baumann (Eds.), *Vocabulary instruction: Research to practice* (2nd ed., pp. 3–14). New York: Guilford.

Kamil, M. L., & Hiebert, E. H. (2005). Teaching and learning of vocabulary: Perspectives and persistent issued. In E. H. Hiebert & M. L. Kamil (Eds.), *Teaching and learning vocabulary: Bringing research to practice* (pp. 1–23). Mahwah, NJ: Erlbaum.

Kieffer, M. J., & Lesaux, N. K. (2007). Breaking down words to build meaning: Morphology, vocabulary, and reading comprehension in the urban classroom. *The Reading Teacher, 61,* 134–144.

Kim, J. S., & Guryan, J. (2010). The efficacy of a voluntary summer book reading intervention for low-income Latino children from language minority families. *Journal of Educational Psychology, 102*(1), 20–31.

Klare, G. R. (1984). Readability. In P. D. Pearson, R. Barr, M. L. Kamil, & P. Mosenthal (Eds.), *Handbook of reading research* (pp. 681–794). New York: Longman.

Klingner, J. K., & Vaughn, S. (1996). Reciprocal teaching of reading comprehension strategies for students with learning disabilities who use English as a second language. *Elementary School Journal, 96,* 275–293.

Klingner, J. K., & Vaughn, S. (2000). The helping behaviors of fifth graders while using collaborative strategic reading during ESL content classes. *TESOL Quarterly, 34,* 69–98.

Krashen, S. (2001). More smoke and mirrors: A critique of the National Reading Panel report on fluency. *Phi Delta Kappan, 83,* 119–123.

Kress, J. (2008). *The ESL/ELL teacher' book of lists.* San Francisco: Jossey-Bass.

Kroll, J. F., & Curley, J. (1988). Lexical memory in novice bilinguals: The role of concepts in retrieving second language words. In M. Gruneberg, P. Morris, & R. Sykes (Eds.), *Practical aspects of memory* (vol. 2, pp. 389–395). London: John Wiley.

Kroll, J. F., & Sholl, A. (1992). Lexical and conceptual memory in fluent and nonfluent bilinguals. In R. J. Harris (Ed.), *Cognitive processing in bilinguals* (pp. 191–204). Amsterdam: Elsevier.

Kuhn, M. R., & Stahl, S. A. (1998). Teaching children to learn word meanings from context: A synthesis and some questions. *Journal of Literacy Research, 30,* 119–138.

Lara-Cinisomo, S., Pebley, A., Vaiana, M., Maggio, E., Berends, M., & Lucas, R. (2004). A matter of class: Educational achievement reflects family background more than ethnicity or immigration. *Rand Review, 28*(3), 10–15.

Laufer, B. (2003). Vocabulary acquisition in a second language: Do learners really acquire most vocabulary by reading? Some empirical evidence. *The Canadian Modern Language Review, 59*(4), 567–587.

Lawrence, J. F., Capotosto, L., Branum-Martin, L., White, C., & Snow, C. E. (2011). Language proficiency, home-language status, and English vocabulary development: A longitudinal follow-up of the Word Generation program. *Bilingualism: Language and Cognition*, 1–15.

Lederer, R. (1996). *Pun and games*. Chicago: Chicago Review Press.

Lederer, R. (1988). *Get thee to a punnery*. Charleston, SC: Wyrick.

Lesaux, N. K., Kieffer, M. J., Faller, E., & Kelley, J. (2010). The effectiveness and ease of implementation of an academic vocabulary intervention for linguistically diverse students in urban middle schools. *Reading Research Quarterly, 45*, 198–230.

Linebarger, D. L. (2000). *Summative evaluation of* Between the Lions: *A final report to WGBH Educational Foundation*. Boston: WGBH.

Long, M. H., & Richards, J. C. (2001). Series editor's preface. In I. S. P. Nation (Ed.), *Learning vocabulary in another language* (p. xiii). Cambridge, UK: Cambridge University Press.

Longman American idioms dictionary. (1999). Harlow, UK: Pearson Education.

Longman diccionario Inglés básico, Ingles-Espanol, Espanol-Ingles: para estudiantes mexicanos. (2004). White Plains, NY: Pearson Longman.

Lorge, I., & Chall, J. (1963). Estimating the size of vocabularies of children and adults: An analysis of methodological issues. *Journal of Experimental Education, 32*, 147–157.

Lovett, M. W., Lacerenza, L., Borden, S. L., Frijters, J. C., Steinbach, K. A., & De Palma, M. (2000). Components of effective remediation for developmental reading disabilities: Combining phonological and strategy-based instruction to improve outcomes. *Journal of Educational Psychology, 92*(2), 263–283.

Lubliner, S., & Hiebert, E. H. (2011). An analysis of English-Spanish cognates as a source of teaching general academic language. *Bilingual English Journal, 34*, 1–18.

MacGinitie, W. H., MacGinitie, R. K., Maria, K., Dreyer, L. G., & Hughes, K. E. (2000). *Gates-MacGinitie reading tests* (4th ed.). Itasca, IL: Riverside Publishing Company.

Malloy, J. A., Marinak, B. A., & Gambrell, L. B. (2010). *Essential readings on motivation*. Newark, DE: International Reading Association.

Mancilla-Martinez, J. (2010). Word meanings matter: Cultivating vocabulary knowledge in fifth-grade Spanish-speaking language minority learners. *TESOL Quarterly, 44*, 669–699.

Mancilla-Martinez, J., & Lesaux, N. K. (2010). Predictors of reading comprehension for struggling readers: The case of Spanish-speaking language minority learners. *Journal of Educational Psychology, 102*, 701–711.

Mancilla-Martinez, J., & Lesaux, N.K. (2011). The gap between Spanish-speakers' word reading and word knowledge: A longitudinal study. *Child Development, 85*, 1544–1560.

Mancilla-Martinez, J., Pan, B. A., & Banu Vagh, S. (2011). Assessing the productive vocabulary of Spanish-English bilingual toddlers from low-income families. *Applied Psycholinguistics, 32*, 333–357.

Manis, F. R., Lindsey, K. A., & Bailey, C. E. (2004). Development of reading in grades K–2 in Spanish-speaking English-language learners. *Learning Disabilities Research & Practice, 19*(4), 214–224.

Marzano, R. J. (2004). *Building background knowledge for academic achievement*. Alexandria, VA: Association for Supervision and Curriculum Development.

McClure, A. A., & Kristo, J. V. (1996). *Books that invite talk, wonder, and play*. Urbana, IL: National Council of Teachers of English.

McKeown, M. G. (1993). Creating effective definitions for young word learners. *Reading Research Quarterly, 28*, 16–31.

McKeown, M. G., & Beck, I. L. (2004). Direct and rich vocabulary instruction. In J. F. Baumann & E. B. Kame'enui, *Vocabulary instruction: Research to practice* (pp. 13–27). New York: Guilford.

McKeown, M. G., Beck, I. L., Omanson, R. C., & Perfetti, C. A. (1983). The effects of long-term vocabulary instruction on reading comprehension: A replication. *Journal of Reading Behavior, 15,* 3–18.

McKeown, M. G., Beck, I. L., Omanson, R. C., & Pople, M. T. (1985). Some effects of the nature and frequency of vocabulary instruction on the knowledge and use of words. *Reading Research Quarterly, 20,* 522–535.

Mezynski, K. (1983). Issues concerning the acquisition of knowledge: Effects of vocabulary training on reading comprehension. *Review of Educational Research, 53,* 253–279.

Miller, G. A., & Gildea, P. M. (1987). How children learn words. *Scientific American, 257*(3), 94–99.

Miller, G. A., & Wakefield, P. C. (1993). Commentary on Anglin's analysis of vocabulary growth. *Monographs of the Society for Research in Child Development, 59*(10), 167–175.

Moats, L., Foorman, B., & Taylor, P. (2006). How quality of writing instruction impacts high-risk fourth graders' writing. *Reading and Writing: An Interdisciplinary Journal, 19,* 363–391.

Molinsky, S. J., & Bliss, B. (2006). *Word by word basic picture dictionary—international* (2nd ed.). White Plains, NY: Pearson Longman.

Muse, D. (Ed.). (1997). *The New Press guide to multicultural resources for young readers.* New York: The New Press.

Nagy, W. E. (1988). *Teaching vocabulary to improve reading comprehension.* Newark, DE: International Reading Association.

Nagy, W. E. (2005). Why vocabulary instruction needs to be long-term and comprehensive. In E. Hiebert & M. Kamil (Eds.), *Teaching and learning vocabulary* (pp. 27–44). Mahwah, NJ: Erlbaum.

Nagy, W. E. (2007). Metalinguistic awareness and the vocabulary-comprehension connection. In R. K. Wagner, A. Muse, & K. Tannenbaum (Eds.), *Vocabulary acquisition: Implications for reading comprehension* (pp. 52–77). New York: Guilford.

Nagy, W. E., & Anderson, R. C. (1984). How many words are there in printed English? *Reading Research Quarterly, 19,* 304–330.

Nagy, W. E., Anderson, R. C., & Herman, P. A. (1987). Learning word meanings from context during normal reading. *American Educational Research Journal, 24,* 237–270.

Nagy, W. E., Anderson, R. C, Schommer, M., Scott, J. A., & Stallman, A. C. (1989). Morphological families in the internal lexicon. *Reading Research Quarterly, 24,* 262–282.

Nagy, W. E., & Herman, P. A. (1987). Breadth and depth of vocabulary knowledge: Implications for acquisition and instruction. In M. C. McKeown & M. E. Curtis (Eds.), *The nature of vocabulary acquisition* (pp. 19–35). Hillsdale, NJ: Erlbaum.

Nagy, W. E., McClure, E. F., & Mir, M. (1997). Linguistic transfer and the use of context by Spanish-English bilinguals. *Applied Psycholinguistics, 18,* 431–452.

Nagy, W. E., & Scott, J. A. (2000). Vocabulary processes. In M. Kamil, P. Mosenthal, P. D. Pearson, & R. Barr (Eds.), *Handbook of reading research* (vol. 3, pp. 269–284). Mahwah, NJ: Erlbaum.

Nash, R. (1997). *NTC's dictionary of Spanish cognates thematically organized.* Lincolnwood, IL: NTC Publishing Group.

Nation, I. S. P. (2001). *Learning vocabulary in another language.* Cambridge, UK: Cambridge University Press.

National Center for Educational Statistics. (1992). *Factors influencing the achievement of American students in grades 4, 8, and 12, in 1988 and 1990.* Washington, DC: U.S. Department of Education.

National Center for English Language Acquisition. (2011a). *How many school-aged Limited English Proficient (LEP) students are there in the U.S?* Retrieved from http://www.ncela.gwu.edu/faqs/view/4

National Center for English Language Acquisition. (2011b). *The growing numbers of English learner students: 1998/99-2008-/09.* Retrieved from http://www.ncela.gwu.edu/files/uploads/9/growingLEP_0809.pdf

National Endowment for the Arts. (2007). *To read or not to read, a question of national consequence.* Washington, DC: Author.

National Reading Panel. (2000). *Report of the National Reading Panel: Teaching children to read.* Bethesda, MD: National Institute of Child Health and Human Development.

National Research Council. (2004). *Engaging schools: Fostering high school students' motivation to learn.* Washington, DC: National Academies Press.

Neuman, S. B. (2006). The knowledge gap: Implications for early education. In D. K. Dickenson & S. B. Neuman (Eds.), *Handbook of early literacy research* (vol. 2, pp. 29–40). New York: Guilford.

Neuman, S. B. (2008). *Changing the odds for children at risk: Seven essential principles of educational programs that break the cycle of poverty.* New York: Teachers College Press.

Neuman, S. B., Caperelli, B. J., & Kee, C. (1998). Literacy learning, a family matter. *The Reading Teacher, 52*(3), 244–252.

Neuman, S. B., & Celano, D. (2001). Access to print in low-income and middle-income communities: An ecological study of four neighborhoods. *Reading Research Quarterly, 36,* 8–26.

Neuman, S. B., & Koskinen, P. (1992). Captioned television as comprehensible input: Effects of incidental word learning from context for language minority students. *Reading Research Quarterly, 27*(1), 94–106.

Nunes, T., Bryant, P., Pretzlik, U., Burman, D., Bell, D., & Gardner, S. (2006). An intervention program for classroom teaching about morphemes: Effects on the children's vocabulary. In T. Nunes, P. Bryant, et al. (Eds.), *Improving literacy by teaching morphemes* (pp. 121–134). London and New York: Routledge.

Oller, D. K., & Eilers, R. E. (2002). *Language and literacy in bilingual children.* Clevedon, UK: Multilingual Matters.

Paribakht, T., & Wesche, M. (1999). Reading and "incidental" L2 vocabulary acquisition. *Studies in Second Language Acquisition, 21,* 195–224.

Paris, S. G., Lipson, M. Y., & Wixson. K. S. (1983). Becoming a strategic reader. *Contemporary Educational Psychology, 8,* 293–316.

Pearson Education Limited. (1999). *Longman American idioms dictionary.* Harlow, UK: Author.

Pérez, E. (1981). Oral language competence improves reading skills of Mexican American third graders. *The Reading Teacher, 35,* 24–27.

Perozzi, J. A. (1985). A pilot study of language facilitation for bilingual, language-handicapped children: Theoretical and approach implications. *Journal of Speech & Hearing Disorders, 50*(4), 403–406.

Petty, W. T., Herold, C. P., & Stoll, E. (1968). *The state of knowledge about vocabulary development.* Champaign, IL: National Council of Teachers of English.

Pinker, S. (2000). *The language instinct: How the mind creates language.* New York: Harper-Perennial.

Pittelman, S. D., Heimlich, J. E., Berglund, R. L., & French, M. P. (1991). *Semantic feature analysis: Classroom applications.* Newark, DE: International Reading Association.

Potter, M. C., So, K. F., Von Eckardt, B., & Feldman, L. B (1984). Lexical and conceptual representation in beginning and proficient bilinguals. *Journal of Verbal Learning and Verbal Behavior, 23,* 23–38.

Pressley, J., Disney, L., & Anderson, K. (2007). Landmark vocabulary instructional research and the vocabulary instructional research that makes sense. In R. K. Wager, A. E. Muse, & K. R. Tannenbaum (Eds.), *Vocabulary acquisition: Implications for reading comprehension* (pp. 205–232). New York: Guilford.

Pressley, M., Dolezal, S. E., Raphael, L. M., Mohan, L., Roehrig, A. D., & Bogner, K. (2003a). Increasing academic motivation in primary-grades classrooms. *Catholic Education, 6,* 372–392.

Pressley, M., Dolezal, S. E., Raphael, L. M., Mohan, L., Roehrig, A. D., & Bogner, K. (2003b). *Motivating primary-grade students.* New York: Guilford.

Pressley, M., Harris, K. R., & Marks, M. B. (1992). But good strategy instructors are constructivists! *Educational Psychology Review, 4,* 3–31.

Proctor, C. P., Carlo, M., August, D., & Snow, C. (2005). The English reading of Spanish-speaking English language learners. *Journal of Educational Psychology, 97,* 246–256.

Proctor, C. P., Dalton, B., & Grisham, D. (2007). Scaffolding English language learners and struggling readers in a multimedia hypertext environment with embedded strategy instruction and vocabulary support. *Journal of Literacy Research, 39*(1), 71–93.

Proctor, C. P., Dalton, B., Uccelli, P., Biancarosa, G., Mo, E., Snow, C. E., & Neugebauer, S. (2011). Improving Comprehension Online (ICON): Effects of deep vocabulary instruction with bilingual and monolingual fifth graders. *Reading and Writing: An Interdisciplinary Journal, 24*(5), 517–544.

Proctor, C. P., Uccelli, P., Dalton, B., & Snow, C. E. (2009). Understanding depth of vocabulary and improving comprehension online with bilingual and monolingual children. *Reading and Writing Quarterly, 25*(4), 311–333.

RAND Reading Study Group. (2002). *Reading for understanding: Toward an R&D program in reading comprehension.* Santa Monica, CA: RAND Education.

Raz, I. S., & Bryant, P. (1990). Social background, phonological awareness and children's reading. *British Journal of Developmental Psychology, 8,* 209–225 .

Read together, talk together [parent video]. (2002a). New York: Pearson Early Learning.

Read together, talk together [teacher training video]. (2002b). New York: Pearson Early Learning.

Richek, M. A. (2005). Words are wonderful: Interactive, time-efficient strategies to teach meaning vocabulary. *The Reading Teacher, 58,* 414–423.

Roberts, F. A. (2008). *The effect of instruction in orthographic conventions and morphological features on the reading fluency and comprehension skills of high-school freshmen* [Unpublished doctoral dissertation]. University of San Francisco, California.

Roberts, T. (2008). Home storybook reading in primary or second language with preschool children: Evidence of equal effectiveness for second-language vocabulary acquisition. *Reading Research Quarterly, 43,* 103–130.

Roberts, T., & Neal, H. (2004). Relationships among preschool English language learners' oral proficiency in English, instructional experience and literacy development. *Contemporary Educational Psychology, 29*(3), 283–311.

Ruddell, M. R., & Shearer, B. A. (2002). "Extraordinary," "tremendous," "exilarating," "magnificent": Middle school at-risk students become avid word learners with the Vocabulary Self-Collection Strategy (VSS). *Journal of Adolescent and Adult Literacy, 45,* 352–363.

Ryder, R. J., & Graves, M. F. (1994). Vocabulary instruction presented prior to reading in two basal readers. *Elementary School Journal, 95*(2), 139–153.

Saddler, B., & Graham, S. (2007). The relationship between writing knowledge and writing performance among more and less skilled writers. *Reading & Writing Quarterly, 23,* 231–247.

Sales, G. C., & Graves, M. F. (2009a). *Listening vocabulary test.* Minneapolis, MN: Seward Inc.

Sales, G. C., & Graves, M. F. (2009b). *Reading vocabulary test.* Minneapolis, MN: Seward Inc.

Sales, G. C., & Graves, M. F. (2009c). Web-based pedagogy for fostering literacy by teaching basic vocabulary. *Information Technology, Education and Society, 9*(2), 5–30.

Sales, G. C., & Graves, M. F. (2012). *Word learning strategies.* Minneapolis, MN: Seward Inc.

Samway, K., & Taylor, D. (2008). *Teaching English language learners.* New York: Scholastic.

San Fransisco, A. R., Mo, E., Carlo, M., August, D., & Snow, C. (2006). The influences of language of literacy instruction and vocabulary on the spelling of Spanish-English bilinguals. *Reading and Writing, 19,* 627–642.

Saunders, W. (1999). Improving literacy achievement for English learners in transitional bilingual programs. *Educational Research and Evaluation, 5*(4), 345–381.

Saunders, W. M., Foorman, B. R., & Carlson, C. D. (2006). Is a separate block of time for oral English language development in programs for English learners needed? *The Elementary School Journal, 107,* 181–198.

Saville-Troike, M. (1984). What *really* matters in second language learning for academic achievement. *TESOL Quarterly, 18,* 199–219.

Scarborough, H. S. (1998). Early identification of children at risk for reading disabilities: Phonological awareness and some other promising predictors. In B. K. Shapiro, P. J. Accardo, & A. J. Capute (Eds.), *Specific reading disabilities: A review of the spectrum* (pp. 75–119). Timonium, MD: York Press.

Schmitt, N. (2000). *Vocabulary in language teaching.* Cambridge, UK: Cambridge University Press.

Schmitt, N. (2010). *Researching vocabulary: A vocabulary research manual.* New York: Palgrave Macmillan.

Schwartz, R. M., & Raphael, T. E. (1985). Concept of definition: A key to improving students' vocabulary. *The Reading Teacher, 39,* 198–205.

Scott, J. A., Blackstone, T., Cross, S., Jones, A., Skobel, B., Wells, J., et al. (1996, May). *The power of language: Creating contexts which enrich children's understanding and use of words.* Microworkshop conducted at the annual meeting of the International Reading Association, New Orleans.

Scott, J. A., Butler, C., & Asselin, M. (1996, December). *The effect of mediated assistance in word learning.* Paper presented at the annual meeting of the National Reading Conference, Charleston, SC.

Scott, J. A., Jamieson-Noel, D., & Asselin, M. (2003). Vocabulary instruction throughout the day in twenty-three Canadian upper-elementary classrooms. *The Elementary School Journal, 103,* 269–286.

Scott, J. A., & Nagy, W. E. (1997). Understanding the definitions of unfamiliar verbs. *Reading Research Quarterly, 32,* 184–200.

Scott, J. A., & Nagy, W. E. (2004). Developing word consciousness. In J. F. Baumann & E. J. Kame'enui (Eds.), *Vocabulary instruction: Research to practice* (pp. 201–217). New York: Guilford.

Scott, J. A., Skobel, B. J., & Wells, J. (2008). *The word conscious classroom.* New York: Scholastic.

Shanahan, T., & Beck, I. L. (2006). Effective literacy teaching for English-language learners. In D. August & T. Shanahan (Eds.), *Developing literacy in second-language learners: Report of the National Literacy Panel on language-minority children and youth* (pp. 415–488). Mahwah, NJ: Erlbaum.

Shibles, B. (1959). How many words does a first-grade child know? *Elementary English, 36,* 42–47.

Silverman, R. D. (2007). Vocabulary development of English-language and English-only learners in kindergarten. *The Elementary School Journal, 107*(4), 365–383.

Simpson-Vlach, R., & Ellis, N. C. (2010). An academic formulas list: New methods in phraseology research. *Applied Linguistics, 31,* 487–512.

Snow, C. E., & Kim, Y. (2007). Large problem spaces: The challenge of vocabulary for English language learners. In R. K. Wagner, A. E. Muse, & K. R. Tannenbaum (Eds.), *Vocabulary acquisition: Implications for reading comprehension* (pp. 123–139). New York: Guilford.

Snow, C., Lawrence, J., & White, C. (2009). Generating knowledge of academic language among urban middle school students. *Journal of Research on Educational Effectiveness, 2,* 325–344.

Stahl, S. A. (1998). Four questions about vocabulary. In C. R. Hynd (Ed.), *Learning from text across conceptual domains* (pp. 73–94). Mahwah, NJ: Erlbaum.

Stahl, S. A., & Fairbanks, M. M. (1986). The effects of vocabulary instruction: A model-based meta-analysis. *Review of Educational Research, 56,* 72–110.

Stahl, S. A., & Nagy, W. E. (2006). *Teaching word meanings.* Mahwah, NJ: Erlbaum.

Stahl, S. A., & Stahl, K. D. (2004). Word wizards all! Teaching word meanings in preschool and primary education. In J. F. Baumann & E. B. Kame'enui (Eds), *Vocabulary instruction: Research to practice* (pp. 59–78). New York: Guilford.

Sternberg, R. J. (1987). Most vocabulary is learned from context. In M. G. McKeown & M. E. Curtis (Eds.), *The nature of vocabulary acquisition* (pp. 89–105). Hillsdale, NJ: Erlbaum.

Swanborn, M. S. W., & de Glopper, K. (1999). Incidental word learning while reading: A meta-analysis. *Review of Educational Research, 69,* 261–285.

Swanson, H. L., Saez, L., & Gerber, M. (2006). Growth in literacy and cognition in bilingual children at risk for reading disabilities. *Journal of Educational Psychology, 98,* 247–264.

Templin, M. C. (1957). *Certain language skills in children, their development and interrelationships.* Minneapolis: University of Minnesota Press.

Terman, L. M. (1916). *The measurement of intelligence.* Boston: Houghton Mifflin.

TESOL. (2006). *PreK–12 English language proficiency standards.* Alexandria, VA: Author.

Thorndike, E. L. (1941). *The teaching of English suffixes.* New York: Teachers College, Columbia University.

Torgesen, J. K., Houston, D. D., Rissman, L. M, Decker, S. M., Roberts, G., Vaughn, S. et al. (2007). *Academic literacy instruction for adolescents.* Portsmouth, NH: RMC Research Corporation, Center on Instruction.

Torres, H. N., & Zeidler, D. L. (2002). The effects of English language proficiency and scientific reasoning skills on the acquisition of science content knowledge by Hispanic English language learners and native English language speaking students. *Electronic Journal of Science Education, 6*(3). Retrieved from http://www2.sjsu.edu/elemetnaryed/ejlts/

Townsend, D. R., & Collins, P. (2009). Academic vocabulary and middle school English learners: An intervention study. *Reading & Writing: An Interdisciplinary Journal, 22,* 993–1019.

Trelease, J. (1989). *The new read-aloud handbook* (2nd rev. ed.). New York: Penguin.

Trelease, J. (2006). *The read-aloud handbook* (6th ed.). New York: Penguin.

Tudor, I., & Hafiz, F. (1989). Extensive reading as a means of input to L2 learning. *Journal of Research in Reading, 12,* 164–178.

Uchikoshi, Y. (2005). Narrative development in bilingual kindergartners: Can *Arthur* help? *Developmental Psychology, 41*(3), 464–478.

Ulanoff, S. H., & Pucci, S. L. (1999). Learning words from books: The effects of read-aloud on second language vocabulary acquisition. *Bilingual Research Journal, 23*(4), 409–422.

Vagh, S. B., Pan, B. A., & Mancilla-Martinez, J. (2009). Measuring growth in bilingual and monolingual children's English productive vocabulary development: The utility of combining parent and teacher report. *Child Development, 80,* 1545–1563.

Van Evra, J. (1998). *Television and child development* (2nd ed.). Mahwah, NJ: Erlbaum.

Vaughn, S., Cirino, P. T., Linan-Thompson, S., Mathes, P. G., Carlson, C. D., Hagan, E. C., Pollard-Durodola, S. D., Fletcher, J. M., & Francis, D. J. (2006). Effectiveness of a Spanish intervention and an English intervention for English-language learners at risk for reading problems. *American Educational Research Journal, 43*(3), 449–487.

Vaughn, S., Linan-Thompson, S., Mathes, P. G., Cirino, P. T., Carlson, C. D., Pollard-Durodola, S. D., et al. (2006). Effectiveness of Spanish intervention for first-grade English language learners at risk for reading difficulties. *Journal of Learning Disabilities, 39*(1), 56–73.

Vaughn, S., Mathes, P., Linan-Thompson, S., Cirino, P., Carlson, C., Pollard-Durodola, S., Cardenas-Hagan, E., & Francis, D. (2006). Effectiveness of an English intervention for first-grade English language learners at risk for reading problems. *The Elementary School Journal, 107*(2), 153–180.

Wasik, B. A., & Bond, M. A. (2001). Beyond the pages of a book: Interactive book reading and language development in preschool classrooms. *Journal of Education Psychology, 93*(2), 243–250.

Watts, S. M. (1995). Vocabulary instruction during reading lessons in six classrooms. *Journal of Reading Behavior, 27*, 399–424.

Watts-Taffe, S. (2006, October). *Teaching vocabulary in grades Pre-K thorugh 3: Inspiring the love of words.* Paper presented at the annual conference of the Ohio Council of the International Reading Association, Youngstown, OH.

Weitz, W. E. (2003). Sustained silent reading with non-native speakers of English: Its impact on reading comprehension, reading attitude, and language acquisition [Doctoral dissertation]. Available from Dissertations & Theses database (Publication No. AAT 3103978).

Weizman, Z. O., & Snow, C. E. (2001). Lexical input as related to children's vocabulary acquisition: Effects of sophisticated exposure and support for meaning. *Developmental Psychology, 37*, 265–279.

West, M. (1953). *A general service list of English words.* London: Longmans, Green, and Company. (Original work published 1936)

White, T. G., Graves, M. F., & Slater, W. H. (1990). Growth of reading vocabulary in diverse elementary schools: Decoding and word meaning. *Journal of Educational Psychology, 82*, 281–290.

White, T. G., Power, M. A., & White, S. (1989). Morphological analysis: Implication for teaching and understanding vocabulary growth. *Reading Research Quarterly, 24*, 283–304

White, T. G., Slater, W. H., & Graves, M. F. (1989). Yes/no method of vocabulary assessment: Valid for whom and useful for what? In S. McCormick & J. Zutell (Eds.), *Cognitive and social perspectives for literacy research and instruction* (pp. 391–398). Chicago: National Reading Conference.

White, T. G., Sowell, J., & Yanagihara, A. (1989). Teaching elementary students to use word-part clues. *The Reading Teacher, 42*, 302–308.

Whitehurst, G. J., Arnold, D. S., Epstein, J. N., Angell, A. L., Smith, M., & Fischel, J. E. (1994). A picture book reading intervention in day care and home for children from low-income families. *Developmental Psychology, 30*, 697–689.

Whitehurst, G. J., Falcon, F., Lonigan, C. J., Fischel, J. E., DeBaryshe, D. B., Valdez-Menchaca, M. C., & Caulfield, M. (1988). Accelerating language development through picture book reading. *Developmental Psychology, 24*, 552–559.

Wigfeld, A., & Eccles, J. S. (Eds.) (2002). *Development of achievement motivation.* San Diego: Academic Press.

Zeno, S. M., Ivens, S. H., Millard, R. T., & Duvvuri, R. (1995). *The educator's word frequency guide.* Brewster, NY: Touchstone Applied Science Associates.

Zevenbergen, A. A., & Whitehurst, G. J. (2003). Dialogic reading: A shared picture book reading intervention for preschoolers. In A. V. Kleeck, S. A. Stahl, & E. B. Bauer (Eds.), *On reading books to children: Parents and teachers* (pp. 177–200). Mahwah, NJ: Erlbaum.

Zhang, Z., & Schumm, J. S. (2000). Exploring effects of the keyword method on limited English proficient students' vocabulary recall and comprehension. *Reading Research and Instruction, 39*(3), 202–221.

Index

About the Authors

Michael F. Graves is Professor Emeritus of Literacy Education at the University of Minnesota and a member of the Reading Hall of Fame. His research and writing focus on vocabulary learning and instruction, and he has written several dozen books, book chapters, and articles on the topic. His recent books on vocabulary include *Essential Readings on Vocabulary Instruction* (2009), *Teaching Individual Words: One Size Does Not Fit All* (2009), and *The Vocabulary Book* (2006).

Diane August is a Managing Director affiliated with the American Institutes for Research in Washington, DC. Previously she was a Senior Research Scientist affiliated with the Center for Applied Linguistics (CAL). Her area of expertise is the development of literacy in second-language learners. At CAL she was a Principal Investigator for several large grants focusing on ELLs and served as the Staff Director for the National Literacy Panel on Language Minority Children and Youth.

Jeannette Mancilla-Martinez is Assistant Professor of Language, Literacy, and Technology at the University of California, Irvine. Her research on the connection between students' language and literacy development, spanning toddlerhood through adolescence, is focused on students with low language and literacy skills, students from low-income homes, immigrant children, and language-minority learners. Her work is featured in such journals as the *Journal of Educational Psychology*, *Child Development*, *Reading and Writing: An Interdisciplinary Journal*, and *TESOL Quarterly*.